113

Experiences in Music for Young Children

To my parents — Lynn and Lauretta Weller
And my children — David, Paul, Carrie, and
Merrill Pugmire

Experiences in Music for Young Children

Mary Carolyn Weller Pugmire

COPYRIGHT © 1977
BY DELMAR PUBLISHERS INC.

LIBRARY OF CONGRESS CATALOG CARD NUMBER: 76-4304
ISBN: 0-8273-0567-2

Printed in the United States of America
Published simultaneously in Canada
by Nelson Canada,
A Division of International Thomson Limited

Jeanne Machado — Consulting Editor
Elinor Gunnerson — Early Childhood Education Series Editor
Veryl Larsen and Paul Pugmire — Photographers

DELMAR PUBLISHERS INC.
2 COMPUTER DRIVE, WEST — BOX 15-015
ALBANY, NEW YORK 12212

Preface

Everyone can use music to teach young children! *Experiences in Music for Young Children* is designed to help adults enjoy musical experiences with children — especially very young children. The music is carefully chosen to appeal to infants, toddlers, and three- and four-year-olds. The skills that help teachers use music more effectively in early childhood education are emphasized.

A two-part approach to music is presented. The parts can be studied together or used independently.

In Part I, the author discusses ways music can be used to teach young children:

- Practical activities are suggested for using music in both structured and spontaneous situations.

- Music — original as well as traditional songs that children love — is printed in a size and form that can be used in the classroom.

- The "how and why" of music in early childhood education is based on methods that have been successfully used in the classroom — most of them by the author.

- Ideas for instructional aids and a system for filing them are given.

The purpose of Part II is to teach or reinforce the basic skills needed by the adult who desires to help children enjoy music:

- A practical approach is taken to the fundamentals of music: melody, rhythm, and harmony.

- Examples are used from music presented earlier in Part I.

- Concepts are keyed to a cassette recording which uses music from Part I.

- The music is simple — using only three chords (I, IV, and V), five key signatures, and four time signatures.

- Emphasis is placed on practice as a means of developing music skills, such as chording.

- The Autoharp is discussed as an instrument adaptable to use with nearly all the music in the text.

Clearly stated objectives introduce each unit. Suggested Activities outline laboratory experiences to guide the students in gaining needed skills and to encourage them to be creative. Review materials follow each unit and can be used by the students to evaluate their own progress since the answers are included.

Mary Carolyn Weller Pugmire is a teacher in early childhood education at Ricks College in Rexburg, Idaho, where she is also supervisor of the Child Development Laboratories. Mrs. Pugmire has taught the primary grades and was a demonstration teacher at Idaho State University in kindergarten and Project Head Start. She studied open concept education in Great Britain and has served on the Governor's Committee for Developmental Disabilities in Idaho. She is a member of the National Association for the Education of Young Children.

The author teaches music classes at the B.Y.U. – Ricks Center for Continuing Education where the text was field tested. She has presented numerous workshops on music. However, her chief interest in this area is to help teachers who feel they cannot use music in teaching young children. She truly believes there should be Joy in music – even in music education. This text is intended to "capture" that joy.

Other texts in the Delmar Early Childhood Education Series include

- Creative Activities for Young Children – Mayesky, Neuman, and Wlodkowski
- A Practical Guide to Solving Preschool Behavior Problems – Essa
- Early Childhood Experiences in Language Arts – Machado
- Administration of Schools for Young Children – Click
- Early Childhood: Development and Education – Mack
- Understanding Child Development – Charlesworth
- Children in Your Life – Radeloff & Zechman

Contents

PART I TEACHING WITH MUSIC

Section 1 Goals and Function of Music for the Young Child

unit 1   influences of music

OBJECTIVES

After studying this unit, the student should be able to

- Describe the effect of music in life situations.
- Sing two simple chants (or songs) of early childhood.
- Describe the challenge of teaching music and music appreciation.

Music affects lives in many ways. It strengthens a mood or changes it. Music reaches every part of the population: rich and poor, young and old, professional musicians and those who listen for pleasure.

Music can be a great influence in the early childhood education center as well as in the home. Most adults who care for young children will admit the *affective influence* of music (how music inspires emotions and changes attitudes). Music can also have an effect on the *cognitive growth* (development of factual knowledge) of the child. A teacher who knows how to help children create and use music has a great advantage.

NATURE OF MUSIC

Man expresses himself most directly with his voice and his body. He has, through the

Fig. 1-1 An assistant teacher guides the musical activities of the children.

1

Joyfully   M. C. Weller Pugmire

Now is the time to sing a song Come join with us and sing a-long

Mu-sic is fun for ev'-ry one So sing the mu-sic clear and strong

Fig. 1-2 *Now Is The Time* (Cassette song 21-C).

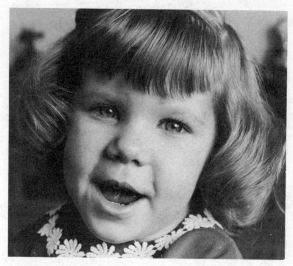

Fig. 1-3. Music is communication.

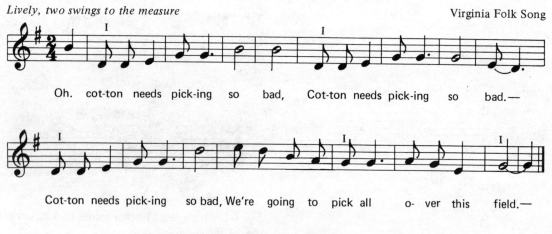

Lively, two swings to the measure   Virginia Folk Song

Oh. cot-ton needs pick-ing so bad, Cot-ton needs pick-ing so bad.—

Cot-ton needs pick-ing so bad, We're going to pick all o-ver this field.—

Fig. 1-4 *Cotton Needs Picking* (Cassette song 22-J).

ages, found extensions of his voice and body as he developed many instruments. He also has invented ways to record his music to preserve it for others. The sounds of music are called *tones* to show that they are different from the sounds of speech.

Music is often referred to as the universal language. Through music, man can express tension and gain a release from this tension. He can arouse feelings of love and tenderness with music as well as anger and distress. This power of music is not limited by any language; it reaches people of many different tongues.

Sound and rhythm are the main elements with which the composer works. The infinite ways that sound and rhythm are combined arouse responses, but no two persons respond exactly alike. The same music may prompt one person to movement while another person remains motionless and enjoys the *esthetic* (beautiful, artistic) sound of the composition.

People have always created music to accompany daily living. Music helps set their pace at work. Times of celebration or sorrow are made more meaningful with the accompaniment of music. Much of the music became *traditional*; it is handed down from generation to generation. This music, called folk music, is often very appealing to young children.

The nature of music demands three roles: the composer, the listener, and the performer.

Fig. 1-5 As the child picks daisies, an adult makes the time happier for him by singing *Daisies Need Picking*.

Not all roles must be fulfilled at one time, but it is interesting to note that the young child performs all three roles.

As he participates in dramatic play, he "composes" and hums his own mood music. Sometimes he asks the teacher to write down a song that he makes up about some event in his life.

His role as a listener often needs to be encouraged. Most children have listened to lullabies and nursery tunes from the time they were born. As they become more mobile, they need help with the skill of listening; their attention span is less constant.

The role of performer is the most common one for the young child. He is capable of performing many varied musical roles to enhance his enjoyment of life. It is the responsibility of those who care for him to see that he is given the opportunity to have a wide variety of experiences.

MUSIC IN EARLY CHILDHOOD

Everyone is familiar with the accompanying chant of childhood, figure 1-6. Perhaps this is not considered music, but from it many songs have emerged — both nonrecorded and recorded. One only has to listen carefully where children are playing to hear the influence of music.

Music has long been an *integral* (purposeful) part of early childhood education programs. Frederic Froebel, the "Father of the Kindergarten," (1782 - 1852) wrote the *Mutter und Kose Lieder* (Songs for Mother and for Nursery)[1] to assist mothers and others who care for children. Froebel gave lectures in which he stressed that songs and verses taught by mothers would help their young children attain complete and healthy development. One song was translated:

[1]Bowen, H. Courthope, *Froebel*, New York: Charles Scribner's Sons, 1909.

Duh - Duh   Duh, Duh - Duh   Duh.   Duh, Duh, Duh, Duh,   Duh Duh

Fig. 1-6 *Chant of Childhood.*

If your child's to understand
Things that other people do,
You must let his tiny hand
Carry out the same things too.
   This is the reason why
     Never still,
     Baby will,
Imitate whatever's by.

In the present when parent involvement is stressed, it is worthwhile to note this emphasis given to mothers by the founder of the kindergarten.

Maria Montessori (1870 - 1952), a great teacher of young children (especially the deprived), believed in "education of the senses." Montessori was convinced that to develop the auditory sense (hearing), the young children must learn to appreciate silence. She then stressed esthetic sounds as opposed to discordant noises. She recommended the ringing of well-toned bells and the use of simple stringed instruments. Montessori believed the music educator should always perform while facing the children.

Montessori created many *musically didactic materials* (teaching tools intended to convey instruction as well as pleasure). Some of these are used today with young children.

The modern well-equipped early childhood center has many music resources: records, phonographs, cassette recorders, ear-

Fig. 1-7 *Itisket, Itasket.*

phones, printed music, and Autoharps. Unfortunately, in many centers, these materials are not used effectively. A staff member who wants the children to gain worthwhile musical experiences uses available resources. However, a person can also provide meaningful musical activities when little equipment is available.

MODERN MUSIC

It sometimes happens that early childhood teachers overlook the music that is played in a child's own home. Whether this music matches her personal preferences or not, this type of music is familiar to the child and for that reason appeals to him. The child's musical tastes can be broadened, but it is often best to begin with the music that is part of his home environment.

In the home, the "musical repertoire" of many small children consists of TV commercials and hymns (or chants). The teacher would do well to become familiar with the most commonly used music of the groups in the community – religious and otherwise. She should initiate her program with familiar music and then use her opportunity for broadening the musical heritage of the children.

THE CHALLENGE OF EARLY MUSIC EDUCATION

Most young children are "born musicians." Teachers must help the child keep and

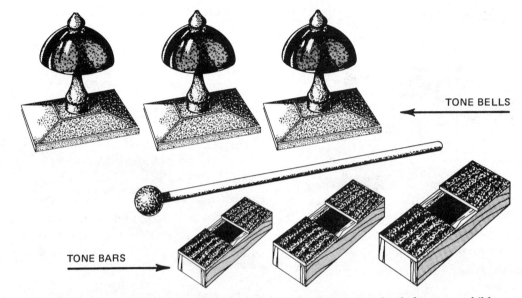

TONE BELLS

TONE BARS

Fig. 1-8 Some Montessori-type materials are used to teach music in schools for young children.

develop the music within him. When the child responds to music, he must be encouraged in every way. The teacher should also help the child learn the fundamentals of music.

A practical approach may be taken to this idea. Everyone knows that the young child likes to be alone or with only one other child at times. Sometimes he likes to be alone or with one friend for musical activities, too. This knowledge may be used in a practical way by building a "House of Music," figure 1-9. Heavyweight cloth is used to make a cover for a cardtable. Cut one piece of material (Piece A) just larger than the top of the table.

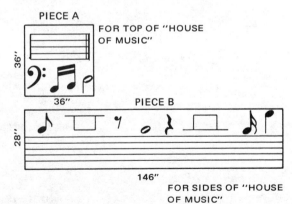

PIECE A

FOR TOP OF "HOUSE OF MUSIC"

36"

36"

PIECE B

28"

146"

FOR SIDES OF "HOUSE OF MUSIC"

NOTE: DIMENSIONS ARE FOR A CARD TABLE 35" SQUARE ON TOP AND 27" HIGH. ADJUST FOR OTHER TABLES.

Fig. 1-9 Diagram of pieces for the "House of Music."

Fig. 1-10 The Opening in the "House of Music" is large enough for the teacher to see inside.

Cut another long strip of material (Piece B) for the sides of the music house. Make a music staff on this with a black felt tip pen. Sew Piece B to Piece A to make the cover as shown in figures 1-9 and 1-10. Overlap the ends of Piece B; then fold back the two ends of Piece B to make an opening. Windows can be cut in the shape of notes and rests. Music symbols are drawn on the music house.

Other ideas are shown in the illustration. Put a phonograph in the house. Other ideas may develop as this "House of Music" is used.

SUMMARY

Music is often called the universal language because it has a definite influence on the lives of people everywhere. Man uses the sound and rhythm of music to express his own emotions. He does this in roles of performer, listener, and creator.

Music has always been used in various early childhood education programs. The challenge is to maintain and develop the child's natural musical responses and expand his knowledge of music. The teacher who understands this and is willing to try to meet this challenge is a valuable asset to any program.

SUGGESTED ACTIVITIES

• Make a list of every place you hear music during the next twenty-four hours. Note the musical experiences where children were present.

• Name the song that was most beloved by you as a child. Recall why this song had special meaning for you.

• As you do a routine task, sing *Cotton Needs Picking*. Adjust the words to fit your own situation. (Example: *Dishes Need Washing*.)

• Make the "Music House" yourself or with class members as a class group project. If possible, place it in the early childhood center where you observe.

REVIEW

A.   Indicate the best choice for each of the following.

1.   The influence of music in an early childhood education program is evident in

   a. The child's cognitive development.
   b. The child's affective behavior.
   c. The assistant's ability to work with young children.
   d. All of the above.

2.   Man expresses himself most directly with

   a. Percussion and wind instruments.
   b. His voice and body.
   c. Ability to record the music he has created.
   d. Stringed instruments.

3.   The principal elements with which the composer of music creates are

   a. Recordings and musicians.
   b. Written music and instruments.
   c. Sound and rhythm.
   d. Inspiration and diligent effort.

4.   The nature of music demands three roles:

   a. Composer, listener, performer.
   b. Technician, writer, tone expert.
   c. Perfect pitch, good voice, ability to read music.
   d. Theorist, song writer, harmonist.

5.   TV commercials

   a. Have no musical influence on young children.
   b. Are poor examples of music for young children to hear.
   c. Make up the main "musical repertoire" of many small children.
   d. None of the above.

6. "Didactic music materials" refers to

   a. Musical instruments that have a sad sound.
   b. Printed music used in Montessori's schools.
   c. Tools for teaching music that are intended to convey instruction as well as pleasure.
   d. Special materials developed for Froebel's kindergartens.

7. The challenge of music education for those who guide young children is

   a. To prepare the child to play instruments.
   b. To teach the child to compose his own music.
   c. To help the child enjoy the singing games of childhood.
   d. To maintain and develop the child's natural responses to music.

B. Match each item in column II with the correct item in column I.

I	II
1. Frederick Froebel	a. Stressed "education of the senses"
2. Cognitive development	b. Changes of feelings or attitudes
3. Affective influence	c. Chant of childhood
4. *Itisket, Itasket*	d. Handed down from generation to generation
5. Maria Montessori	
6. *Cotton Needs Picking*	e. Folk song which seemed to help the work get done faster
7. Folk music	f. "Father" of the Kindergarten
8. Tone	g. Attainment of factual knowledge
9. Hardware	h. Equipment such as phonographs and tape recorders
	i. Vocal or musical sound

C.   Briefly answer each of the following.

   1.   Relate the influence of Frederick Froebel in early childhood education. Emphasize the musical influence.

   2.   Describe some of the ideas Maria Montessori developed to help young children with musical experiences.

   3.   List instances of the child's varied roles as composer, listener, and performer.

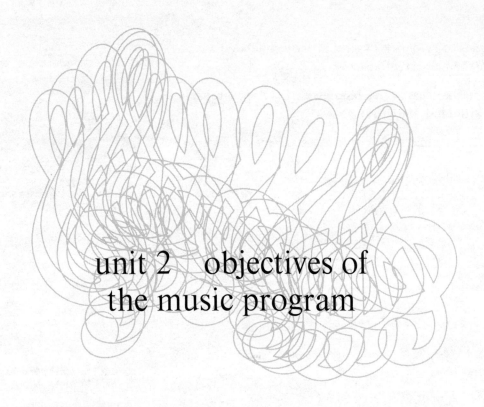

unit 2 objectives of the music program

There are many *models* (types) of early childhood education programs. The role that music plays ranges from being the main part of the curriculum to being an afterthought. Although goals of music education are determined by the type of program, there are common considerations to be found in the formation of the goals:

- Enjoying music

- Developing listening skill

- Encouraging responses

- Building a base for musical experiences

- Fostering creativity

An overview of these goals is important. As the assistant becomes more aware of the range of possibilities for musical guidance, she begins to achieve these goals in her own teaching.

OBJECTIVES

After studying this unit, the student should be able to

- List five objectives of the music program.

- Name one activity an assistant teacher can do to achieve each of these goals.

- List the skills developed in a music program.

- Make a resource file for music materials.

ENJOYMENT OF MUSIC

"Singing a song is fun to do" is the message of the song *Fun To Do*, figure 2-1. Music should be enjoyed! Yet many students preparing to become teachers, assistants, and mothers seem to regard music as the part of early childhood education that is the most awkward for them. This need not be so. Therefore, it is important for the student to examine her own attitudes concerning music.

Rebecca Stevens

Cecilia Johns

Fig. 2-1 *Fun to Do.*

M. C. Weller Pugmire

M. C. Weller Pugmire

Fig. 2-3 *Fly, My Pretty Balloon* **(Cassette song 22-C).**

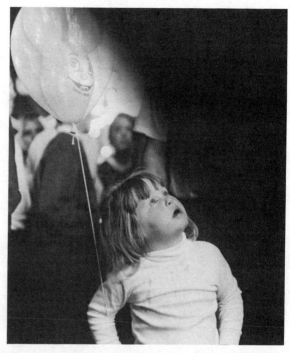

Fig. 2-2 The teacher shares the child's excitement about the carnival by singing *Fly, My Pretty Balloon.*

She should desire to further the children's enjoyment of music, not destroy it. She should try to make music boost the child's *self-concept* (the way a person feels about himself). If the child has had a special outing with his family to the carnival, the adult shares the excitement and says, "I know a song about balloons that I'll sing just for you. I bet you'll want to learn it, so we can teach the others." The child beams and the song, *Fly, My Pretty Balloon* becomes a favorite..

"Make-up" songs are useful to increase enjoyment; *Little Wheel A-Turning* is a favorite, figure 2-4. The catchy tune lends itself to words that fit the "here-and-now" events of the child's world.

> *"There's a little dog a-barkin' at our door"*
> *"There's a great big sun a-shinin' overhead"*

Young children love the familiar. The teacher who sincerely wants children to enjoy music finds out which songs and dances they already know. She seeks opportunities, also, to help the children learn some new music.

Music can bring enjoyment to the child with special problems. Many of the happiest moments such children seem to have is when they are responding to music. Parents as well as teachers and assistants need to be shown ways to help their children enjoy music. Many of the suggestions in this book can be taught to parents.

DEVELOPING LISTENING SKILL

The skills of music are generally listed as listening, singing, moving, and playing instruments. Creating, reading, and writing music are also skills, but their use is limited in early childhood education. All of the skills are dependent on the ability to listen. The teacher should ask herself how she rates as a listener. In our world, we are bombarded with noise. We learn to "tune out" much of this. But in so doing, we often lower our listening capacity, too.

The skill of listening is emphasized many times throughout the text. However, the story of "Magoocump — The Listening Bus" should give the teacher and the assistant some ideas of chances for further listening, figure 2-5.

Traditional Negro Folk Song

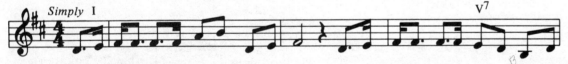

There's a lit-tle wheel a turn-ing in my heart, There's a lit-tle wheel a-turn-ing in my

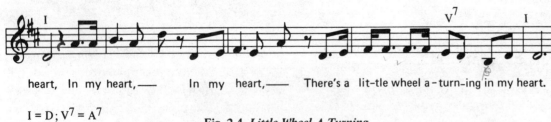

heart, In my heart,—— In my heart,—— There's a lit-tle wheel a-turn-ing in my heart.

I = D; V⁷ = A⁷

Fig. 2-4 *Little Wheel A-Turning.*

Fig. 2-5 Illustrations for "Magoocump."

Magoocump – the Listening Bus

The children in the school were restless. "Come on," said Miss Rosie, "let's go for a ride in Magoocump."

The delighted children surrounded the pretty teacher and together they went into the yard. There stood their masterpiece – Magoocump – a refrigerator box that they had turned into a "bus." But oh! this bus was special.

The project had started when they were returning from a trip to the zoo. The children were talking about the sounds they had heard the animals make. When they stopped, Miss Rosie asked them to listen for sounds around them. Just then, they crossed Magoocump Creek. "Magoocump, Magoocump," sang the children, as they laughed at the sound of the word. The next day the big box on the porch became "Magoocump," the listening bus.

Now the children and Miss Rosie piled into the box. "Who has a special word to sing?" asked Miss Rosie. "My mother planted rhododendrons!" cried Jeremy. "Let's sing about it!"

> "Rhododendrons
> Rhododendrons
> Pretty, pretty, rhododendrons"

"Let's listen for sounds," said Miss Rosie. The children were very still. "I hear a horn honking," said Paula. "Shh!" said Marie, "Listen to the bird. My Mom says the bird is singing, 'Our town is a pretty-little-place'."

The children were delighted because Marie sang *pretty-little-place* very fast and it did sound like the bird's song.

"I hear the footsteps of someone special," said Miss Rosie. The happy children left Magoocump. It was time to go home.

ENCOURAGING RESPONSES TO MUSIC

When children (and adults) listen to Tchaikovsky's *None But the Lonely Heart*, played on a violin, they respond differently than they do to an orchestration by Herb Alpert's Tiajuana Brass. The mood of the music is different. The power of music to affect mood should be strongly considered. Often only a limited selection of music is used, keeping the children from becoming familiar with a variety of "mood music" and having a chance to respond in more ways.

If You're Happy is a song with which the teacher can experiment, figure 2-6. With the children around her, she sings the song completely one time. Then she invites the children to join with her. After the children know the first verse, other verses are added:

> "If you're sad and you know it, wipe your eyes" (brush eyes with back of hand).
> "If you're . . . , make a frown"

The teacher ends on some quiet action so that the children are ready to go on to another activity.

Simple props help the children express mood. Thin, colorful scarves are excellent for this. Any music that conveys movement can be used. The teacher and the assistant usually dance with the children, gently making their scarves "flow," for just a short period of time. Then they move to one side and encourage the children with smiles and nods of approval.

Encouraging *music appreciation* (responding to music in a positive way) is part of early education. Of course, there can be negative responses, too. Sometimes, a small child does not wish to listen to certain music. It makes such a child irritable. Each child hears differently. How he learns to respond to music determines the type of music he will like.

BUILDING A FOUNDATION FOR MUSICAL EXPERIENCES

The very youngest children in the early childhood education center respond to the basic music elements – rhythm, melody, and harmony. The older children can understand and enjoy a fair amount of knowledge about the structure of music. There is a "readiness" factor operating as a child gains musical knowledge just as there is reading and number "readiness."

Rhythm is all around us. *Rhythm* (a recurring pattern of strong and weak pulses in the flow of sound) is heard in the ticking clock, the noises of a child's running feet, or the patter of the raindrops on the window.

An adult can become more aware of rhythm patterns by listening for them. She can make these rhythm patterns by clapping her hands and leading a group of children to do this, too.

Melody (an agreeable succession of sound) is usually what students regard as the most important part of music. Perhaps this is true. The experience of having a melody "play in one's mind" is a common occurrence. An interesting melody appeals to children. It is usually thought that all songs for children must have short and very simple melodies. This is not necessarily true. The song *Give, Said the Little Stream*, figure 2-7, is long but has a melody that is "catchy." Many children enjoy this song.

When searching for melodies to use, teachers should ask the children for song titles. Usually, the song that is remembered is the one with a pleasing melody. Teachers often ask other teachers for suggestions about selections.

Harmony (the combination of musical notes into chords) is basic to music structure, but it is not stressed as much as rhythm and melody in the early years. Young children can learn to recognize chords as the teacher plays. More importantly, they can play an Autoharp and get a first hand experience with chords and how they change or progress.

The assistant should prepare herself to use the Autoharp with the children. Most schools have an Autoharp; it is often on a shelf gathering dust. This should not happen. It is easy to learn to use the instrument, and its use helps the children gain a sense of harmonic structure.

Fig. 2-6 *If You're Happy.*

Many music texts enumerate other elements of music. However, these three basic elements — rhythm, melody, and harmony — include all the others. The student who gains mastery of these concepts has built a foundation for musical experiences.

FOSTERING CREATIVITY

A master teacher defined creativity as "the first time a child uses a certain media." Usually, creativity is considered to have an element of doing something original with an old idea, but for the purpose of early childhood education, the first definition has merit.

When a child who hears a musical selection exclaims, "Oh, that sounds like the willow tree in my backyard when the wind blows!" and stretches forth his arms and moves to the music, swaying with the "wind," he is probably doing something that has been done by children through the ages. For this particular child, however, it is a creative experience. How fortunate is the child who works and plays in an environment where this is possible.

All of the goals of music education are closely related. This is especially true of creative experiences. The child just discussed was enjoying the music. He was certainly listening to hear the "wind." He was responding in a joyful mood, and the rhythm of his response was possible because he had had experience with rhythm before.

Public Domain

Give, said the little stream, Give, Oh! give, give, oh! give.

Give, said the little stream, as it hurried down the hill. I'm

small I know, but wherever I go, the fields grow greener still.

Singing singing all the day, Give away, Oh! give away.

Singing, singing all the day, Give, Oh! give away.

I = D; IV = G; $V^7 = A^7$

Fig. 2-7 *Give, Said the Little Stream* (Cassette song 21-A).

BUILDING A RESOURCE FILE

In order to achieve these music goals more easily, the student should begin to develop a file of music materials. This probably will be a section of a general early childhood education file, although it can be a separate file.

There are several ways to build a file. Color coding is common. For example, all music materials are marked with a blue rectangle in the upper left-hand corner. The materials are filed in blue file folders or regular manila folders marked in blue. Whenever material is taken from the file, it can be replaced easily.

A number system is more effective. An example of a number file is shown. The numbers 80 to 89 are the numbers assigned to music in the teacher's general file. These numbers are written in the upper left-hand corner of the materials filed. (Any series of numbers could be used.)

80 – Music, General

81 – Music Elements
    81A – Melody
    81B – Rhythm
    81C – Harmony

82 – Music Skills
    82A – Listening
    82B – Singing
    82C – Movement
    82D – Playing Instruments
    82E – Creating Music

83 – Songs for Early Childhood Education
    83A – Action
    83B – Folk and Ethnic
    83C – Self-concept
    83D – Fun and Fancy
    83E – Songs for the Very Young

84 – Music in Related Areas
    84A – Art
    84B – Health and Nutrition
    84C – Language Arts
    84D – Math
    84E – Music
    84F – Science
    84G – Social Studies
        84G-1 – Holidays
    84H – Transition; Clean Up

85 – Music Plans and Concept Development

86 – Musical Dramatizations and Games

87 – Music Appreciation
    87A – Cultural and Ethnic Influence
    87B – Musicians

88 – Musical Development in Children

89 – Instructional Aids

A combination type filing system may also be used. In this case, the story "Magoocump, the Listening Bus," would be marked with blue in the upper left-hand corner of the pages as well as number 82A (for Listening Skill).

Some of the resource materials will be three-dimensional (the chiffon scarves for example). These would be placed in a separate box marked with a blue "89" and labeled appropriately.

SUMMARY

Although goals for a particular early childhood education center are developed by the personnel of that program, certain defined objectives usually guide early music education. All of these goals are interdependent, but fostering creativity is very dependent upon all of the other goals. It is important that the child learn to enjoy listening to music because, of all the musical skills, listening is the most important. As the child listens, he responds. Actually, his mood can be changed or reinforced with music.

In order to achieve these goals, the teacher should build a file of music materials. These materials should be coded so they can be easily refiled after they are used.

SUGGESTED ACTIVITIES

- With a group of classmates, conduct a "buzz session" to gain ideas for achieving the five goals of the music program.

- Make a listening bus, like "Magoocump," with a group of children. Go for a listening ride, if possible.

- Make up a verse to *Little Wheel A-Turning*. Sing this song to your classmates. Have them join with you.

REVIEW

A.   Match each item in column II with the correct item in column I.

I	II
1. Early childhood education models	a. The way a person feels about himself
2. Self-concept	b. Help the children express mood
3. *Little Wheel A-Turning*	c. Story stressing the listening skill
4. Simple props	d. Types of programs
5. "Magoocump"	e. "Make-up" type song
6. Music appreciation	f. Responding to music in a positive manner
7. Color coding	g. Method of marking materials for refiling

B.   Indicate the best choice for each of the following.

1. Concerning children with special learning problems:

   a. Music is not important in their lives.
   b. There is no place in the curriculum of special education programs for music.
   c. Music is very important to them.
   d. Only specially prepared music should be used in special education programs.

2. Which of the following statements are true?

   a. "Music appreciation" infers that a person will respond positively to music.
   b. Music can alter the moods of young children.
   c. Young children are "consumers" of music in our society.
   d. The way a child responds to music determines the type of music consumer he will be.

3. Rhythm is

   a. Alternating loudness and softness in music.
   b. The same as dynamics.
   c. A recurring pattern of strong and weak elements in the flow of sound.
   d. Concerned mainly with timbre.

4. Melody is

   a. Always the top row of notes on the musical staff.
   b. An agreeable succession or arrangement of sounds.
   c. Learned most effectively when played on the piano.
   d. The same as a descant.

5. In order to be enjoyed by young children, a melody must

   a. Be short.
   b. Be simple.
   c. Have an element of appeal.
   d. Be on the lower half of the staff.

6. Harmony is

   a. Stressed during the early years.
   b. Not recognizable by young children.
   c. The theoretical explanation of music.
   d. The combination of musical notes into chords.

7. Which of the following are true statements about creativity?

   a. Study of theory is necessary in order to have creativity in music.
   b. Creativity means the first time a child uses a certain media.
   c. Creativity is interdependent with other musical goals.
   d. Creativity means doing something original with an old idea.

C. Name a musical activity for reinforcing or changing each mood listed. Indicate whether the mood is reinforced or changed.

Happy	Sleepy	Dejected
Sad	Patriotic	Bored

D. Briefly answer each of the following.

   1. List the music skills generally stressed in early childhood education.

   2. What are the basic elements of music?

   3. What is the reason for color coding or numbering materials to be filed?

   4. If the number filing system given in the text is used, what does the number "82C" mean?

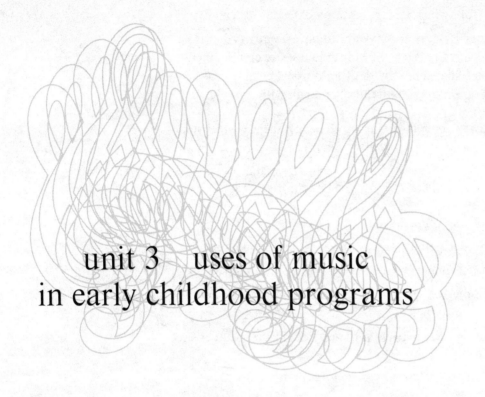

unit 3 uses of music
in early childhood programs

OBJECTIVES

After studying this unit, the student should be able to

- Describe five instances when music is an excellent activity.
- Direct a small group of children from one area to another through the use of music.
- Name two ways that parents can be involved in the music program.

Music can be a powerful tool in early childhood education as well as a subject that brings greater enjoyment to life. The teacher who uses music in every possible way has an advantage. She finds that in many situations the children respond more readily to music than to words. Music adds a new dimension to many of her teaching tasks. She can use music in practical ways such as helping a sad child gain a happier outlook on life and fostering his/her creative expression.

The National Association for the Education of Young Children (N.A.E.Y.C.) has published a booklet entitled "Curriculum Is What Happens." Music is always happening in the lives of young children. The baby moves his entire body in response to music. The toddler dances to the tune on the radio. The four-year-old sings one TV commercial after another. Because of this natural interest, most early childhood programs have some planned music experiences.

STRUCTURED MUSIC PERIOD

There is usually some time during each day when children gather in a group for music experiences. Very young children may respond to a favorite record. Nursery school children sing action songs, moving fingers and arms. Older children learn many new songs *by rote*, (listening to the whole song and then singing with the teacher).

The type of program usually determines when the music period is conducted. Some common times are listed:

- The period following "clean-up" when the children have finished their share of the tasks and come to a designated area for music.

- A specified time during a play period when a teacher comes to the "music place" and those interested join her for music activities.

- A short time following the children's arrival in the morning, especially if the children come together in a bus.

Fig. 3-1 The children move to the music. Note the child dancing with the doll.

The content of the structured music period is usually determined by the goals of the program and the interest of the children. If a child brings his pet, the children may sing *Mary Had A Little Lamb*. While the interest is high, the teacher leads into other musical experiences. Some plans emphasize basic elements of music; others aim to broaden the children's enjoyment of music.

SPONTANEOUS MUSIC ACTIVITY

The teacher who has the skill to employ music in situations that arise spontaneously is rewarded with more pleasant teaching experiences. Several situations illustrate this:

- The children sway back and forth and sing with the teacher as they wait for their turn to be pushed in the swing.

- The children are finger painting with blue and green paint. "Oh, I want to make the sea!" exclaims a child. The teacher puts Debussy's *La Mer* on the phonograph and the children paint to the music.

- The children are talking about the concert in the park where one of their big sisters will perform. The teacher plays Ella Jenkin's *Call and Response* record, and the children participate in a "concert."

- One child is fearful of going to the well-child clinic. The teacher makes a nurse

Fig. 3-2 The "smile" visual aid may be made larger when used with children. When turned upside down, it represents a frown.

cap for the child, and they sing *Let's Pretend*.

- A little boy is sad because his mother has been gone for several days. Sensing this, the teacher sings a short lullaby to him and then produces her "smile visual-aid" from her resource file and sings *Smiles*, figure 3-3.

The spirit of spontaneous musical activity is contagious. When a group of children are interacting poorly, the teacher can start singing in which the class "makes up" their own words. The atmosphere may soon be better. The children will be thinking of words, not arguments. Sometimes the children will initiate such an activity on their own impulse!

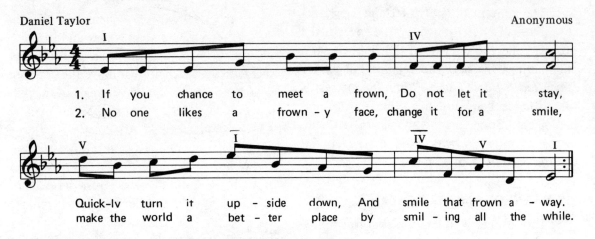

Fig. 3-3 *Smiles* (Cassette application song F).

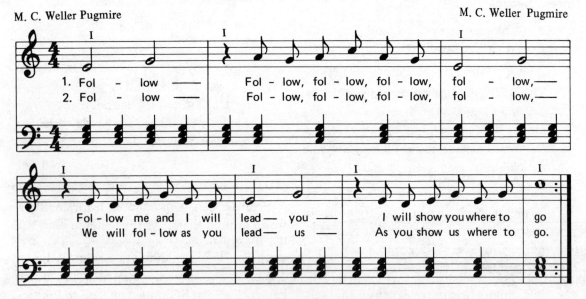

Fig. 3-4 *Follow Me* (Cassette song 23-C).

MUSIC – A TOOL FOR WORKING WITH GROUPS

The ability to use music as a means for group control is valuable. The teacher primarily desires that her students enjoy music and have opportunities for creative expression. Keeping these goals in mind, she uses music in various ways.

Transitions (children moving from one area to another) can be made more smoothly with music. *Follow Me*, figure 3-4, is a follow-the-leader type song in which the teacher starts walking through the room motioning children to come and join her. She leads them to the desired place, singing:

> *"Follow me and I will lead you.*
> *I will show you where to go."*

The children sing:

> *"We will follow as you lead us,*
> *As you show us where to go."*

The young child enjoys the role of being teacher's special helper to lead the transition. This is shown in *Add On*, figure 3-5. If the children have not seen caravans of travel trailers, show them a picture. Trailers and mobile homes are well known to many young children today. One child is a "trailer." He takes another child ("trailer") by the hand. Other children then join as part of the "caravan" and are led "down the road." In practice,

M. C. Weller Pugmire   M. C. Weller Pugmire

1. Have you seen a car-a-van of trail-ers go-ing down the road?
2. Have you seen a group of chil-dren who are play-ing "Add—On?

Have you seen the trail-ers go-ing some-where in a line?
Have you seen the chil-dren add-ing on—— to the line?

One adds on to the end of the line. An-oth-er adds on to the end of the line.
One adds on to the end of the line. An-oth-er adds on to the end of the line.

Yes, we've seen a car-a-van of trail-ers go-ing down the road.
Yes, we've seen a group of chil-dren who are play-ing "Add—On".

Yes, we've seen the trail-ers go-ing some-where in a line.
Yes, we've seen the chil-dren add-ing on—— to the line.

Fig. 3-5 *Add-On* (Cassette song 24-G).

they go to another part of the room. The accompaniment to this song is easy and the children love it. Songs of this type are especially valuable if the teacher must move the children to another room in a building as part of the regular schedule. It also gives the children chances to practice leadership.

Adults use music for relaxation; music helps children relax, too. If the teacher is working in a program where rest periods are part of the daily schedule, she should choose the music for this period carefully. Helping a child relax as he listens to music will help him with the "art of living" in today's world. The teacher should bear in mind that children love to hear familiar music over and over, but she should also introduce new music during rest time. Many of the classics are fine for this purpose.

Group singing while children are being transported on a field trip is a helpful function of music. It often serves to improve group unity.

MUSIC IN RELATED AREAS

Music can help children learn about the world around them. As the children play with wheels, the teacher may sing about them, figure 3-6. The teacher prepared for this, yet it was not part of a structured music period. She knew this teaching opportunity would arise when children were playing with the

M. C. Weller Pugmire   M. C. Weller Pugmire

1. The wheels are turn-ing, turn-ing, turn-ing, turn-ing round and round. —
2. They help when we are mov-ing, mov-ing things a-cross the ground.—

Fig. 3-6 *Wheels* **(Cassette song 22-H).**

Words and Melody by Rita S. Robinson

1. Cab-bage!   Car-rots!   Co-co-nuts!
2. Milk and!   Cheese and!   Whole-wheat bread!

Crunch-e-ty,   Crunch-e-ty,   Crunch-e-ty,   Crunch!
Munch-e-ty,   Munch-e-ty,   Munch-e-ty,   Munch!

Ap-ples!   Cel-'ry!   Toast-ed nuts!
Ma-ma's   chil-dren   are well fed!

Crunch-e-ty,   Crunch-e-ty   Crunch-e-ty,   Crunch!
O! what a   Crunch-e-ty   Munch-e-ty,   Lunch!

I = F; IV = B♭; V^7 = C^7

Fig. 3-7 *Crunchy Lunch* **(Cassette application song C).**

wheels. Other opportunities for planned musical experiences may be utilized:

- Periods when children are helping to prepare food. Children sing the *Crunchy Lunch* song, figure 3-7.

- In a learning center, such as a "play store." Children sing as they engage in *dramatic play* (that type of play in which children learn about the world by assuming roles.)

- Activities that foster *perception*, awareness of objects through the senses. Movement to music is often more intriguing to the child than going through a set of prescribed exercises.

Fig. 3-8 The child may sing as she prepares the food. Eating is the best part, but music adds to the activity.

- Language arts activities (which involve communication of all types — such as speaking, reading, and writing.) Children who learn to sing with expression will learn to read with expression.

- Number and math activities. "Counting" songs are popular with children. Musical activities emphasize shapes and one-to-one relationships (one object for each number).

PARENT INVOLVEMENT

Enjoyment of music is an area common to children and adults. Therefore, music can become an important part of parent involvement in the early childhood program.

First, the teacher needs to find the interests and talents of the parents in the program. This can be accomplished during home visits, with a questionnaire, or while talking with the parents at the center. Fathers should be considered, too! Many fathers who feel uncomfortable with nothing to do will play the piano or show how different sounds are made on a wind instrument. Children respond to parents' efforts even though their musical talents may not be extensive.

Parent involvement in music activities has a practical implication for teachers. It can extend their own musical experience.

Many teachers who do not play the piano or guitar (though all should learn to play simple accompaniments) are very pleased to have the help of parents with musical abilities.

There is another aspect of parent involvement in music for even the very youngest children that should be mentioned. Jean Piaget, the reknowned Swiss psychologist, has called the age from birth until two the *sensory-motor stage* (that period when the child learns through movement and the use of his senses). If parents realize that music is another way to foster the development of their child, an important message has been communicated. However, teachers may need to be prepared to make suggestions regarding the child's home musical environment.

SUMMARY

Music has five main functions in the early childhood learning environment. A structured period can be planned to teach the children songs and basic musical elements, as well as to increase their enjoyment of music. Spontaneous musical activity helps to create a more pleasant and effective learning environment. Music can also be used as a tool for working with groups. The possibilities for this function of music range from keeping a large group of children profitably occupied, when necessary, to helping a small group with social interaction. Parents can become involved in many music appreciation activities. Indeed, music can be used in every area of the curriculum as a means to achieve the total goals of early childhood education.

Fig. 3-9 Children respond to parents' efforts to share their musical talents.

SUGGESTED ACTIVITIES

- Choose a short musical activity that you already know well. Teach this activity to a group of your classmates. Comment on the following after the completion of this activity:

  a. Describe the musical activity that you taught.
  b. What is its function in the early childhood learning environment?
  c. Were you well prepared to present this activity?
  d. Was it difficult for you?   (If your answer is "yes," tell why.)
  e. List skills that you must gain and knowledge you must have before you can effectively teach music to young children. (This list should be referred to at the end of the course.)

Note to the "Musically Unsure Student":

If you need help, ask for it. Perhaps a classmate can aid in your presentation and you can act as assistant. Your instructor might recommend a self-directing record for children such as A Visit to My Little Friend (Children's Record Guild) for you to use.

Try to gain confidence in yourself. Every person working with young children can develop the ability to direct many musical experiences.

Note to the "Musically Trained Student":

Help others where needed! Since working with parents and volunteers is such an important part of early childhood education, direct a musical activity in which fellow students assume the roles of volunteers. For example, teach a song about grandmothers. Then have the "grandmother volunteer" sing a song she remembers from her childhood. (Your "children" will have a good listening experience.)

- Use *Follow Me* or *Add-On* to move a group of students from one area to another. When you finish, discuss whether using music for transition is more effective at times than just using words.

- List three songs you know that are suitable for young children. After each title write a possible function of the song in the early childhood center.
- Survey your class or a group of parents to determine their music interests and talents.

REVIEW

A. Briefly answer each of the following.

1. Name two factors that determine the content of the structured music period.
2. Name three situations in which spontaneous musical activities might occur.
3. Define dramatic play.
4. Describe one situation where music is used during dramatic play.
5. What is one important relationship of music to future reading ability?
6. Name two ways parents can be involved in musical activities.
7. How could parents use music during the sensory-motor stage of child development?

B. Match each item in Column II with the correct item in Column I.

I	II
1. Structured music period	a. The teacher must take the children to another room for quiet activities.
2. Spontaneous music activities	b. The teacher wants the children to learn a new Halloween song.
3. Transition	c. The teacher sings a soft song with a child who needs individual attention.
4. Music in related areas	d. Helps the teacher extend her musical experience.
5. Parent involvement	e. A song is used to teach the children basic scientific facts about snow.

C. Indicate the best choice for each of the following.

1. Which of the following usually determines the content of the structured music period?

   a. The skill of the teacher and the assistants.
   b. The goals of the program and the interests of the children.
   c. The number of children and teaching personnel.
   d. The amount of equipment and money available for the music program.

2. When the song *Follow Me* is used to move children from one area to another, it is being used as

   a. A song to teach children tone patterns.
   b. A transition song.
   c. A song denoting cultural heritage.
   d. A song to make good use of the children's time.

3. When children learn a song by "rote," the following happens:

   a. The teacher writes the music and presents it to the children.
   b. The children learn the song by the method right for them.
   c. The words are printed on a chart or blackboard.
   d. The children listen to the whole song and then sing it with the teacher.

4. The song *Add-On* can be used to

   a. Develop leadership role in the child.
   b. Make a transition smoother.
   c. Develop a child's self-concept as he is the "teacher's special helper."
   d. All of the above.

5. Music can help in the math area as the children learn counting songs and about one-to-one relationships, a math concept that means

   a. There is one note sung for every word.
   b. There is one child to sing every phrase in the song.
   c. Music teachers must have a good background in mathematics to be effective.
   d. There is one object for each number.

6. Jean Piaget is

   a. A famous composer.
   b. A compiler of the folk music of Europe.
   c. A reknowned Swiss psychologist.
   d. A writer of many children's songs sung all over the world.

Section 2 Individual Differences

unit 4   developmental influence of music

OBJECTIVES

After studying this unit, the student should be able to

- Describe infants' musical responses.

- Name four toddler characteristics that influence musical activities.

- List several characteristics of preschoolers that affect their music education.

- Develop two appropriate musical activities for young school children.

Teachers should understand how a child develops. This will help them guide the child in music. Lists of developmental characteristics (sometimes called *norms*) are the result of hundreds of observations. Records are kept that tell what the children did at certain ages. From these observations, charts are made to show how most children behave at a certain age. However, each child is an individual and may not perform an action by a certain age. Still, he is "normal." A teacher can use information about norms to help her develop musical activities that are suitable for young children.

THE INFANT

The baby requires human touch. Without it, he cannot develop normally. Often, as mothers show their affection through hugging, cuddling, rocking, and crooning, lullabies result. Babies respond to this rhythm and sound from the earliest months.

Some babies need more rhythmical movement than others. These babies take a crawling position and rock their cribs back and forth before they go to sleep (at eight or nine months). When they can pull themselves to the standing position (at ten to twelve months), they bounce with rhythm in their beds. Most babies do respond to definite rhythms, and playing music is one way to enrich their lives.

The sound of music brings a response from the baby. The five-month-old hears and picks up the musical toy. By the eighth month, the baby responds to his name and loves to hear it sung. By the tenth and eleventh months, his games are more advanced, and he tries to imitate the simple actions that correspond to nursery songs.

The infant babbles (random sound produced by infants) through his first year. Babbling often has a definite rhythm. The infant's language progresses to repeated syllables and a few words at the end of the first year. Sometimes the baby seems to "sing" as he babbles and starts to talk, but actual singing develops later.

The teacher or aide has the chance to encourage parents to work with their infants.

Sometimes parents do not realize the value of singing to their infants. Communication takes place between parent and child when rhythm and melody are encouraged. This is enjoyable and helps the baby.

THE TODDLER

The child's second year is called toddlerhood. It is a time when the child is learning to do things for himself. He starts walking. He plays alone most of the time (*solitary play*), but sometimes plays beside another child (*parallel play*). There is really no interaction between these "playmates." They merely enjoy each other's company. Most musical activities, however, are on a *one-to-one basis* (one person works with one child).

Rhythm and movement are big parts of the toddler's life. Moving objects gain his attention more than still ones. As he watches a swing, his whole body moves. The most common toddler response to music is dancing. Any type of music is suitable; however, popular music on radio or TV is very stimulating.

The toddler likes to "show off," and watching adults are delighted. When he gets the attention he wants, he often does not know what to do with it. It is confusing to hear, "You're cute!" and then later, "You're spoiled." Adults must avoid voicing such confusing comments.

Fig. 4-2 As a mother rocks her baby, lullabies result. Baby and mother respond with pleasure.

Fig. 4-1 *Sleep, Baby, Sleep* (Cassette song 21-E).

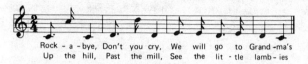

Fig. 4-3 Song sung by Pamela at seventeen months old.

Rock - a - bye, Don't you cry, We will go to Grand - ma's
Up the hill, Past the mill, See the lit - tle lamb - ies

The toddler loves to bang on pots and pans. This may seem ugly noise to some, but it is an experience with sound that toddlers love. The toddler loves to have an adult swing him and sing to him. Families often have traditional songs they sing as they do this.

The grandma of the family swings the delighted Pamela. Pamela listens. If Grandma stops, Pamela fills in the next word. This shows that Pamela is developing her listening skills.

The toddler likes the sound of songs he knows and begs for "mo." He can learn simple actions to the songs that someone teaches him. A toddler has a *symmetry of action* (does most things with both sides of his body). Usually, he reaches with both hands. The song *Up, Up in the Sky,* figure 4-4, illustrates this point.

The toddler's vocabulary is growing. He understands much more than he can say. He likes to play with words and sounds and tries to sing songs with nonsense words. As he learns a song, he hums and sings a word here

Author Unknown

An Old Melody

Up, up in the sky where the lit - tle birds fly. Down down in their nests where the lit - tle birds rest. With a wing on the left And a wing on the right. Well let the dear - bir dies sleep all the long night. When the round sun comes up, And the dew floats a - way, Good morn - ing bright sun - shine the - lit tle birds say.

Fig. 4-4 *Up, Up in the Sky*.

and there. The toddler learns quickly. If he enjoys music at age two, he will probably love music throughout his life.

1. UP, UP IN THE SKY

2. WHERE THE LITTLE BIRDS FLY

3. DOWN, DOWN IN THEIR NESTS. WHERE THE LITTLE BIRDS REST.

4. WITH A WING ON THE LEFT

5. AND A WING ON THE RIGHT. WE'LL LET THE DEAR BIRDIES SLEEP ALL THE LONG NIGHT.

6. WHEN THE ROUND SUN COMES UP

7. AND THE DEW FLOATS AWAY

8. "GOOD MORNING" BRIGHT SUNSHINE THE LITTLE BIRDS SAY.

Fig. 4-5 Simple actions a small child may learn to accompany the song, *Up, Up in the Sky*.

THE PRESCHOOLER

The preschool stage includes children from two to five. Some in this stage are twice as old as others! Therefore, there is a big difference in their ability to do musical activities. Teachers should consider this as they plan activities. Most preschoolers can carry a tune. Simple rhythm patterns can be followed by clapping them out, even though the children's coordination is irregular.

The preschooler usually likes to do the action to a song. Sometimes he gets so involved with the actions, that he does not sing. Often it surprises the teacher to find that the child sings every word of the song at home and does the actions, too.

There are two things to know about play activities that affect music. During this stage, the child becomes much better at *cooperative play*. This play involves two or more children who are interacting. He can begin group musical activities, although he still has periods of solitary play when he often plays a simple phonograph. *Dramatic play* (when children "try on" different roles in life) is common. This is seen when the children sing as they play "house." Boxes and chairs become trains and planes, and creative movements and rhythm patterns develop. The children play spaceman and sing TV commercials they have heard. They will also sing songs about space that someone has taught them. A

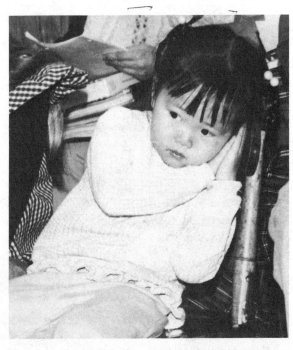

Fig. 4-6 This little girl is so involved with the actions of the song that she does not sing. Yet she sings every word of the song at home.

cowboy hat leads a child to play a cowboy, singing *I'm Goin' to Leave Old Texas Now*, figure 4-7.

The preschooler matures socially through music. He learns a song such as *Here's a Ball for Baby*, figure 4-8, to teach to his little sister or brother. He entertains himself with a humorous song. He cleans his playroom more willingly if he sings as he works. During this time, his vocabulary increases to about two thousand words.

1. I'm goin' to leave ——— old——— Tex – as now,
2. They've plowed and fenced ——— my——— cat – tle range,
3. I'll take my horse, ——— I'll——— take – my rope,
4. Say *a – di – os* ——— to the Al – a – mo,

They've got no use ——— for the long – horn cow. ———
and the peo – ple there ——— are ——— all so strange. ———
And hit the trail ——— up ——— on a lope. ———
And turn my head ——— toward——— Mex – i – co. ———

Fig. 4-7 I'm Goin' to Leave Old Texas Now (Cassette song 22-G).

Unknown   *Unknown*

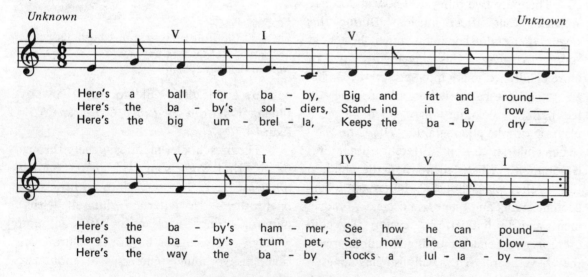

Here's a ball for ba – by, Big and fat and round ———
Here's the ba – by's sol – diers, Stand – ing in a row ———
Here's the big um – brel – la, Keeps the ba – by dry ———

Here's the ba – by's ham – mer, See how he can pound———
Here's the ba – by's trum – pet, See how he can blow———
Here's the way the ba – by Rocks a lul – la – by ———

Fig. 4-8 Here's a Ball for Baby.

THE YOUNG SCHOOL CHILD

As the child takes part in kindergarten, he finds he can do many things. He likes all kinds of play — solitary, parallel, and coopera- tive; he likes all kinds of musical activities, too. Examples can be seen as he plays the phonograph by himself. Then he is by another child in the music corner to look and play with the rhythm instruments even though he might not interact with the other child. Fi- nally, he takes part in musical games and dramatizations and enjoys them.

The five-year-old has increasing control over his body. He does not seem to have to use so much effort to control it as younger children do. He marches easily and learns the music of the great marches.

The big event for the six-year-old is learn- ing to read. He enjoys having a music book to look through and reads some of the lyrics. Music books should be available at schools and day care centers, as well as at home. The six- year-old is very active. Sometimes he tries to do more than he is able to do and seems clumsy. However, being able to move freely helps him enjoy music.

As the child turns seven, he often wants music or dancing lessons. If he takes lessons, those who care for him should encourage him as much as possible. If he cannot take lessons, he often gains some skill from the classroom teacher and his parents.

SUMMARY

The teacher should know how the child develops. Lists of "norms" have been made to help her. The child develops musically. The infant gains from having people sing to him. The toddler is learning very fast to enjoy music, and his language development affects his singing. He likes to dance; he "shows off" and loves the attention. The preschooler makes rhythm and melody a part of his life. He learns to do musical activities with others. The young school child can do many more things with music. Sometimes he tries to do too much and seems to be clumsy. As he learns to read, he likes to look at music books. At all the age levels, it is hoped that music will be an important part of the child's life.

1. HERE'S A BALL FOR BABY. BIG AND FAT AND ROUND.

2. HERE'S THE BABY'S HAMMER. SEE HOW HE CAN POUND.

3. HERE'RE THE BABY'S SOLDIERS STANDING IN A ROW.

4. HERE'S THE BABY'S TRUMPET. SEE HOW HE CAN BLOW.

5. HERE'S THE BIG UMBRELLA. KEEPS THE BABY DRY.

6. HERE'S THE WAY THE BABY ROCKS A LULLABY.

Fig. 4-9 Illustration for actions to use with song *Here's a Ball for Baby.*

SUGGESTED ACTIVITIES

- Arrange to meet with a group of mothers of infants and toddlers. Teach them the action songs in this unit and let them know the value of such songs.

- Visit a day care center. Note the language and body movements of several toddlers and preschoolers. Record each child's name, age, and how his language and body movements affect his musical activities.

- Visit a nursery school while the children are playing. Look for examples of music activities in the play. Also look for characteristics described in this unit.

- Arrange to work with a group of five-year-olds. Let them march to a very good march record or to a march played on the piano. Record the interest and responses of each child.

- Get a simple children's music book from a local library. Help a six- or seven-year-old read the words to the music. Talk about the pictures in the book. Record the child's responses.

REVIEW

A. Indicate the best choice(s) for each of the following.

1. Developmental characteristic lists are determined by

    a. Studying animal behavior.
    b. Recording actions of hundreds of children.
    c. Reading child development textbooks.
    d. Developing musical habits.

2. Information about developmental characteristics

    a. Is often misleading.
    b. Should help the teacher determine if a child is normal.
    c. Helps the teacher sing better.
    d. Can aid the teacher when used as a guide.

3. Which items correctly describe infants?

   a. Some need more rhythmic movement than others.
   b. They require music to live.
   c. Their babbling often has rhythm to it.
   d. They usually like toys that make sounds.

4. Parallel play means

   a. Two children playing together intently.
   b. Stacking musical toys.
   c. Children playing by each other with no real interaction.
   d. Children playing exactly the same.

5. Which items correctly describe the toddler?

   a. Moving objects gain his attention more than still ones.
   b. He likes to "dance."
   c. He likes to have an adult swing him.
   d. He understands more than he can say or sing.

6. Cooperative play means

   a. Cooperating with the teacher.
   b. Getting play materials from a cooperative learning center.
   c. The interaction of two or more children.
   d. Cooperation between teacher, aide, and child.

7. Dramatic play is defined as

   a. Taking a role in a planned production.
   b. "Trying on" different life roles.
   c. Playing with older children.
   d. Involving a teacher.

8. The toddler's symmetry of action tells the teacher

   a. To keep activities simple.
   b. To have music in the center of the room.
   c. To let the toddler do actions with both hands.
   d. That action is important to the toddler.

9. When the toddler dances

   a. It will spoil him to give him attention.
   b. It is a characteristic of this age.
   c. He should be given dancing lessons.
   d. His parents should show him how to do it.

10. Which items correctly describe the preschooler?

    a. His coordination is not very good.
    b. He is a natural musician.
    c. He can entertain himself fairly well.
    d. He is interested in taking music lessons.

11. The preschooler

    a. Is developing a taste for humor.
    b. Needs complex props for dramatic play.
    c. Has no sense of humor.
    d. No longer feels his family is important.

12. Which items are true about the young school child?

    a. He takes part in all types of play.
    b. He has a greater control over his body.
    c. He begins to dislike music.
    d. His interest in music and dance should be encouraged.

B.   Match each item in Column II with the correct item in Column I.

I	II
1. List of developmental characteristics	a. Solitary play
2. Playing alone	b. One-to-one interaction
3. One person working with one child	c. "Norms"
4. Child does things with both sides of his body	d. Parallel play
5. Playing side by side with no real interaction	e. Symmetry of action
6. Random sound production; often has rhythm	f. Cooperative play
7. Two or more children who are interacting	g. Dramatic play
8. "Trying on" different roles in life	h. Babbling

C.   Name a musical response characteristic of each age level mentioned in the text: infant, toddler, preschooler, and young school age. Include rhythm and movement as well as singing.

D.   Briefly answer each of the following.

1. Discuss the development of language as it affects singing in each of the following age levels:

   a. Infancy.
   b. Toddlerhood.
   c. Preschooler.
   d. Young Schooler.

2. How can day care center workers encourage parents to give music experiences to their children?

3. How can day care center workers encourage young school children in their interest in music.

4. When does a child usually first show interest in taking music or dancing lessons? Briefly discuss the value of such lessons.

unit 5   preferences of children and teachers

OBJECTIVES

After studying this unit, the student should be able to

- Define culture and discuss its influence on musical preferences of children and teachers.
- Discuss the teaching of values through music.
- List ways to help the musically unsure person and the musically talented child.
- Describe and perform roles in the team teaching of music.

Each teacher has likes and dislikes. The teacher needs to understand that she has definite musical preferences. She can teach some music skills with more ease than others. When she realizes this, it will be easier for her to recognize that her students have different preferences and talents, too. However, the teacher has a great opportunity to broaden her students' musical background, and that is exciting.

INFLUENCE OF CULTURE

Culture has been defined as the ways of our lives that are part of our "flesh and bones." That is, most of us do not even realize that the ways that we accept as natural and "right" have been learned in our surroundings. Music may be used as an example: when we hear music from the Far East that we have not heard before, it sounds strange and unappealing to us; but a child who has been exposed to that kind of music since birth would probably have the same uncomfortable feelings when hearing the music we usually play.

Cultural influences have brought about some strange musical happenings. In the simple cultures of the past, the very young child took part in tribal singing and dancing. The young child learned to use his fingers in such fine skills as beading and weaving. Young children were expected to sit for long periods of time to do these activities and sing. The child in our culture, however, is not usually

Negro Spiritual

No - bo - dy knows the trou - ble I've seen, No - bo -dy knows my

sor - row no - bo - dy knows the trou - ble I've seen, Glo - ry hal - le - lu - jah!

Fig. 5-1 *Nobody Knows the Trouble I've Seen.*

Cowboy Song

Home, home on the range,— Where the deer and the an - te - lope

play, Where sel - dom is heard a dis - cour - ag - ing word, And the

skies are not cloud - y all day. ——

Fig. 5-2 *Home on the Range.*

required to work and is not included in the musical activities of adults.

In our culture, the child lives without economic responsibility. His fingers are not developed for fine work and fine instruments. He is much older when he learns to play an instrument than were children in some simpler cultures.

Different groups of people have music that seems to "belong" to them. This is called their *cultural heritage*. The Negro spirituals (figure 5-1), the songs from the mountain regions, and the songs of the cowboys (figure 5-2) are examples. This is special music, and children should be given opportunities to hear it.

The author had a very meaningful, cultural experience with this. In her kindergarten classroom, she had always built a tepee that reached the ceiling. As teacher, she presented Indian chants (figure 5-3), and the children used them and the tepee for dramatic play.

One year, the author had several Indian children from a nearby reservation in her class. She decided not to use the tepee because it was not authentic. As the year went on, the young Indian children came to her and asked when she was going to make the tepee so that they could "play Indian." Needless to say, the tepee was put up! The Indian children were excellent dramatic players. The Indian parents brought real Indian tools and treasures to the

Indian Chant
Adapted by M. C. Weller Pugmire

Fig. 5-3 *Kĭ – Yĭ – Yĭ* (Cassette song 23-E).

classroom; they sang Indian chants for all the children. There were no complaints about the tepee not being authentic. In following years, when there were no Indian students, the Indian parents still came to her classroom to sing and dance for the delighted children, and the children sang the songs throughout the rest of the year.

Although children feel most comfortable with the music of their own culture, they should be exposed to other music. The teacher will often find people who are willing to share the songs of their culture. The older people of the community like to teach the songs they loved as children. Even "Old World" songs in foreign languages do not frustrate young children because they use language as a "toy" at their age.

TEACHING VALUES THROUGH MUSIC

Those who choose the musical activities for children need to be aware that values are taught through music. The values that are taught depend on the teacher's *philosophy* (basic beliefs) of education. Some teachers believe they should not teach any material that shows their own personal beliefs. However, this is done without the individual realizing it. An example is in the choosing of music at Christmas time. If the teacher picks no songs about Santa Claus and does not encourage her children when they sing about Santa Claus,

M. C. Weller Pugmire

1. A - mer - i - ca, A - mer - i - ca, I'm glad that I live here. I'm
2. Oh, Can - a - da, Dear Can - a - da I'm glad that I live here. I'm

glad that I can play and sing, that I have no need to fear So I'll
glad that I can play and sing, that I have no need to fear So I'll

sing hur-ray for the U. S. A. God gave me this land of the free I will
sing hur-ray for dear Can-a - da God gave me this land of the free I will

try to do what He wants me to for peace and lib - er - ty
try to do what He wants me to for peace and lib - er - ty

Fig. 5-4 *For America, For Canada* (Cassette application song E).

she shows that she lacks support for the Santa Claus myth.

It can happen that a teacher may use a musical activity without realizing that it will conflict with the values taught in a child's home. The parents may complain, but the teacher should not get upset. She should use the incident to communicate with the parents. Often, greater understanding of the child results.

Many early childhood centers are run by agencies that have definite beliefs and values. Teachers in these situations should be aware that students learn most rapidly during their early childhood years and that value systems are formed at this time. Teachers in church schools guide value development through music; military day care centers teach appreciation of the armed services and patriotism. Actually, learning values through music continues throughout the child's life.

EMOTIONAL REACTIONS DIFFER

Most responses to music are very personal. Some people have had the experience of hearing music that made them feel happy and full of joy and have found that the same music irritated another listener. As the teacher learns about the individual differences of her children, she will consider their emotional reactions to musical selections. She will use music to help her children express their feelings —

sometimes through drawings made while they listen to music.

THE MUSICALLY TALENTED CHILD

While determining individual preferences of each child, the teacher may find a child who has a great deal of natural music ability or a great interest in music. The teacher should give special help to this child. Some suggestions are listed:

- Let the child play the piano. Often the piano is regarded as a piece of furniture instead of a musical instrument. Very young children often surprise adults by "picking out a tune by ear." The child

Fig. 5-5 "I Never Wory" (drawn by a four-year-old).

should be encouraged if he has this talent. His parents should be made aware of it, of course.

- Individual attention should be given to the musically talented child. Perhaps some one-to-one activities can be arranged — such as a visit to hear a local musician practice. The teacher herself cannot do this, probably, but she can arrange for a volunteer or high school student to do it.

- Help the child (and other children as well) learn of careers in which music plays a major role. People who hold such jobs could be invited to the early childhood classroom. The teacher could see that the child had a chance to use dramatic play to "try on" the roles of these musical workers.

- Help the child gain a respect for music and for the talent he has.

WAYS TO HELP THE MUSICALLY UNSURE TEACHER OR ASSISTANT

So often music is the area of early childhood education where teachers and assistants lack confidence because they consider themselves to be poor musicians. Teachers who prefer to teach subjects other than music because they feel unsure of themselves should ask the following questions. Hopefully these questions

will help them see that they have more ability to help children enjoy music than they think they have.

- Am I a good listener? How did I get that way? Do I listen to records or the radio? Why do I enjoy it? Do I learn the words to a song as I listen to it? How can I use my ability as a good listener to help a child be a better listener?

- Am I a good dancer? How do I respond as I move to music? Do I ever dance alone around my house? What inspires me to dance or move to the music I hear? Was I in a high school drill team or similar club where we moved to a drum beat? How could I use my ability to respond to music with movement to help the children I teach?

- Do I play any musical instrument? If so, am I sharing this ability with the children? If I played only for a short while, am I using that knowledge of the instrument to help the children learn how instruments work and what sounds they make?

- Does music ever excite me or depress me? Have I taken the time or effort to understand my reactions? If I did this, would it help me understand the children's responses to music?

The biggest help for the musically unsure student is to learn more about music and to try out many musical activities and ask for help. Many people with musical talents have learned to use their time wisely in order to practice. Thus they find time to help others.

WAYS TO HELP THE MUSICALLY UNSURE CHILD

Most children who do not want to take part in musical activities are expressing their preferences as an individual. Often, it is not the music that they are objecting to by not

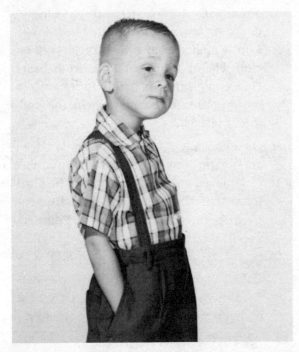

Fig. 5-6 "I don't want to sing today — and what's more, I'm not going to!"

participating; it is just a part of growing and developing. The child can say, "Look at me, I don't want to sing today, and what's more, I'm not going to!" Sometimes, the child who is not taking an active part simply wants to listen or to observe the other children. Often the teacher can help the child most by not forcing him to take part with the group. She can help him on an individual basis. Eventually, he may participate, but until then, the teacher can look for his strengths in other musical activities.

The child who speaks another language besides English at home (*bilingual child*) should be considered. Maybe he would prefer to sing in his "home" language, and have his parents come to school to sing with him. This is an excellent experience for all of the children.

TEAM TEACHING IN MUSIC

There are many teaching roles in music for the teacher to consider. She may find that she prefers one role to another or that she is exceptionally good at one. The various teaching roles may be performed by a music teaching team as follows:

- *Innovator* — This is the person who looks for new musical activities for the classroom. She decides ways that these ideas could be used.

- *Researcher* — This person seeks out the music that is part of the cultural heritage of the area. She also finds out the type of music that is heard in each child's home.

- *Media-Manager* — This person takes care of the instructional aids used to teach music and stimulate musical activities. She also makes new materials and knows where to order commercial materials.

- *Follow-through Expert* — This person keeps track of the music activities that have been taught because she knows the children love to repeat activities and songs. She also sees that the parents' suggestions are carried through, if possible.

- *Musical Leader* — This person actually teaches the new songs, games, and other activities.

- *Evaluator* — This person knows the goals of the music program very well. She keeps a written record to see that the goals of the music program are being reached for each child.

Sometimes one teacher finds that she is called upon to perform all six roles. She should realize what a big job this is! She should try to have parents and/or volunteers do some of these jobs.

EVALUATION FORM	
Child's Name	Parent
Address	Date
Goal 　Enjoyment 　Listening 　Responses 　Building Musical Foundation 　Creativity	
Suggestions for Parent Involvement	

Fig. 5-7 Sample form to be used to record individual progress toward the goals of the music program.

SUMMARY

People have different emotional reactions to music. Culture has very definite influences on their musical preferences. The teacher helps the children learn about their own musical heritage and about that of others. The musically unsure teacher and child try to find musical interests of their own. The teaching of music demands many roles, and the teacher should find out which roles she prefers. She should guide others to help her in a teaching team.

SUGGESTED ACTIVITIES

- With a group of classmates and/or parents list all the musical activities in your area that are influenced by culture. If possible, do this in two different settings so that you can look for additional cultural influence between the two sessions.

- Name some of the songs that are part of the cultural heritage of your area. If possible collect the music and words to the music and add them to your file.

- Name every emotion you can think of.

- List careers in which music plays a major role.

- Go through the unit and answer the questions. Write down the ways that your answers might help you to be a better music teacher.

- Play this game: Form a "musical teaching team" with five other members of your class. Determine which role each will perform. Have a meeting to determine the planned musical experiences for one week in a classroom. After a short break, have another meeting to report on the effectiveness of your role on the musical team during the week. (This is done most effectively if each group member is prepared to take all roles in the game. As the game progresses, she can then add to the discussion in a more meaningful way.)

REVIEW

A. Indicate the best choice for each of the following.

1. Culture is

a. Attending musical concerts.
b. The ways of our lives that are part of our "flesh and bones."
c. The ways of our society that we accept as natural and "right."
d. Both b and c.

2. In simpler cultures, children

a. Were not around music.
b. Were responsible for musical performances.
c. Often took part in adult musical activities.
d. None of the above.

3. The teacher should

a. Ignore the cultural heritage around her and emphasize standard music.
b. Encourage parent involvement to bring cultural heritage to the class.
c. Emphasize cultural heritage only if she has children of that culture in the class.
d. Develop her own culture.

4. Emotional responses to music

    a. Are usually the same for most people.
    b. Should be avoided because they can upset the child.
    c. Can be different for each person.
    d. Are not important in the study of music.

5. The musically talented child

    a. Cannot be identified in the early years.
    b. Usually overreacts emotionally to music.
    c. Should be given individual help and encouragement.
    d. Is hard to handle.

6. Teaching values through music

    a. Is sometimes done without the teacher realizing it.
    b. Is the wrong thing to do.
    c. Works against the musical goals.
    d. Is very hard to do.

7. The biggest help for the musically unsure student is to

    a. Take private singing lessons.
    b. Learn to play an instrument.
    c. Join a dance club or drill team.
    d. Learn more about music and try as many musical activities
       as possible.

8. Music sung in other languages

    a. Often helps the bilingual child.
    b. Should be avoided in early education.
    c. Is good because young children use language as a "toy."
    d. Both a and c.

B. Match the item in Column II with the correct item in Column I.

<table>
<tr><td align="center">I</td><td align="center">II</td></tr>
<tr><td>1. Reveal emotions experienced while listening to music</td><td>a. Bilingual child</td></tr>
<tr><td>2. Speaks another language in his home</td><td>b. Cultural heritage</td></tr>
<tr><td>3. Music that "belongs" to a group of people</td><td>c. Children's drawings
d. Innovator</td></tr>
<tr><td>4. Knows about the cultural heritage of the area</td><td>e. Researcher
f. Media-manager</td></tr>
<tr><td>5. Takes care of audiovisual aids</td><td>g. Follow-through expert</td></tr>
<tr><td>6. Finds new musical activities</td><td>h. Musical leader</td></tr>
<tr><td>7. Determines if goals are being reached</td><td>i. Evaluator</td></tr>
<tr><td>8. Sees that the parents' suggestions are used if possible</td><td>j. Philosophy of education</td></tr>
<tr><td>9. Actually teaches the musical activities</td><td></td></tr>
<tr><td>10. Basic beliefs about teaching</td><td></td></tr>
</table>

Section 3 Planning and Conducting Music Experiences

unit 6 the structured music period

OBJECTIVES

After studying this unit, the student should be able to

- Write a lesson plan in which a concept of music is taught.
- Write a lesson plan using music to teach another part of the curriculum.
- Choose a lesson "starter" to teach a group of children.

The *structured music period* is planned music time. It is often held to teach the child a *concept* (an idea or thought) about music. Sometimes the structured music period is used to teach a concept in other lessons, such as social studies or science. The student should remember that there are many types of schools for the young child. In some types, there are many structured periods. In others, there are few. However, almost always there are times when an idea in music needs to be taught.

There is a difference between teaching and learning, of course. Each child must *learn* (get knowledge in a subject or skill in an art) for himself. Those who *teach* (show others how to do something) can help. The *lesson plan* is a guide which leads to better teaching.

The beginning student will often ask why she should write out a lesson plan. The experienced teacher knows that she organizes her lesson better and knows what concepts she is developing as she makes a plan. It also helps her in her future teaching as she builds up her file with good plans.

Many schools have their own outlines for lesson plans. The one presented in this text, figure 6-1, helps the student gain the skill necessary for writing lesson plans.

LESSON PLAN FOR MUSIC

It makes a difference in the lesson plan whether it is to be given to large or small groups

51

of children. The place of the lesson is also considered. (A change of place adds interest, but the child often needs regular places and routines.) First, the question is asked, "What is it that I want the child to learn?" The answer is written in *A — Concept to Learn*. Next, the teacher thinks about how much each child already knows about the general idea in the plan. She writes this in *B — What the Children Already Know*. The next part, *C*, is very important. The teacher needs to check to see if each child is learning. In order

---

MUSIC LESSON PLAN

Date and Approximate Time   Number in Group

Area of School   Teacher

Name of song or Music

A.   Concept to Learn

B.   What Children Already Know

C.   Learning Check:

At the end of this lesson, each student should be able to

D.   *Procedure to Follow*   E.   *Material to Use*

    1.   1.
    2.   (ETC.)   2.   (ETC.)

F.   Evaluation of Plan

Did each child do the action described in C? (Note those who did not)

G.   Suggestions for Future Teaching:

Fig. 6-1 Sample Music Lesson Plan.

---

to do this, she needs to provide a learning opportunity that she can check by observing or hearing. The student will note that the same "learning check" is suggested for this lesson plan as is used at the beginning of each of the units in this text, *C — At the end of the lesson, each child should be able to. . .* Using the information just recorded, the teacher then plans for *D — Procedure to Follow*. At each step she lists *E — Materials to Use*. After she finishes teaching the plan, she fills in *F — Evaluation of Plan*. Her final comments are listed in *G — Suggestions for Future Teaching*.

CONCEPT LESSON PLAN FOR MUSIC

An example of a plan for teaching a concept lesson in music is shown. The children in this school have become interested in music, and the teacher wants them to learn more about printed music. The class has already had one structured lesson about printed music.

This lesson plan has been used several times with three-, four-, and five-year-old children. A bad feature of the lesson is that it becomes more of an art experience than a music experience. The good part of this lesson is that children want to do this activity for several days. Each child did pass the learning check. Parents became involved. Many played the music the child had "made" on the piano or asked the teacher to play it for them.

USING MUSIC IN A RELATED AREA

An example of a plan for using music to teach a lesson is also described. The main point of this lesson is to teach manners. This is part of the social studies curriculum; that is, the child is being helped to get along with others. Music is used as a tool in this lesson. This lesson plan also has proved successful with young children. They sing the song and "play school" with the "good manner animals." As the children use good manners through the school year, the song can be sung. It is more effective than just talking about good manners.

STARTING A LESSON

The student can see that in each of the two plans an object is used to start the lesson. This object directs the attention of each child in the group to the same place. In the first lesson, the child looked at the new chart. In the second lesson, the child looked at the toy monkey. These objects attracted the child's interest. The teacher used this interest to help the child want to learn. This is called *motivation*. The good teacher knows ways to gain the child's interest.

A "lesson starter" could be a person. A new volunteer in the classroom who likes to sing could present the song, *Manners Can Be Fun*, for the first time. The fact that the aide

LESSON PLAN TO TEACH A MUSIC CONCEPT

A. Concept to Learn — Notes are put on a staff so that people can make music.

B. What Children Already Know — They have learned the term, "staff." They have seen lots of printed music.

C. Learning Check — At the end of this lesson, each child should be able to
  - Paste notes correctly on a music staff.
  - Tell the teacher (when she plays his notes on the piano) that notes are put on a staff so that people can make music.

D. *Procedure to Follow:*	E. *Materials to Use*
1. Show the new chart. Let the children see the notes of the song. Listen to their comments, especially those about the printed music on the chart.	1. Large chart with music to a song the children enjoy printed on it.
2. See if the children remember the term, *staff*. Point to the staff on the chart and the staff on the flannelboard.	2. Flannelboard with a staff on it.
3. Put black felt notes on the music flannelboard. Use the term, *notes* and have the children tell where they have seen notes. Lead into brief discussion that notes are used to make music.	3. Black felt notes.
4. Have children paste notes on paper with a staff on it. Give help so that the stems of the notes go straight up or down. (Show example on chart, figure 6-2.)	4. White butcher paper with staff drawn on it. Notes cut from construction paper. Glue or paste.
5. Play the notes on the piano. Have each child tell the teacher (or answer questions) that notes are put on a staff so that people can make music. (Figure 6-3.)	5. Piano

F. Evaluation of Plan

  Did each child do the action described in "C"? _____

  Notes: Many children were not able to get the stems of the notes straight up or down. Some previous experience would have helped as this seemed to take away from the music learning.

G. Suggestions for Future Teaching

  Leave the notes, staff paper and glue out for "free-choice time" on the day following the lesson. Review lesson again in the next week.

  Next time point out what "notes" are many times before trying this activity.

LESSON PLAN TO USE MUSIC TO TEACH A CONCEPT IN A RELATED AREA

Name of Song: *Manners Can Be Fun*

A.	Concept to Learn — Manners help us get along with other people.
B.	What the Children Already Know — Names of the poster board animals used to teach the song. Some ideas about manners.
C.	Learning Check — At the end of this lesson, each child should be able to • Name five good manners that children can practice.

D. *Procedure to Follow*	E. *Materials to Use*
1. Hold a stuffed monkey. When the children's attention centers on the monkey, sing the whole first verse of *Manners Can Be Fun*, figure 6-3. (Not too fast!)	1. Stuffed animal (monkey)
2. Ask children to sing with you. Hold up monkey made from picture in text.	2. Monkey made from poster board, figure 6-4. (Words can be put on back of monkey illustration.)
3. Have a brief talk with children on manners. Let them tell the teacher that manners help us get along with others.	3. None
4. Teach the other four verses.	4. Beaver, elephant, rabbit, frog made from pictures in this text.
5. Have each child tell the names of the five good manners that the animals stand for. When he does, pin an animal cutout on him as a reward.	5. Small cutouts of the animals.

F.	Evaluation of the Plan Did each child do the action in "C"? _____No_____ (James and Sue lost interest)
G.	Suggestions for Future Teaching It would be better to teach the song in two sessions. Five verses were too many!

Fig. 6-2 **The teacher helps the child paste the notes so that the stems go straight up or down.**

LaFawn Holt

M. C. Weller Pugmire

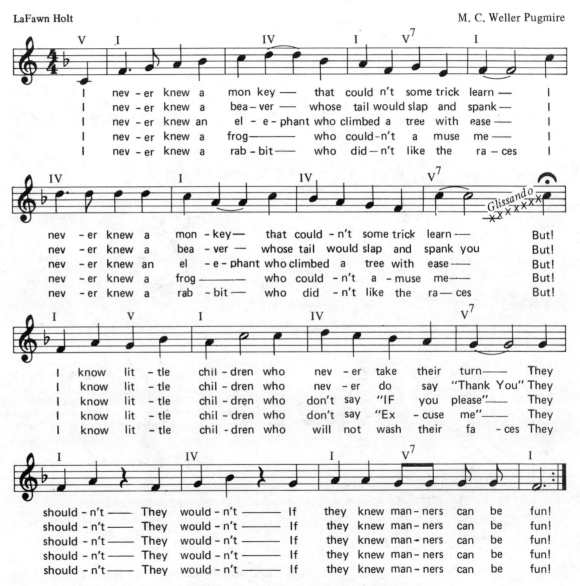

I nev – er knew a mon key —— that could n't some trick learn ——
I nev – er knew a bea – ver —— whose tail would slap and spank ——
I nev – er knew an el – e – phant who climbed a tree with ease ——
I nev – er knew a frog —— who could-n't a muse me ——
I nev – er knew a rab – bit —— who did – n't like the ra – ces

nev – er knew a mon – key — that could – n't some trick learn —— But!
nev – er knew a bea – ver — whose tail would slap and spank you But!
nev – er knew an el – e – phant who climbed a tree with ease —— But!
nev – er knew a frog —— who could – n't a – muse me —— But!
nev – er knew a rab – bit —— who did – n't like the ra – ces But!

I know lit – tle chil – dren who nev – er take their turn —— They
I know lit – tle chil – dren who nev – er do say "Thank You" They
I know lit – tle chil – dren who don't say "IF you please"—— They
I know lit – tle chil – dren who don't say "Ex – cuse me"—— They
I know lit – tle chil – dren who will not wash their fa – ces They

should – n't —— They would – n't —— If they knew man – ners can be fun!
should – n't —— They would – n't —— If they knew man – ners can be fun!
should – n't —— They would – n't —— If they knew man – ners can be fun!
should – n't —— They would – n't —— If they knew man – ners can be fun!
should – n't —— They would – n't —— If they knew man – ners can be fun!

Fig. 6-3 *Manners Can Be Fun* (Cassette song 25-F).

Fig. 6-4 "Good manner animals" to go with song, *Manners Can Be Fun.*
(Illustrator: LaFawn Holt)

is new will hold the children's interest. (The teacher is still in charge, of course.) A sailor father could sing a song about the sea. A visitor from another country could do a dance learned at home.

The most used lesson starters are songs or finger plays that are well known. The music to *Here We Go 'Round the Mulberry Bush*, figure 6-5, could be used. The last action used would be "This is the way we wash our faces." The teacher could lead into the manners lesson by saying, "One reason we wash our faces is so that others will enjoy looking at us. We look better when we're clean!"

She would hold up the rabbit and sing that verse of *Manners Can Be Fun*.

ENDING THE LESSON

The student can also see that in each of the two plans, the lesson was ended by giving each child a reward for doing the action in "C". In the first plan the child's reward was hearing the music he had "made" played on the piano. In the second lesson plan, the child was given an animal cutout when he named the five good manners. One of the best rewards is the teacher's sincere pride in the child. This can be shown with a smile, a nod of the head, or a simple word of praise.

Here we go round the Mul-ber-ry bush, The

Mul-ber-ry bush, the Mul-ber-ry bush.

Here we go round the Mul-ber-ry bush, So

ear-ly in the morn-ing.

Fig. 6-5 *Here We Go 'Round the Mulberry Bush.*

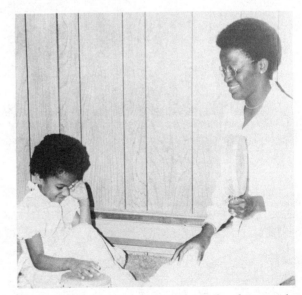

Fig. 6-6 The child is helped by a smile of approval.

Sometimes the teacher thinks it is not worth the time it takes to do parts "F" and "G" of the lesson plan. However, if she wants to be the best music teacher she can be, she will do this. It will help her see the good and bad points of her lesson.

One more thing should be checked as the teacher evaluates her lesson. She should ask herself who did most of the talking. The best teachers get the children to participate. The best teachers show the way instead of talking so much themselves.

SUMMARY

The structured music period is a planned time in which a concept is taught. Each child must learn the idea for himself. Many schools have their own outlines for lesson plans. However, a plan for teaching a concept about music and a plan for using music to teach in other areas are given. These can be used as guides.

Teachers can use "lesson starters" to motivate the child to learn. These can be objects, people, or a familiar song. The person who wants to be a really good teacher will evaluate her own work. She will try to get each child to take part. At the end of her lesson, she will check to see how well she has done.

SUGGESTED ACTIVITIES

- Choose a simple musical concept. Write a lesson plan using the form in the text. Teach this plan to a group of children (or class members). Evaluate when lesson is over.

- Make the "Good-Action Animals" shown in the unit. (Enlarge them with an opaque projector, if available.) Put these in your file.

- Choose some part of the curriculum to teach, using music. Write a lesson plan using the form in the text. Teach this plan to a group of children or class members. Evaluate when lesson is over.

- Arrange to teach a short music lesson in a local school. Use a "lesson starter" to motivate the children's interest.

REVIEW

A.   List all the actions related to music that you can think of.

(Example: Hum) For each of these actions finish the statement "At the end of this lesson, each child should be able to. . ." as if it were part of a lesson plan. (Example: Hum the first part of *America*.)

B. For each area of the curriculum (math, social studies, science, and language arts), list musical activities that may be used to teach in these areas.

C. Match each item in Column II with the correct item in Column I.

I

1. An idea or thought
2. An object, person, or song used to attract the child's attention.
3. To get knowledge or skill in an art
4. A planned music experience
5. Guide to organized teaching
6. Show others how to do something
7. Noting the good and bad points of a lesson
8. To get the child to want to learn

II

a. Structured music period
b. Teaching
c. Concept
d. "Lesson starter"
e. Learning
f. Lesson plan
g. Motivation
h. Evaluation

D. Briefly answer each of the following.

1. Why does the experienced teacher write lesson plans?

2. Name at least two facts that will make a difference when teaching a lesson.

3. Name several "lesson starters."

4. Name several "rewards" that can be given to children.

5. How much should a teacher talk during a structured lesson?

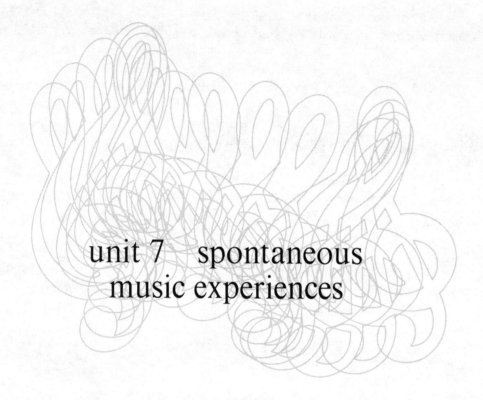

unit 7   spontaneous music experiences

OBJECTIVES

After studying this unit, the student should be able to

- List three spontaneous music experiences for infants and toddlers.
- List six examples of spontaneous music activities for the child aged three to seven.
- Write anecdotal records while observing a musical experience.
- Make a "prop box" that will encourage musical activities.

The *spontaneous music period* is one that happens on the "spur-of-the-moment." An event takes place, or a child shows interest, and the time is right for a music experience. Since the zest to learn is there, the child often seems to learn faster at this time than in a structured period.

One cannot say, however, that the spontaneous music period is unplanned. The teacher who understands young children knows that certain events will happen at some time and that interest will be shown. She must be prepared because the teacher who is ready to make use of the child's interest when it is shown finds a quick learner. Her file has aids for teaching that are ready. She looks for events that will lead to music experiences. She listens for questions that show interest in music.

The spontaneous music time can be compared with the structured music time discussed in unit 6. The lesson on the concept that notes are put on a staff so that people can make music could be taught when the children show interest in the new chart. Some will argue that this interest will not be shown all the time. Others answer that when such interest is shown, the child is more likely to learn.

SPONTANEOUS EXPERIENCES FOR INFANTS AND TODDLERS

Many of the activities in this book have been for the child from age three to age seven.

M. C. Weller – Pugmire

M. C. Weller – Pugmire

2 beats per measure

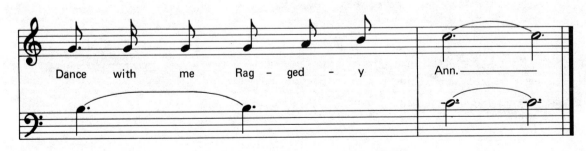

Fig. 7-1 *Raggedy Ann* (Cassette song 23-A).

Spontaneous music experiences are very important for infants and toddlers, too. Teachers should be very aware of them! Look for them!

The infant begins rocking and cooing to the country music played in a house next to the center. The assistant notices this and finds some good country-western music to play.

The toddler, who loves large toys, may come to the center with a big Raggedy Ann doll. The teacher or assistant can say, "Look how Raggedy Ann moves. She flops." The teacher and children pretend to be Raggedy Ann while they sing *Raggedy Ann*, figure 7-1. The assistant puts music on the phonograph and moves Raggedy Ann to the music. The toddlers move, too!

In a new shipment of toys for the center is a wooden pull toy. The assistant notices that when the toddlers pull the toy on different surfaces, such as on tiles or on a wooden floor, a different sound is made. "Listen to the sounds," she says to the toddlers. Together, they find different surfaces to make different sounds. They pull the toy on a smooth cement sidewalk and across a piece of cardboard.

A child finds an old mallet (used to beat a drum) at the bottom of a toy box. He starts banging on the floor. The assistant finds different drums, cereal boxes, and pans for him to bang. She shows him how to pound softly as well as loudly.

SPONTANEOUS EXPERIENCES FOR THE CHILD AGED THREE TO SEVEN

Many things happen during the play of children three to seven that bring about spontaneous music times. These may be called spur-of-the-moment experiences. The student should again note that many of these can be predicted.

Dave is holding a garden hose. He says, "I help my Daddy water the lawn." The assistant says, "I know a good song about that." She sings *When We're Helping,* figure 7-3. Later, after snack time, she and Dave teach the song to the other children. This song is sung whenever the children are helping.

Six-year-old Jay shows more interest in music than the other children. He asks many questions. One day he asks about the treble clef sign 𝄞 and the bass clef sign 𝄢. The teacher tells him that the treble clef sign shows that the music is to be sung by women and children. The bass clef sign shows that the music is to be sung by men. She and Jay go to the piano and she plays notes from the treble clef and then notes from the bass clef. Other children gather around the piano. The teacher asks questions to see that each child understands. "Can we make this kind?" ask the children. The teacher has staffs drawn on butcher paper. She shows the children how to make the treble clef sign:

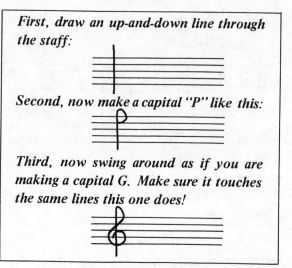

First, draw an up-and-down line through the staff:

Second, now make a capital "P" like this:

Third, now swing around as if you are making a capital G. Make sure it touches the same lines this one does!

Three-year-old Chico bursts into the nursery school to tell about his new shoes. The

Fig. 7-2 The child's actions can be a spur to music.

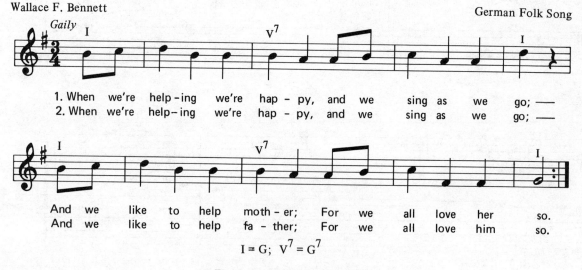

Wallace F. Bennett

German Folk Song

Gaily

1. When we're help-ing we're hap-py, and we sing as we go;——
2. When we're help-ing we're hap-py, and we sing as we go;——

And we like to help moth-er; For we all love her so.
And we like to help fa-ther; For we all love him so.

$I = G; \quad V^7 = G^7$

Fig. 7-3 *When We're Helping.*

M. C. Weller Pugmire

M. C. Weller Pugmire

Lively

Look at Chi - co,— Look at Chi - co,— He has new

shoes. he jumps high - er,— he runs fast - er,— 'Cause he has new shoes.

Marching Tempo

New shoes are such fun to wear, they take you quick-ly ev 'ry where.

New shoes make you feel so grand, Just like you could lead a band! Look at

Return to lively temp

Chi - co — Look at Chi - co,— He has new shoes. He is

danc - ing,— He is pranc - ing — 'Cause he has new shoes.

Fig. 7-4 *Look at Chico's New Shoes*: **Fit the child's name in the song. (The very young child can sing the first two lines.) (Cassette song 22-0)**

teacher says, "Time to sing *Look at Chico's Shoes*," figure 7-4. The teacher knows she has to be careful if there is a child present who may not have any new clothing during the year; however, almost every child has something new to wear at some time during the year.

Community events encourage spontaneous singing and dancing. Paul is happy about going skating with his big sister. The assistant puts on the record of *The Skater's Waltz* and the children move to the music, pretending they are skating.

Jan's mother has twins. Reports of new babies are common, but twins are very special. The teacher remembers a song that can be used. In honor of the new twins, the whole group sings *Two to...*, figure 7-5. Doll play is encouraged. The children play with two dolls rather than one.

The children are playing "campfire." They have dressed up in old clothes. Their teacher sings the campfire song, *Kum Ba Yah*, figure 7-6. The song is sung slowly. It is different than most children's songs. The teacher helps them understand how music can express feelings.

Lee wants to tell about her dream. The assistant knows that four-year-olds sometimes have feelings of fright about dreams. She listens. She teaches Lee the song, *You Tell Me Your Dream*, figure 7-7. Later Lee's mother says that she often sings the song at home, now.

Fig. 7-5 *Two to . . .* (Cassette song 25-E).

Bad dreams do not seem to bother her quite as much.

ANECDOTAL RECORDS

An *anecdotal record* is a brief written account of what a child does at a certain time. Anecdotal records are made for many reasons. One purpose is to help the staff understand the child better. Such records show whether or not a child is doing a certain thing. For ex-

2. Someone's crying, Lord, Kum ba yah!
3. Someone's singing, Lord, Kum ba yah!
4. Someone's praying, Lord, Kum ba yah!

*Pronounced: "Koom-bah-yah."
(Kum ba yah– Come near me.)

Fig. 7-6 *Kum Ba Yah* (Cassette application song D).

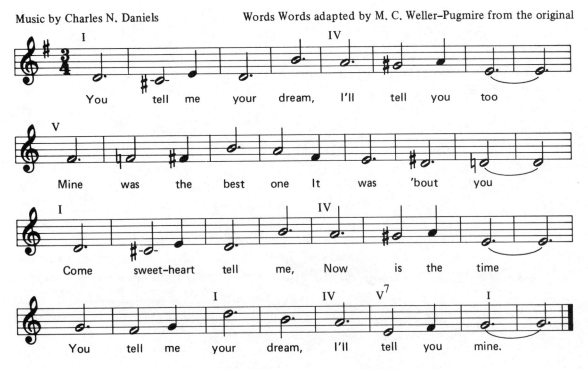

Music by Charles N. Daniels

Words Words adapted by M. C. Weller–Pugmire from the original

You tell me your dream, I'll tell you too

Mine was the best one It was 'bout you

Come sweet-heart tell me, Now is the time

You tell me your dream, I'll tell you mine.

Fig. 7-7 *You Tell Me Your Dream* **(Cassette song 21-D).**

Fig. 7-8 When the child wakes up it will be time to sing *You Tell Me Your Dream.*

9-26-7

John was singing. Kurt poked him three times. Kurt did not look at John while he poked him. John then moved up and pushed Bing aside. Bing objected. The group had to stop singing while Miss Smith quieted the boys.

Fig. 7-9 Example of an Anecdotal Record.

ample, the staff may think John is always causing trouble during music periods. An assistant is asked to write records of his actions during several music periods. She writes only what she sees and hears. (She does not use terms such as, "I think" or "I feel.") After making records for several days, she may find it is Kurt who is poking John. Then the problem can be solved, because the staff has something to use to help both John and Kurt, figure 7-9.

Anecdotal records can show a child's progress. Ann, for example, is very shy. The staff makes a plan to help Ann join the group for music time. A daily anecdotal record kept for a week or two shows if the plan is working.

One of the best uses for anecdotal records is for parent-teacher interaction. Parents like to know what their child does at school. A brief report of facts about their child's actions is often appreciated. One mother tells of an assistant in a nursery school who wrote down a chant that her son kept singing. The mother tells how much this anecdotal record meant to her. It was a time of stress in her home. Her son's chant made her smile. The fact that he called his nine-year-old sister "Sister-Mama" showed her something about how they were getting along.

Not all assistants or teachers can write down the notes to a child's chant, but they can write down the words. They can be aware that action for anecdotal records often takes place during unplanned music periods.

Two ways to find time to make anecdotal records are (1) to carry a pencil and some 3″ x 5″ cards in a pocket and (2) to have pads of note paper and pencils mounted on the wall. Then, when a child does something that the teacher wants to record, she can jot it down while it is on her mind. Later, she can file it in the child's folder to be used by the staff or given to the parents.

Some records that a teacher or assistant makes should be kept confidential. An example is any information that might hurt the child or family. A child may even sing something that should be held in confidence. This is part of the ethics of teaching.

PROP BOXES FOR MUSIC

Prop boxes have objects in them that motivate children's dramatic play. A music prop box has things in it to start dramatic play about music. Some of the things that might be in such a prop box are baton ("stick" for leading music), music stand, old music, instruments the children can play with, and old tuxedo jackets.

The children would have to have some musical background to use such a prop box. They might have had a field trip to hear an orchestra, or they might have watched a children's concert on TV. Many spontaneous music experiences could come from this play. The

teacher could show them about the baton and have the children learn the word.

Another prop box might stress playing "marching band." Old hats from band uniforms would be in this box. Records of good marches could be there. These items lead to marching movements.

Old band hats, tuxedos, and other props can be bought at rummage sales very inexpensively. People will sometimes give these to a school. It is good if the different prop boxes are the same size. This makes storage easier. Boxes that held fruit are good. They can be obtained free at a food store. Local business places often have boxes of the same size that

their supplies come in. They usually will give these boxes to a school, if they are asked.

SUMMARY

A spontaneous music period is one that takes place on the "spur-of-the-moment." The person who knows children can predict many events that will happen through the year that will lead to music times. Infants and toddlers learn from experiences of this type. Preschoolers have things happen in their play and work that "spur" music times. Helpful anecdotal records can be written during music periods. Prop boxes can be made to encourage the children in desired musical activities.

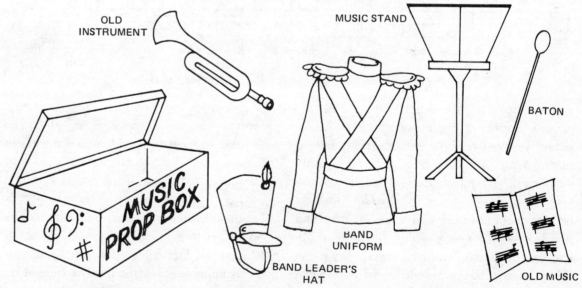

Fig. 7-10 A music prop box has things in it to start dramatic play about music.

SUGGESTED ACTIVITIES

- With members of your class, list events that have happened to you during the past twenty-four hours that might encourage a musical activity. Use imagination! Write down the musical activities.

- Observe a group of children in a day care center during play time. Note every activity that might have led to a spontaneous musical experience.

- Observe a music period with young children. Write an anecdotal record for the parents of one or two of the children.

- Practice making treble clef and bass clef signs.

- Ask each member of the class to bring one or two items for a musical prop box. Tell what activity the item might start.

Note: If you are working with children or will be soon, make a musical prop box to use with them.

REVIEW

A. Match each item in Column II with the correct item in Column I.

I	II
1. Writing (brief) that tells something a child has done	a. Spontaneous
2. "Spur-of-the-moment"	b. Anecdotal records
3. "Stick" used to lead music	c. Mallet
4. Used to beat a drum	d. Prop boxes
5. Have objects in them to motivate dramatic play	e. Baton
6. Treble clef sign	f. 𝄢
7. Bass clef sign	g. 𝄞
8. Event that brings about a spontaneous music time	h. "Spur Experience"

B.   Indicate the best choice(s) for each of the following.

1. The spontaneous music experience

   a. Is entirely unplanned.
   b. Is a spur-of-the-moment music time.
   c. Is not a worthwhile activity.
   d. Is better for older children.

2. The teacher who understands children

   a. Knows certain events will happen and interests will be shown.
   b. Knows structured music periods are always best.
   c. Knows infants and toddlers are too young for music.
   d. Knows she can best prepare when interests are shown.

3. Spontaneous music experiences for toddlers and infants

   a. Are not worth the effort.
   b. Are important.
   c. Must be planned.
   d. Must be done by the music teacher.

4. Spontaneous music times for children aged 3 to 7

   a. Are often brought about through play.
   b. Must be planned.
   c. Cannot ever be predicted.
   d. Have little musical value.

5. Music prop boxes

   a. Are wound up to be played.
   b. Are used to store music equipment.
   c. Motivate dramatic play about music.
   d. Are used mainly for toddlers.

6. When making anecdotal records, a person

   a. Must not know the child.
   b. Must first study psychology.
   c. Should write her own feelings about the child.
   d. Should record only what she sees or hears.

7. Which statements are true about anecdotal records?

   a. Can help the staff understand a child better.
   b. Are used only in teaching music.
   c. Are sometimes used for good teacher-parent interaction.
   d. Can show a child's progress.

8. A good way to find time to make anecdotal records is to

   a. Carry 3" x 5" cards and write them immediately.
   b. Assign someone else to do it.
   c. Wait until the children go home.
   d. Write them the next morning before school.

C. Suggest an appropriate musical activity for infants and toddlers based on each of the following "spur" experiences.

   1. A gift of money is given to the day care center to buy toys.

   2. The infants and toddlers seem to relax more when soft music is played.

D. Suggest an appropriate musical activity for children 3 to 7 based on the following "spur" experiences.

   1. Jim reports his mother had a new baby.

   2. Lou brings a songbook that has songs from a popular TV show.

   3. Jane's father is a disc jockey. The children visit his studio.

   4. Lynn brings to school a ukelele that is smaller than the teacher's.

5. The children notice signs of spring.

6. The high school band practices in front of the center.

E. Briefly answer each of the following.

1. Discuss the reasons for and against the spontaneous music period.

2. When should anecdotal records be kept confidential?

3. Why are prop boxes used?

Section 4 Music Areas and Activities

unit 8 the "music corner" and related areas

OBJECTIVES

After studying this unit, the student should be able to

- Arrange a given space for musical activities.
- Name one musical activity for each major holiday.
- List musical activities for each area of the curriculum.

The use of space is challenging to the early childhood educator who must decide which areas to use for specific activities. Space should be provided for activities that will help achieve the musical goals.

Available space is varied according to the physical facilities used. Perhaps a small corner in a home is all that is available. Other programs may be located in an entire basement of a church or community center. Sometimes, open space may have to be limited. Outdoor space may be available. In any case, the space must be analyzed for its most effective use.

The time spent in creating an atmosphere for musical learning is time well spent. The child who knows he has room to create and listen to music will do so more often than one who does not. The child's gain is the teacher's reward for making the effort to design the space effectively.

DESIGNING ENVIRONMENTS

Information about setting up learning areas is important. Too many articles for the child to handle cause confusion. Pictures become "part of the wall" to a child, after three or four days. Frequent change or rearranging is necessary, and a routine time for changing an area is beneficial. However, this should not hinder spontaneous change by a teacher in a learning center.

Tables, shelves, and bulletin boards are usually considered when arranging a room. The ceiling, walls, and empty floor space should be considered, too. Mobiles can be hung from the ceiling and light fixtures. (Sometimes parents or the children can make these.) Walls can be painted, wallpapered, or have textured materials on them. Sometimes furniture or other play units need to be moved together to leave empty spaces.

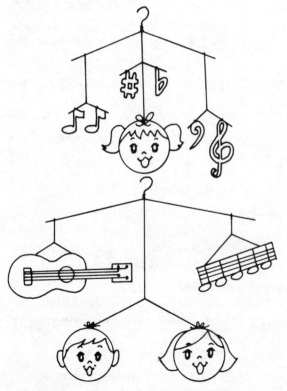

Fig. 8-1 Examples of musical mobiles.

These suggestions can be applied to the music corner. As often as twice a week, the assistant can change the pictures. Cutouts of notes and rests, made from textured materials are good. Simple musical charts can be made and displayed. Pictures that relate to music lead to singing and free movement activities.

The age level of the children influences the contents of the music corner. Younger preschoolers (two and one-half to three-year-olds) can be taught to use records and a simple record player. All of the records can be kept in a record cabinet or closet, with a few at a time displayed on a table at the child's level. Interest in the records is more intense if the display is changed often. For older children, more ideas leading to musical discoveries can be developed in the music learning center.

THE MUSIC AREA THROUGH THE YEAR

Holidays are not usually emphasized in early childhood education; however, they are part of the children's "here and now" existence. Showing how the music corner can be used at holiday times gives added ideas to those who are creating music learning centers.

Labor Day

As Labor Day is a time of final summer activities, songs and movement about summer fun are featured in the music corner. Older children draw pictures; younger children bring small articles from home to remind them of summer activities; everyone sings:

Fig. 8-2 A child's drawing of "A-fishing We Did Go."

> *A-fishing we did go.*
> *A-fishing we did go.*
> *We got our good wish,*
> *To catch a big fish.*
> *A-fishing we did go.*
>
> *Tune: A-Hunting We Will Go*

Veteran's Day

A container holding small flags on sticks for each child is on the table for Veteran's Day. Children march with the flags to quality recordings of march music.

Halloween

For Halloween, the assistant and the children cut ghosts (freehand) from butcher paper. The assistant encourages children to make up "eerie" ghost songs. These songs are recorded on a cassette and played back for the children.

Thanksgiving Day

A *mural* (large wall picture) entitled "We're Thankful We Can Sing" is made for Thanksgiving Day. Each child draws his picture on the mural. The name of his favorite song is printed by his picture. At music time, each child leads the class in singing his song.

Christmas

The children learn the song *The Sparkling Christmas Tree* early in the holiday season. The classroom Christmas tree is placed where

Fig. 8-3 *The Sparkling Christmas Tree* **(Cassette song 22-F).**

the children can "dance" around it. When this song is sung or played, the children move freely around the tree. They stop when the music tells them to look at the tree; then they continue moving.

Hanukkah

A menorah (traditional candle holder) is placed in the music area for Hanukkah. A Jewish parent tells the story of the menorah, a miracle. The children sing a song about Hanukkah time, figure 8-4.

New Year

A large staff and the notes of a chant may be drawn on a piece of butcher paper for New Year's Day. Words are drawn that correspond with each note. (See illustration) The children chant the words during the music period as the teacher points to the notes. (This is a readiness activity for reading music.)

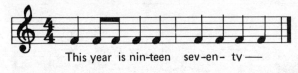

This year is nin-teen sev-en-ty——

Valentine's Day

The Autoharp is placed in the music corner. The teacher shows each child how to make a chord by pressing on the "C Maj" button with his right hand while he strums with a

pick held in his left hand. The following song is taught during music period:

(Strumming is indicated by underlining)

> Valentine's Day is a <u>spec</u>ial time
> For <u>mak</u>ing things,
> It's <u>true</u>.
> <u>Hearts</u> and
> <u>Doilies</u>,
> <u>I'll</u> make mine for <u>you</u>.
>
> Tune: *Little, Tom Tinker*

M. C. Pugmire

The assistant helps each child accompany himself on the Autoharp as he sings. Of course, hearts and doilies are available for the children to create valentines.

Note: Once this activity is mastered, the children will want to make up their own words for other holidays.

President's Day

The patriotic feeling of this holiday usually gives an uplift to the children and the

M. C. Weller – Pugmire

Burn lit – tle can – dles, burn, burn, burn,

Turn, lit – tle drei – del. turn, turn, turn.

Shine lit – tle can – dles, shine, shine, shine.

This is hap – py Han – u – kkah – time.

Fig. 8-4 *Happy Hanukkah Time* (Cassette song 23-D).

Fig. 8-5 *President's Day* (Cassette song 24-F): Even the young child can learn to play the chords of the simple accompaniment.

M. C. Weller Pugmire

M. C. Weller Pugmire

Fig. 8-6 *Mother, You're Special* **(Cassette song 25-C): The very young child would sing only the last two lines.**

school. The song *Presidents' Day*, figure 8-5, has an easy-to-play rhythmical accompaniment that starts before the singing does. Some of the children will be able to play this. Show those who are interested in the piano how to do it. Let them try. Interested children who are five or older seem to do this quite easily. The song becomes a favorite.

Easter

Since the weather is usually milder at the time of Easter, this is a good time to go for a walk to listen for the sounds of nature. A collection of items found on this walk can be brought back and placed in the music corner for later discussion. (Examples: Twigs that crackled underfoot, leaves from the bushes that rustled, a bird's feather that reminded them of listening for a bird's song.)

Mother's Day

A simple but appreciated gift for mother is a song, *Mother, You're Special,* figure 8-6. The song could be written on a chart for the music corner. A sign is placed by the chart, "We'll sing this song for our mothers on Mother's Day."

A song for grandmothers is nice, also. Most children have a grandmother (or two) who is very dear to them, figure 8-7.

Father's Day

Imitating the movements that fathers make while they work is an enjoyable activity for the children near Father's Day. The teacher plays *Here We Go 'Round the Mulberry Bush,* figure 6-5, on the piano. Her assistant says, "Miguel, show us what your Dad does." Miguel imitates his father driving a truck. "Let's all drive trucks," says the assistant. The children sing, "This is the way Dad drives a truck." (Of course, this activity, can be extended to include Mom's work, too.) Pictures of fathers and mothers working can be placed in the music corner.

A song for grandfathers may be used also, figure 8-8. The children may pretend they are the two different kinds of grandfathers mentioned in the song.

Fourth of July

The Fourth of July is a good time to let the children have bands and parades with rhythm instruments. Pictures of parades are placed in the music corner. At first, place only the rhythm sticks on the music table. Change the rhythm instruments each day for several days. Encourage the children to have their own parades or concerts.

Note: These ideas can be filed separately under 84G-1 — Holidays of the Community.

MUSIC IN RELATED AREAS

The list of music activities throughout the curriculum is nearly endless. The alert teacher enjoys the opportunity of making music a part of the entire curriculum. Music can be part of all the learning centers.

Science

The children show interest in the plants growing in the science area. The teacher asks them if they will sing a song with her about growing seeds, such as *Oats, Peas, Beans and Barley Grow.* Soon the children join in the song, and later, discussion may take place.

Mathematics

The teacher discovers that the children love to sing counting songs. She collects and

M. W. Weller Pugmire   Composer Unknown

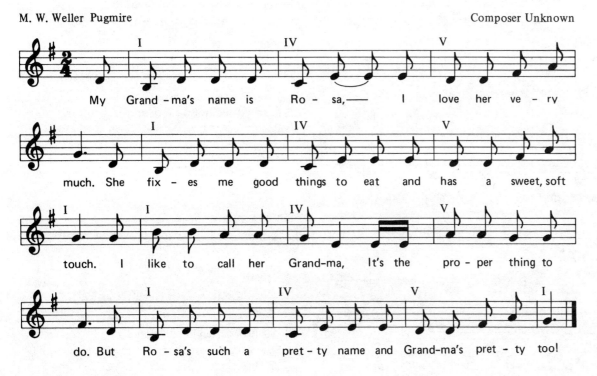

Fig. 8-7 *Grandma's Name:* **Fit the name of the child's grandmother into the song.**

M. C. Weller Pugmire

My Grand–pa, my Grand–pa, He walks with a cane. But
My Grand–pa, my Grand–pa, He plays ball with me. And

he's al–ways smil–ing. And he nev–er com–plains.
he's al–ways smil–ing. As I sit on his knee.

Fig. 8-8 *My Grandpa* **(Cassette song 24-E).**

M. C. Weller Pugmire

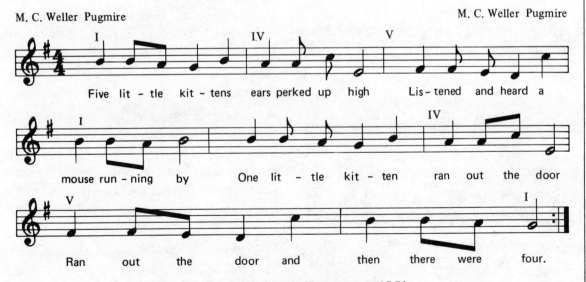

Five lit–tle kit–tens ears perked up high Lis–tened and heard a

mouse run–ning by One lit–tle kit–ten ran out the door

Ran out the door and then there were four.

Fig. 8-9 *Five Little Kittens* **(Cassette song 25-D).**

Five Little Kittens

Five little kittens; ears perked up high
Listened and heard a mouse running by
One little kitten ran out the door
Ran out the door and then there were four.

Four little kittens, paws in a row
Listened and heard a mouse-sound so low
One little kitten ran up the tree
Ran up the tree and then there were three.

Three little kittens, eyes opened wide
Listened and heard a mouse-sound outside
One little kitten ran saying, "Mew"
Ran saying "Mew" and then there were two.

Two little kittens silky and soft
Listened and heard a mouse in the loft
One little kitten ran in the sun
Ran in the sun and then there was one.

One little kitten left all alone
Listened and heard a mouse by a stone
One little kitten ran for some fun
Ran for some fun, and then there were none.

Fig. 8-10 "Five little kittens — ears perked up high, listened and heard a mouse running by. One little kitten ran out the door. Ran out the door and . . ." " . . . then there were four."

files many. The children especially like *Five Little Kittens,* and the teacher finds illustrations for this song.

Language Arts

Listening is important to both the music and language arts areas. The teacher strives to build listening skills by using music effectively. Many of the techniques used to build reading readiness are made more interesting with music. Rhyming is an example. The teacher and children sing *Twinkle, Twinkle Little Star.* The teacher stops singing on "star," "are," "high," and "sky."

As children learn to recognize the spelling of their names, the names are printed on cards

and sung by the teacher. Then the children copy her singing (the pitches, rhythm, and words).

Rich – ard   Ma – ry   Car – o – lyn

Social Studies

Children talk and sing about their families. They visit places in their community and sing about the workers they meet. The children are too young to grasp the concept of the bigness of the United States, but they enjoy singing or hearing *America, the Beautiful.*

Fig. 8-11 Playing and singing in the snow are fun.

MUSIC OUTDOORS

The saying "If possible, do it outdoors!" is often used in early childhood education. A long, safe, extension cord is a necessity in school so that the phonograph can be used outdoors. Rhythm instruments are often used outdoors. Children march and dance more freely with no walls and roof to limit them. Remember that outdoor play takes place in winter, too. Playing and singing in the snow are fun. Many good songs are about the snow.

Persons guiding outdoor activities have a responsibility to get the music materials inside to their proper places. The children will learn to help because they enjoy sharing responsibilities.

SUMMARY

Deciding how to use space in an early childhood center is a challenge. Space should be planned for musical activities. The "music corner" is the center of musical activities. A variety of materials used there helps the children enjoy music much more.

In order to be effective, the music learning center must be changed often. Space should be analyzed for different and improved usage. The age level of the majority of the children must be considered. The music corner can be used throughout the year.

Music is used in every area of the curriculum. Musical activities can often be carried on outdoors.

SUGGESTED ACTIVITIES

- Make several large musical notes (♪ ♩ ♩ 𝅝) from different textured materials. (Use fur, foam rubber, black sand paper, and other varied textures.) Place these on a wall where children can feel them. Record comments of the children and student teachers. (File textured notes for later use.)

- Choose a room available to you. Determine ways to rearrange the furnishings so that empty space is available for movement activities.

- With classmates, develop ideas for each holiday. Write these on index cards. File them in your musical resource file.

REVIEW

A. Indicate the best choice for each of the following.

1. Which of the following should be considered when developing space for musical activities?

a. Walls and ceilings.

b. Empty spaces.

c. Tables, shelves, bulletin boards.

d. All of the above.

2. Storing materials, then bringing them into the center again

    a. Is not a good thing to do.
    b. Should be done only for toddlers.
    c. Will encourage use of the material.
    d. Should be done only for five-year-olds.

3. The musical skill emphasized in the Halloween activity with the tape recorder is

    a. Movement.   c. Playing instruments.
    b. Singing.   d. Creating.

4. When the assistant points to the notes of the chant about the New Year, she is

    a. Encouraging the children to listen.
    b. Helping the children with "musical reading readiness."
    c. Furthering the goal of enjoying music.
    d. Establishing a favorable music mood for the New Year.

5. Which of the statements about the Autoharp are true?

    a. Only the assistant should play the Autoharp.
    b. Even very young children can play a simple accompaniment on the Autoharp.
    c. The young child can be shown how to use a pick to strum the Autoharp.
    d. The Autoharp is sturdy enough to be used by children in the music area.

6. All materials in the music corner

    a. Must be strictly musically oriented.
    b. May be related to musical activities in any way.
    c. Must be unbreakable.
    d. Must be changed every day.

7. Concerning Mother's Day

   a. A song sung by the child to the mother is an appropriate gift.
   b. A song is a fine gift if accompanied by something else.
   c. It is better not to let the child disappoint the mother if he sings "off-key."
   d. Hand prints are the gift most mothers want.

8. Language arts and music

   a. Are not related.
   b. Can be used together to build desired concepts.
   c. Have different goals in the curriculum.
   d. Must be taught indoors.

B. Match each item in Column II with the correct item in Column I.

I	II
1. Permits use of phonograph outdoors	a. Younger preschoolers (2 1/2-3)
2. Can use simple phonograph	b. *The Sparkling Christmas Tree*
3. Traditional candleholder for Hanukkah	c. Long extension cord
4. Song that encourages free movement	d. Five-year-olds
5. Can usually match tones	e. Menorah
6. Helps reach goals of social studies program	f. Discovery
7. Takes place in music corner	g. Song about community workers

C. Briefly answer each of the following.

1. You are assigned to set up a music corner in a nursery school. The children range in age from three to five years old. It is March but Easter comes during April. You have the following equipment available:

Small table, child-size
Butcher paper and felt pens
Phonograph that children can play
Records, unbreakable
Rhythm instruments
Autoharp
Materials from your own home

Using any or all of these materials, describe how you would ar-range a music corner that would help meet the goals of a music program for young children.

2. List four facts about setting up any learning center.

3. List ways that the walls and ceilings of a learning center can be utilized.

4. Why would the use of textured musical symbols for the walls be recommended?

5. Discuss the use of empty floor space in the school.

6. Why are outdoor musical activities emphasized?

unit 9 singing

OBJECTIVES

After studying this unit, the student should be able to

- List four factors that improve the quality of singing.
- Teach a song by the rote method.
- Teach a song by using a recording.

Singing is basic to music. In order to sing, a person must be able to hear the musical tones and make them. He must be able to say the words to the song.

Almost every person can sing. Deaf and mute children may not be able to sing, but they can appreciate the lyrics of songs. A group of college students acted as assistants in a class of deaf children. They reported how excited the children seemed to be to learn the sign language for some songs that were sung a great deal in the area.

The most important quality for singing with children is enthusiasm. Children do not really care how the teacher's voice sounds. If she likes to sing and lets this feeling show, they will love to sing, too!

SINGING SKILL

Singing improves with practice. Very few children are *monotones* (those who sing words without changing the pitch). Some younger children at first sing several tones lower than the teacher, but soon they come closer to the *pitch* (highness or lowness of the musical sound).

There are uncertain singers, even among the very young. If they are encouraged to sing, they improve, however. The teacher can help them match tones and rhythm patterns.

Any person — old or young — sings better when smiling. The effect may be psychological in nature — but it works! Singing is improved by the act of smiling.

The mechanics of singing are important. When singing, the teacher should set a good example. Points to be considered are listed.

- Breathing in the right places (at the end of phrases). Breathing deep from the diaphragm (midriff) also helps.

- Paying attention to *dynamics* (the loud or soft part of the melody).

- Knowing the correct *tempo* (the speed at which a song is sung). She may use a slower tempo while she is teaching the song, but then she increases it to the right tempo.

- Using expression. The tones she uses give an expressive quality to singing. Using her eyes effectively helps, also.

A teacher need not let these things overwhelm her. Rather, she should strive for quality as she sings, realizing that enjoyment of singing is the most important fact.

RANGE OF THE CHILD'S VOICE

When the preschooler becomes able to "carry a tune," his most comfortable range is middle C to G. Some toddlers may have a much wider range. Generally speaking, though, songs in which most of the notes fall within this span are best, figure 9-2.

As the children grow older, the range of their voices widens. In kindergarten, children can sing from middle C to the next high C quite easily, figure 9-3. However, one of the main causes for children failing to like a song or sing it well is that the song contains too many high notes.

TEACHING A SONG BY ROTE

Many short songs are taught to the children by *rote* (learning by memory or imitation alone). The following steps are used in teaching *Hush, Little Baby,* figure 9-4, by rote.

Fig. 9-1 Children (and teachers) sing better when they smile!

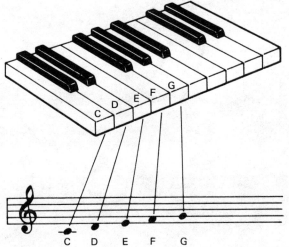

Fig. 9-2 Range of the voice of the young beginning singer (C to G).

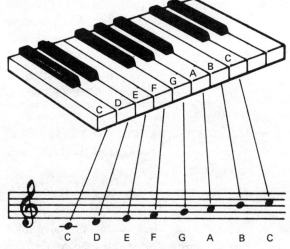

Fig. 9-3 Range of the voice of the kindergarten child (Middle C to C above).

85

- The song is chosen because the teacher knows it appeals to children.
- With the children around her, the teacher sings the song all the way through.

  Note: Some teachers prefer to sit on the floor with the children. Some teachers prefer to sit on a small chair. Eye-to-eye contact is possible in these ways.

- She sings the song through again; this time she uses visual aids to focus each child's attention.

  Example: Pictures of a baby, mockingbird, and diamond ring are placed on the flannelboard, figure 9-5.

  If some children sing with her, it is fine.

- She suggests that all the children sing with her.
- If the children sing the melody or words wrong, she sings that part separately. She uses her hand to indicate whether the melody goes higher or lower. The words are discussed.
- The song is sung again. It is sung several days in a row, so that the children come to know it well.
- The accompaniment can be added. The teacher faces the children. She uses an Autoharp or other stringed instrument for accompaniment, or she plays the piano "from the side" so that she can still see the children.

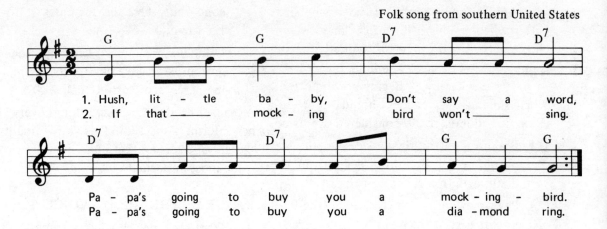

Folk song from southern United States

1. Hush, lit - tle ba - by, Don't say a word,
2. If that mock - ing bird won't sing.

Pa - pa's going to buy you a mock - ing - bird.
Pa - pa's going to buy you a dia - mond ring.

Fig. 9-4 *Hush, Little Baby.*

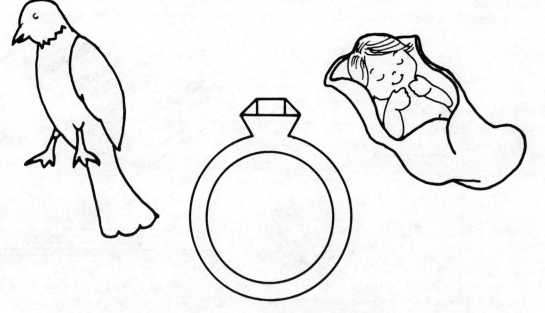

Fig. 9-5 Figures for visual aids for *Hush, Little Baby.*

TEACHING A SONG WITH A RECORDING

Sometimes the assistant feels more secure at first using a recording to teach a song. Either a high quality professional recording is used or a teacher or parent makes a cassette recording. The method used is very much like the rote method:

- The teacher plays the recording all the way through. She might use something to gain attention at first when using a recording. (Example: A three-dimensional mockingbird and a ring might be used for *Hush, Little Baby*.)

- She plays the recording again, urging the children to sing softly the parts they choose. She shows she is listening to the recording as she sings.

- She encourages the children to sing with the recording.

- She gradually turns the sound softer on the recording.

- She and the children sing the song without the recording.

The student will not find this method as effective as presenting the song herself. However, it does have some advantages. Often the recording artists are men; it is good for young children to hear the lower male voice. The talent of the recording artist sets a good example of tone quality. (Remember, though, children prefer their own teacher's voice!) Sometimes the orchestra plays without words on a recording. This is an additional musical experience for the child.

COLLECTING SONGS

Every teacher of young children should build a file of songs she is prepared to use. Some teachers prefer to place a copy of their most used songs in plastic pages in a binder. Then the music is always available in one place ready to use.

SONGS FOR EARLY CHILDHOOD

There are many types of songs available for the early childhood educator. The following classification could be used:

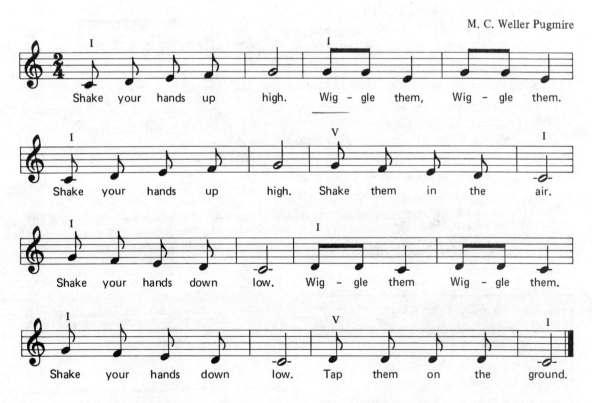

Fig. 9-6 *Shake Your Hands Up High* (Cassette song 21-F).

87

- Action songs (File: 83A)

- Folk and Ethnic songs (File: 83B)

- Self-concept songs (File: 83C)

- "Fun and Fancy" songs (File: 83D)

- Songs for the Very Young (File: 83E)

Action songs are very popular with both children and teachers. They usually fill the goal of enjoyment of music. They help the child relax. Note that the action song *Shake Your Hands Up High*, figure 9-6, is written within the range of the young singer's voice. This allows him to enjoy the actions more.

There are many folk songs that are excellent for children. Some common ones are *Yankee Doodle, Farmer In the Dell* and *Kookaburra*, figure 9-7. *Swing Low, Sweet Chariot* is an easy spiritual for children to sing and play. There are many others.

Self-concept songs tell something about the individual child. A birthday song is a good example. Self-concept songs are often "make-up" songs.

> *Your birthday time is here.*
> *It is a day to cheer.*
> *Rah! rah! dear* _____
> *Your birthday time is here.*
>
> *(Tune: The Farmer In the Dell)*

Fig. 9-7 *Kookaburra* (Cassette application song A).

Fig. 9-8 *Missus Mac, Mac, Mackle* — A nonsense song that "works."

"Fun and fancy" songs have special meaning in early childhood. Mother Goose songs such as *Jack and Jill* and *Humpty Dumpty* are loved by the child. Many fun and fancy songs are based on nonsense. But remember that the young child likes to use words as "toys." Often the child who hesitates to sing cannot resist joining in the singing of a song full of nonsense. The song *Missus Mac, Mac, Mackle* has been the means of getting many children to take part, figure 9-8.

A separate category is used for songs for the very young — that is, infants and toddlers. Lullabies and similar songs are included. Very simple songs that toddlers like to sing should be sought. These songs help the very young enjoy singing more as they grow older. *Jingle Bells* and *Eensy Weensy Spider* are examples, figure 9-9.

Sometimes the reason a teacher gives for choosing a song is that the song is "cute." Although enjoyment of music is important, teachers need to realize that many types of songs are available and seek to broaden their resources for singing.

SUMMARY

Singing is a basic skill of music. The most important quality for singing with children is enthusiasm. Smiling is important to teacher and child. The singing of both the teacher and the children improves with practice.

The teacher should consider the mechanics of singing so that she can encourage a better quality of music. The teacher should collect songs to use with the children. They should be varied and within the range of the child's voice. Action, folk and ethnic, self-concept, and nonsense songs should be among those in her file. Some of the songs can be taught by the rote method; sometimes, there is an advantage to using a recording to teach a song.

Traditional

Een - sy, ween -sy spi - der went up the wa - ter spout

Down came the rain and washed the spi - der out;

Out came the sun and dried up all the rain; And the

een - sy, ween- sy spi - der went up the spout a - gain.

I = C; IV = F; V = G

Fig. 9-9 *Eensy Weensy Spider.*

SUGGESTED ACTIVITIES

- With your classmates, write down the names of all the action songs you know. Secure copies of the music if possible. Illustrate the actions if you do not know the song well.

- Make up and sing to your class a curriculum song concerning some idea of current interest to the children in your area.

- Sing a song to a member of your class that would be classified as a self-concept song for that person.

- Learn *Missus Mac, Mac, Mackle*. Find someone (preferably a child) who does not like to sing. Try to get this person to sing the song with you. Let your enjoyment of the fun and fancy song show!

- Teach a song by the rote method, using suggestions in text.

- Teach a song with a recording, using suggestions in the text.

- Singing improves with practice. Sing children's songs you know for ten minutes a day during the next five days. Apply suggestions found in the text. After five days, decide whether you feel your singing has improved.

REVIEW

A. Match each item in Column II with the correct item in Column I.

I	II
1. Loudness or softness of the melody	a. "Fun and fancy" song
2. Range of beginning singer's voice	b. Monotone
3. Singing successive words on the same pitch	c. Dynamics
4. Highness or lowness of sound	d. Tempo
5. The rate of speed at which a song is sung	e. Pitch
6. Often helps the hesitant singer to participate	f. Middle "C" to "G"
7. Help improve quality of singing	g. Smiles

B.   Indicate the best choice(s) for each of the following.

1. The most important quality for singing with children is

    a. A good voice.   c. Enthusiasm.
    b. Musical training.   d. Sense of correct pitch.

2. Which are true statements about singing?

    a. Singing improves with practice.
    b. Almost every person can sing.
    c. Singing is a basic musical skill.
    d. The teacher must have a good voice to lead singing.

3. A main reason for children failing to like a song or sing it well is

    a. It does not have wide enough range.
    b. It has too many fast notes.
    c. It has too many slow notes.
    d. It has too many high notes.

4. Teachers sit on the floor or a small chair to teach singing because

    a. It allows for more eye-to-eye contact.
    b. It is more comfortable.
    c. It allows better positions for breathing.
    d. She is usually instructed to do so.

5. In kindergarten, the most common range of a child's voice is from

    a. Middle "C" to "G."

    b. Middle "C" to the "C" above.
    c. "G" below middle "C" to "G" above.
    d. Middle "C" up to fifteen notes above.

6. *Shake Your Hands Up High* is

    a. An action song.   c. A self-concept song.
    b. An ethnic song.   d. A fun and fancy song.

7. *Missus Mac, Mac, Mackel* is

a. An action song.   c. A self-concept song.
b. An ethnic song.   d. A fun and fancy song.

C.   Briefly answer each of the following.

1. List four things a teacher can do as she learns a song that will improve the quality of singing.

2. List three advantages of teaching a song by using a recording.

3. What are the five types of songs for young children suggested in the text?

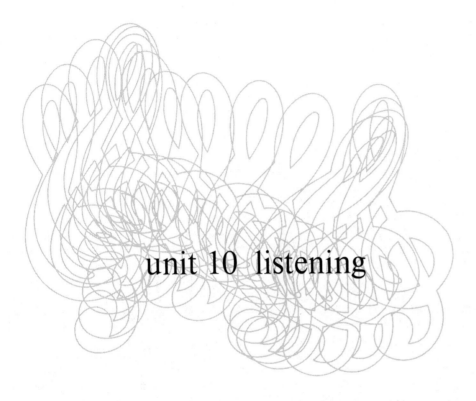

unit 10 listening

OBJECTIVES

After studying this unit, the student should be able to

- Demonstrate four activities to improve listening skill.
- List the advantages and disadvantages of using the rest period as a listening time.
- Discuss effective use of a phonograph and records.

Listening is different from hearing. When people *listen*, they take an active part. They know they are doing it. When people *hear,* they do not have to take an active part. Any teacher or mother knows this. She hears a child talking to her. Her mind is on something else. She thinks to herself, "What was it that he said?" She is hearing but not really listening. Every child should be listened to and should be helped to learn to really listen. It will help him enjoy music — and life — more.

THE TEACHER AS LISTENER

Before a teacher can expect others to learn to listen, she must learn to be a good

Fig. 10-1 Every child should have the opportunity to listen to music and respond to it.

listener. Often, by the time men and women become teachers, they have learned to shut out much of the noise around them. This often is necessary, but things of value may be shut out, also.

Each student should take several walks with a child. She should help the child listen for sounds. During one walk, the sounds of nature can be stressed. Some sounds to listen for are a bird's song, the wind through the leaves on the trees, the swishing of tall grass, and the chirp of an insect. The purpose of a second walk could be to listen to sounds of the town. Listen to the sounds of cars and trucks, the piped-in music in the food store, the calls of boys riding bikes. Record the sounds if possible.

Is there some type of music you do not like? What would you do if you were in charge of children who liked this music best because it was played in their homes? Play some music that you do not care for very much. Listen and try to hear why this music appeals to many others.

The *color of sound* is not always heard. Think of a four-year-old child singing *Nobody Knows the Trouble I've Seen*. Then think of one of the great black singers performing it. The music is the same; the color of the sound is different. The same can be heard when listening to sounds. A French horn and a flute can produce the same notes. The color of the

sound is not the same, though. One set of tones can be described as "full." The other set may be said to be "thin," or "shrill."

When children are five or older, they can usually match tones. Sometimes teachers need to practice this. For most people, it is a matter of listening to the tones. Learn the song, *We'll Have a Happy Day Today*, figure 10-2. Match tones on the song. Try this with a five

or six-year-old. When the child can do this, he is said to have *auditory skill*; that is, he uses his hearing in a way that leads to producing certain sounds.

LISTENING ACTIVITIES

There are many games, songs, and activities to help the child become a better listener. A mother notices that when her baby is about

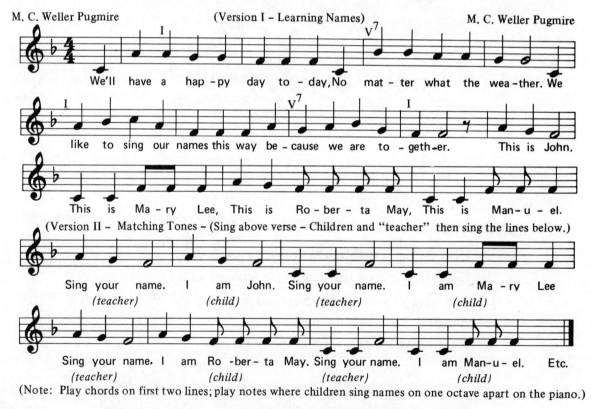

Fig. 10-2 *We'll Have A Happy Day Today* (**Cassette application song B**).

three months old, he reacts in different ways to various sounds she makes. These reactions become stronger as he gets older. She notices that some music makes him relax and other music bothers him. At the end of the first year, she can make a drum for him that he will love. A round box can be covered with a material which has a deep pile. The mallet can be made by securely gluing the ends of a tinker toy or thin dowel into two rubber balls. The mother can sing:

Lis -ten my   ba -by, let's play the drum

The toddler loves to hear music boxes. Sturdy ones can be bought. Some of these are made so the child can see the insides work. Bells fascinate the young child. It is good to have two bells alike so that he can compare sounds.

The matching of sounds helps the child with listening. Items can be hung from a wooden clothes dryer so they make interesting sounds. Two of each may be used so that the child can compare the sounds, figure 10-3. Some articles that can be used are horseshoes, long nails, small pans, pan lids, plastic discs, and funnels.

Another game for comparing sounds is made by using empty 35mm film cans. These can be obtained from a film processer. Two cans are filled with a substance like salt. The cans are taped shut with cloth tape. Other pairs of cans can be made that contain pennies, thumb tacks, gravel, golf tees, and other things. The child shakes the cans and matches the two that have the same sound.

A song that children love is called *Cymbals*, figure 10-4. The children should be shown how to hold the cymbals with their hands through the loops on the back. They should listen as the teacher brings the cymbals directly together; then, as the cymbals are brought together with an up and down sweep of the arms. It should be done softly, then loudly. The children should do this, then sing the song using the soft clash and loud crash in the right places. Later in life, he will listen for the sound of the cymbals in music.

The child can learn that silence is important to listen for in music, too. In order to make the "Snap!" in the *Snapdragons* song, figure 10-5, the children have to quit singing. The kindergarten and first grade child enjoys

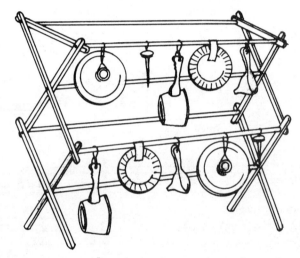

Fig. 10-3 A wooden clothes dryer can be used to make a game in which children match sounds.

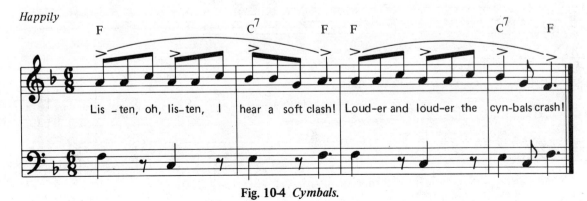

Happily

Lis -ten, oh, lis-ten, I | hear a soft clash! | Loud-er and loud-er the | cyn-bals crash!

Fig. 10-4 *Cymbals*.

M. C. Weller–Pugmire

Fig. 10-5 *Snapdragons* (Cassette song 22-E).

seeing this song written on a chart. The teacher can show him that *rests* are musical symbols that tell him there is no sound there. He may like to make musical rests on chart paper.

An action game for listening is available on the *Way-Out Phonograph Record*. It has a different sound than most records, and children in many areas enjoy listening to it. In the "Elastics" game, the children stretch like elastics. When they hear the elastics snap back, they relax and start stretching again as they listen for the next snap.

Fig. 10-6 The teacher may help the children paste "rests" on paper.

USE OF THE PHONOGRAPH AND RECORDS

As early childhood centers are visited, one can often observe music being played on the phonograph with no one paying attention to it. It is doubtful that the children are learning to listen to this kind of music. They are probably "tuning it out" if it is played all the time or above the noise of children playing. It is better to have spontaneous music periods that stress listening.

Some teachers show shock when it is suggested that a simple phonograph that the children use themselves should be considered as an item to buy each year. These really do not cost more than the crayons and pencils that are bought once a year. This does not imply that the children should not treat the phonograph with care. It does say that an inexpensive phonograph used by child after child will wear out. Indeed, having a simple phonograph for children to use is a good way to teach them to care for the machine and the records.

A phonograph with excellent tone should be in every classroom, to be used only by the staff, and should be kept in repair. Records are selected with care, and they are used! A list of the records is kept where all the staff can see it. Records are handled only by the outside edges and are returned to their covers. When a record is worn out, it is replaced.

REST TIME AS A LISTENING PERIOD

Many centers have a rest period. In all-day programs this involves children napping in the early afternoon. In some nursery schools and kindergartens, the children lie down on a rug or mat for fifteen or twenty minutes in the middle of the session.

The teacher or assistant may use this as an effective listening time if she plans for it. There are many records that have rest songs and lullabies on them. Sometimes the background music from motion pictures is soothing and is very good music. Perhaps the music has been presented in a lesson. Now, the children can listen as they rest.

The adult should try to make this a special time. She can help the children enjoy the listening period by listening herself, instead of rushing off to do some other chore. A suggestion of what to listen for will help. Something special can be used. At Halloween time, a candle can glow from a pumpkin as music is played. At Christmas time, a very small Christmas tree with tiny lights could be turned on as a signal for listening to Christmas music during rest time. These special effects appeal to children.

In some half-day sessions, the children do not like rest periods. If they do not and if the teacher has tried without success to make it special, perhaps it should be done away with. Bad feelings toward the skill of listening should

be avoided! A period of quiet activities that features listening would be better.

SELECTIONS TO FOSTER LISTENING

There are two main types of music for listening. One type is called *program music*. In this, the music makes the listener think of a special story, or a picture, or an event. The *Nutcracker Suite* tells about a nutcracker under the Christmas tree that is turned into a prince and takes the child on a tour of his exciting kingdom. This is program music. The other type is *pure music*. It has no story to tell; one listens to its themes and rhythms. To encourage children to listen, they should first be exposed to program music and the accompanying story.

This book is different from many texts in that very few records are recommended. This is because many students do not have specific records available in every school. Many libraries lend records. The story of the music is given on most jackets of the records. There are also many fine books that tell the stories that go with the music. The teacher should check the resources at the local library.

When the teacher wants to purchase records for listening, she can consult books or catalogs of the companies that sell records. If she lists for them the records she already has, record companies will sometimes recommend other music for listening.

Children who learn to listen begin to enjoy pure music. If a selection has themes that are very easy to hear, the child becomes familiar with them and wants to listen to them again and again.

SUMMARY

Listening implies that the person thinks about what he hears. Many children and teachers find that they are dulled to the sounds around them. The teacher wants to help the child know the pleasure that comes from listening to good music. Thus she makes the effort to become a better listener herself.

There are many games, songs, and other activities that help children become better listeners. Children enjoy games in which sounds are compared and seem to be helped by them.

Sometimes the phonograph and records could be used in better ways to help children learn to listen. A center should have an inexpensive phonograph for the children to use and a very good one for the staff to operate.

Rest time can be used as a listening period. Program music is used first. Later, the children learn to enjoy pure music.

SUGGESTED ACTIVITIES

- Each member of the class should bring a recording of music for children's listening. After playing the selection, the student should lead the discussion of the value of her choice.

- Make one of the listening games suggested in this unit. Try using it with a child.

- Arrange to visit a person who plays an electronic organ. Have him demonstrate the many sounds that can be made. Try to identify some of the sounds. For example, the organ can make a banjo sound. Does it sound like a banjo to you? Have the organist show how he gets people to listen to him by the way he uses the sounds of the organ. Evaluate the experience. Describe how it helped you be a better listener.

- Invite an effective music teacher to talk to the class about listening activities. Make notes that will help you in your own teaching.

- Fill out a chart similar to the one suggested below.

The Teacher As A Listener

1. Have you taken time lately just to listen to sounds around you?

   Will you take a walk (try to take a child)?

   Were you more aware of sounds at the end of your walk?

   _____

   _____

2. Can you tell what common schoolroom sounds are?

   Will you take the "school-sound" test and write your reaction?

   After writing your re-action, do you think you are more aware of sounds around you?

   _____

   _____

3. List one type of music you do not like.

   Do you ever listen to this? Will you listen to some of this music now?

   After trying this, could you see some value to it?

   _____

   _____

4. Are you aware of the *color* of sound?

   Will you try to listen to different voices and in-struments to learn more about tone color?

   After your listening effort, were you more aware of the *color* of sound?

   _____

5. Have you tried tone matching?

   Will you try tone match-ing? Will you help a five-year-old try?

   Did you feel you could match tones better after you did this?

   _____

   _____

REVIEW

A. Match each item in Column II with the correct item in Column I.

<table>
<tr><td align="center">I</td><td align="center">II</td></tr>
<tr><td>1. Makes one think of a story or picture or event</td><td>a. Musical rests</td></tr>
<tr><td></td><td>b. "Color" of sound</td></tr>
<tr><td>2. Thinking about what is heard</td><td>c. Program music</td></tr>
<tr><td>3. Has no story; music themes and rhythms are important</td><td>d. Pure music</td></tr>
<tr><td></td><td>e. Auditory skill</td></tr>
<tr><td>4. Use of hearing that leads to making special sounds</td><td>f. Listening</td></tr>
</table>

5.

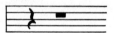

6. The "full" or "thin" quality of tones

B. Briefly answer each of the following.

1. Do you agree with the statement, "A good listener thinks of what he hears?" Why or why not?

2. Give reasons for and against using the children's rest period as a listening period.

3. Give two suggestions for helping children listen to music as rest time begins.

4. Name your favorite selection of pure music. Why do you like it?

5. List ways to use the phonograph effectively.

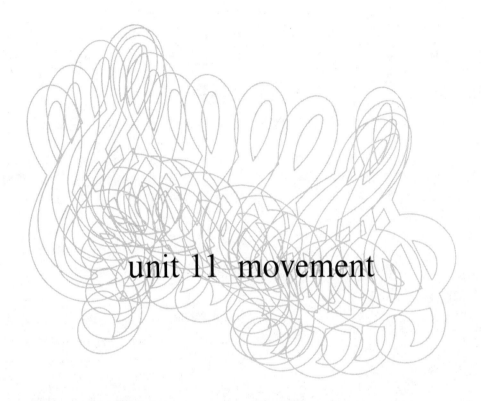

unit 11 movement

OBJECTIVES

After studying this unit, the student should be able to

- State a definition of motor perception.
- Explain the importance of free movement.
- Create movement activities.

Singing is the most common musical activity, but movement shows the joy of music. The whole body responds to music; yet, many children do not have the opportunity to express themselves through movement.

Why do some children miss this opportunity? One reason may be the stress placed on physical fitness. A child needs to be physically fit, but doing repetitious movements for this reason alone tends to destroy the joy of freely moving to music. There are other ways to build physical fitness.

In the past few years, researchers have found that a child's *motor perception* (knowledge or impressions gained through movement of the body) affects his ability to read and do other learning tasks. We must not rob him of his right to respond to music with freedom and expression, nor of his right to learn to read.

RESPONDING TO MUSIC

It used to be "right" to teach children *note values* (♪♪ = ♩) and *time signatures*

and ask them to move to music, supposing their movements would show what they had learned. Now, teachers know that it is after the young child moves in his own way that the elements of music (such as note values and time signatures) are learned more easily.

Teachers and assistants need to move to music with the children. Some of the older students may feel a bit shy about this. They may worry what others think. It has been stated before that the young child is a born

Fig. 11-1 The teacher's attitude helps the child express his feelings in movement to music.

musician. This includes responding to music with movement. The child does not care if his music teacher is young or old, fat or thin. If she has the attitude that moving to music is fine, the child feels free to express his moods.

The "Pas de Deux" from the *Nutcracker Suite*, by Tchaikovsky, has a simple melody, but the *orchestration* (the parts played by the various instruments to support the main musical theme) is very beautiful. Play the music and listen. Then, play it again. In a relaxed manner, with your eyes shut, move your arms and the upper part of your body in response to the music. Bend and reach; when you feel like it, bend your whole body. If you do this a few times, you will discover how moods can be expressed.

Some male students may feel more at ease as they move in the free manner described above if they choose the "Marche" from the *Nutcracker Suite* as a beginning experience. The snap and tone of this music may lead to more "masculine" movements.

Young boys enjoy moving to music and would gladly follow their male teachers. Both boys and men should be encouraged to express their feelings through movement to music.

THE WAY THE BODY MOVES

We often do not think of the many ways the body can move. Look at your fingers. Move them as many ways as you can. You can pat, pinch, touch, snap, point, pull, push, and rub.

Now look at other body parts. Your hands and arms can swing, reach, wave, lift, pinch, and shake. Your leg and foot movements are the kick, stamp, and wiggle. Children — even the very young — move in many, many ways. In this way, they learn to direct their bodies through space

Basic Body Movements

There are nine basic *locomotor movements*. These are

- Walking
- Running
- Jumping
- Hopping
- Galloping
- Leaping
- Sliding
- Rolling
- Skipping

The child without physical handicaps learns to do these easily. As he learns, he gains a body awareness that helps him in life.

Music with strong rhythm helps promote a child's natural feelings for movement. The simple music shown in figure 11-2 can be played very fast so that the child wants to run. He may sing as he runs, "Children, let's go running on this cloudy day, this cloudy day." The line of music can be played with a *staccato* (having a "break" between each note of music) touch so that the child wants to jump or hop.

Children of nursery school age can walk, run, jump, and hop. The child of four or five can leap, gallop, and slide. The music itself tells him to follow the teacher who is doing these movements. Then the teacher can stop while she encourages the children to go on and do the movements with the music.

Rolling is the one basic locomotor skill that is not usually done to music. However, some young children have said they thought it would be fun! Perhaps someone reading this text knows a way for children to use the basic skill of rolling within the limits of a good music program.

Skipping is a movement that shows joy. Many children do not like to skip, however, because a teacher made hard work of learning to skip. The child of five or six can usually learn to skip the hard way by going step-hop with one foot and then step-hop with the other foot. The following method often works better. The children walk in a circle. The teacher chants joyfully.

> *Walk, walk, walk, walk —*
> *A beautiful day, a beautiful day*
> *As you walk —*
> *Rise higher and higher*
> *Up on your toes!*
> *Up on your toes!*
> *Higher, higher, higher, higher*
> *Look, look! You're skipping!*

The teacher and aides walk in the circle with the children. When the teacher chants, "Up on your toes!", the adults lift their heels up and rise up on their toes. Then everyone does this. Sooner or later, the child skips!

Many records are available that have music to motivate the children to do basic movements. Using the piano also helps. The music to indicate leaps or galloping and sliding can be as fast or slow as the group needs.

Sometimes the child likes to have some small thing to help him as he moves. Headbands with "bunny ears" may help him do the "Bunny Hop." Similar headbands can be used to motivate him to leap like a deer.

Let the child take off his shoes and socks (if he wishes) and move freely to the music.

M. C. Weller Pugmire

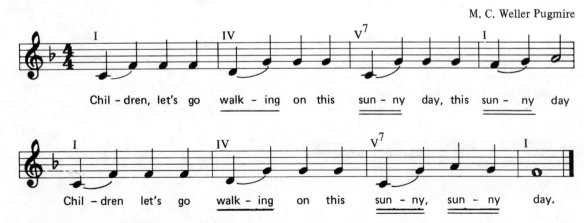

Fig. 11-2 *Let's Go Walking* (Cassette song 22-A): **The words underlined once can be changed to other movements. The words underlined twice can be changed to different weather.**

Fig. 11-3 Music with strong rhythm will help the children move in many ways.

In Strict Rythm

I = E♭; IV = A♭ V = B♭

Fig. 11-4 *Do As I'm Doing* (Cassette song 22-M).

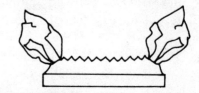

FOR DEER EARS: TIE CORNERS OF A PAPER SACK. STAPLE SACK (WHICH HAS BEEN CUT TO DEPTH) TO HEADBAND MADE OF TAGBOARD.

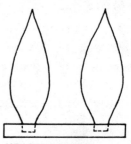

HEADBAND FOR BUNNY EARS. MAKE EARS FROM STIFF CONSTRUCTION PAPER.

TO MAKE BUNNY EARS. CUT FREEHAND. FOLD EDGES OVER. STAPLE TO HEADBAND.

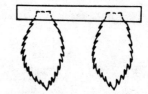

LAMBS' EARS. CUT EARS FROM "FURRY" MATERIAL. STAPLE TO HEADBAND.

Fig. 11-5 Sometimes, having a headband will help the child move more freely.

Put on a record that he hears on television, and he will move as he may have seen those on television do. He will gain a sense of space relationships as he is encouraged to move through the available area. This will help the child's total development.

CREATING MOVEMENT ACTIVITIES

The teacher often makes up her own movement activities. Soon, the children help her by creating short poems or new words to an old song. The first type of activity can be movement to short poems which can be chanted or sung:

> *"Like a bee,*
> *Flying so free."*
>
> *"Flip, flop*
> *Like a mop."*
>
> *"Like a broom,*
> *Sweeping the room."*

A second type of movement activity involves being aware of sounds. The teacher collects items that will make different sounds. Children through the ages have marched to a pan and its lid being clapped together. A spoon rubbed across the back of a potato masher makes an unusual sound which often causes children to wiggle in response.

A third type of movement involves the use of records that are considered adults'

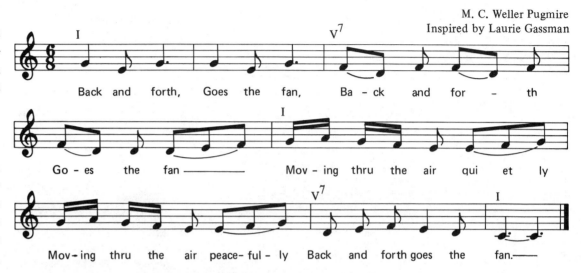

M. C. Weller Pugmire
Inspired by Laurie Gassman

Back and forth, Goes the fan, Ba - ck and for - th
Go - es the fan ——— Mov - ing thru the air qui et ly
Mov - ing thru the air peace-ful - ly Back and forth goes the fan.———

Fig. 11-6 *The Fan* (Cassette song 22-D).

records. One teacher had a child who would not talk to her; he talked to the other children, but he seemed too shy to talk to the teacher. One day he brought the Herb Alpert Tiajuana Brass record, *Taste of Honey* to her. "Let's dance!" he said. It "broke the ice" between the teacher and the child. *Taste of Honey* became a favorite with the group.

A fourth type of movement activity is the creation of new words for an old song:

> *"Hopping, hopping, Yankee Doodle*
> *Jumping, jumping, Yankee Doodle*
> *Sliding, sliding, Yankee Doodle*
> *Yankee Doodle Dandy"*
>
> *(Move freely to the last line)*

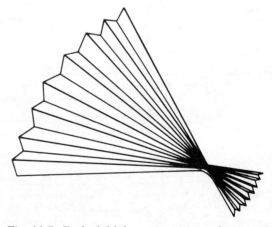

Fig. 11-7 Each child decorates a piece of paper while listening to the swaying sound in *The Fan*. He folds the paper as shown here to make the fan and uses it as he moves to the music.

The tune used should have a strong beat and should be known by all the children.

Another activity involves the use of movement activities brought by the child from home. Waving a fan is an example. The children make their fans by folding paper. *The Fan,* figure 11-6, is the song used. Each child waves his fan and moves in a swaying motion as the class sings the song.

SUMMARY

The teacher must be aware of the ways in which the body moves. She develops basic body movements in an early education music program, and she gives the children opportunities for creative movement. Creative movement allows children to express their feelings (such as joy and loneliness). It helps the child gain body awareness. Teachers can create many activities to encourage children to move freely to music.

SUGGESTED ACTIVITIES

- Have each member of the class bring a record of music that encourages physical responses. Play this music in class and move to it.

- Play the "Pas de Deux" and "Marche" from the *Nutcracker Suite*, by Tchaikovsky. Follow suggestions in the text. Write how you felt as you allowed yourself to respond.

- Play the march from "Pomp and Circumstance" by Elgar ("Land of Hope and Glory"). First have class members do the traditional steps used at school graduations. Then see how many different movements can be done to the beat of the music.

- Complete a chart similar to the one shown for creating movement activities for young children.

Type of Activity	Beginning	To finish, do this:
Make up jingle or chant	"Like a kangaroo. . .	_____
Find different sounding instruments	Look around home and find. . .	_____
Recordings	Look for a recording to inspire movement	_____
Make up words to a song with strong rhythm	"Over in the meadow. . .	_____

REVIEW

A. Name every movement you can think of that the listed parts of the body can do.

    1. Fingers   3. Hands and arms

    2. Legs and feet   4. Head

B. Name one activity (other than the one in the text) for each of the basic movements listed below.

    1. Walking   6. Leaping

    2. Running   7. Sliding

    3. Jumping   8. Rolling

    4. Hopping   9. Skipping

    5. Galloping

C. Match each item in Column II with the correct item in Column I.

                I   II

    1.    a. Motor perception

                             b. Time signatures and note values

    2. Parts played by various instruments to support the main musical theme   c. Orchestration

                             d. Locomotive movements

    3. Basic skills   e. Staccato

    4. Knowledge or impressions gained through movement of the body   f. Step, hop; step, hop

    5. Having a "break" between each note of music

    6. The hard way to learn to skip

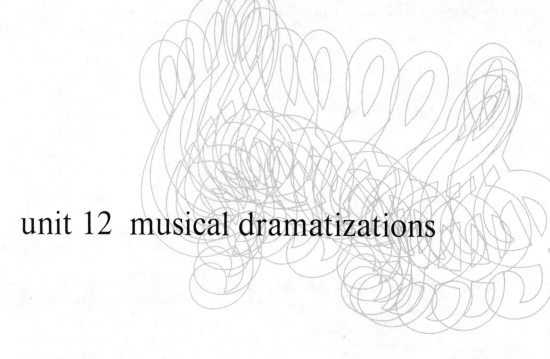

unit 12 musical dramatizations

OBJECTIVES

After studying this unit, the student should be able to

- List three reasons for having musical dramatizations.
- Discuss creativity in musical dramatizations.
- Name several techniques used to direct a musical dramatization.

There is a place for stories set to music (*musical dramatizations*) in the early childhood years. Dramatizations can be created by teachers or by students, although many records can be bought that have musical stories. Dramatizations are printed in most of the basic music series books, which often have beautiful pictures to use. Such music is also in other children's music books.

REASONS FOR MUSICAL DRAMATIZATIONS

Musical dramatizations help reach the goals of the music program. An example is the well-known story *Caps for Sale* by Esphyr Slododkina. Young children act out the story. Then music is added to it. The teacher offers suggestions such as *Monkey See, Monkey Do,* figure 12-1. When the monkeys say, "Tsk, Tsk, Tsk," a child accompanies on the piano by playing a black note (gracenote) followed quickly by a white note. The children dance in the "tree" like monkeys as they tease the peddler. Some main goals are reached:

- Enjoying music and drama

- Listening for mood music and instrumental parts.

- Helping the teacher create a special accompaniment, thus having built a foundation for later experiences with the piano.

Some main skills are taught:

- Singing with a purpose.

- Free movement inspired by the story.

Parent involvement is possible. Parents hear about the drama from their child, and ask about it. The teacher encourages the parents to read *Caps for Sale* by Esphyr Slododkina. The teacher presents the song *Monkey See, Monkey Do*, by Stephen Scott, at a parent-involvement meeting; she encourages parent-child singing at home.

Musical dramatizations give children opportunities to be leaders and to be followers. The teacher encourages the shy child in the part he has. She helps others to be followers in the musical dramatization.

Some educators do not like musical dramatizations because they feel many do not encourage creativity. The stories seem to demand that the child act out in the same way, every time. An imaginative teacher, however, can prevent this from happening.

A Structured Musical Dramatization

Many early childhood centers have a highly recommended record, *A Visit to My Little Friend*, by the Children's Record Guild. In this dramatization, the child uses a different movement each "day" to visit his friend. At the end of the "week" he sings a song, "My Thumbs and Fingers Keep Moving." Then, he rides home on his pony as the music tells him to do.

Fig. 12-2 **The children sing "Tsk, Tsk" as they enact** *Caps for Sale.*

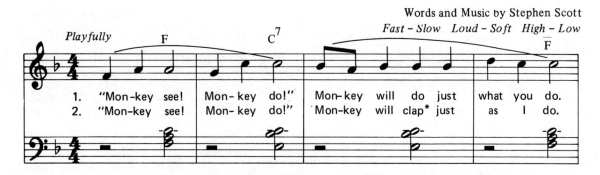

Words and Music by Stephen Scott

Fast - Slow   Loud - Soft   High - Low

*dancing, walking, waving, etc.

Fig. 12-1 *Monkey See, Monkey Do.*

LION

GIRAFFE

MONKEY

SEAL

BEAR

HIPPOPOTAMUS

Fig. 12-3 Animal faces to be made into two-sided masks.

Children usually learn the story and actions from the record at first, developing their listening skills as they do so. Next, they follow the record by themselves. This process illustrates how the listening skill can be strengthened by an excellent record.

The Creative Musical Dramatization

Many commercial recordings foster creativity effectively. Children are urged to

- Soar like a seagull.

- Curl up like a chick in a shell.

- Stretch their arms to the sun like the green leaves on a plant.

When a Walt Disney production plays at a theater and many of the children see it, the teacher develops a musical story experience from it. A TV program has a special feature on the circus. In her file of materials, the teacher finds her animal masks. These masks are especially good for young children because they do not cover the face. They are made by making two "faces" such as those shown in figure 12-3. A piece of stretchy cloth is stapled or taped between the two masks. This makes a cap effect for the child's head and leaves his face uncovered, figure 12-4. Music about animals and the circus is found. The children and teacher create the dramatization. She helps the children to express ideas that are new to them and to put these ideas to music.

ONE SIDE OF MASK

STRETCHY MATERIAL
OVER HEAD

CHILD'S
FACE
SHOWS

OTHER SIDE
OF MASK

TIED UNDER CHIN

Fig. 12-4 This mask makes a "cap" effect. The child's face is completely uncovered.

The beginning student often thinks these ideas may not work, but she is urged to try them. First, she should try the ideas with a small group of interested children, because participation is better there than in a large group. Then, she may try a well-planned project with a large group.

DEVELOPING A MUSICAL DRAMATIZATION

There are times when the children seem tired of all of their activities, possibly caused by a long period of bad weather. One child tells stories and shows pictures of her recent trip to Yellowstone Park. "Let's all go to Yellowstone," says the teacher. All of them put small chairs into the form of a "station wagon." The teacher sings

> *"Merrily we drive along, drive along,*
> *drive along.*
> *Merrily we drive along, singing happily."*

"We're in the pines now," says the teacher. "See the wind blowing them gently. Let's pile out of the car and pretend we're trees blowing in the wind." (The teacher puts a record on with a swaying motion to it.) She helps a child by gently urging him to join the others, but she does not insist. She compliments or smiles directly at a child who is leading in the action. "Time to get back in the car and go on," says the teacher. "Merrily we drive along!"

Further along, she says, "There's Yellowstone Lake. Let's get out and *Row, Row, Row Your Boat*," figure 12-6. "Sing and row! Now let's get back in our car!"

"Look at all the colors in the geyser basin!" cry the children.

Fig. 12-5 The teacher with a positive attitude, who desires to help the children gain all they can, will usually have creative music experiences in her group.

"While we're driving, let's play a game called *Sing the Colors*. Who can sing yellow? Good, Jeff. Let's all sing that!"

Yel-low is hap-py and bright and gay.

We're in Yel-low-stone Park to - day.

"Out of the car, children!" cries the excited teacher. "Old Faithful Geyser is about to go up! Who can make it go higher and higher on the piano?" The assistant shows one child how to play higher and higher up the keyboard. The children stretch taller and taller. "Now who can make Old Faithful drop down into her tunnel in the ground?" The assistant shows the child how to play lower and lower on the black keys. The children sink to the ground as the child plays. "Back into the car we go," says the teacher.

The possibilities for extending the above musical journey are endless. (The trip can be adapted to a familiar locale.) The assistant could suggest that the children make move-

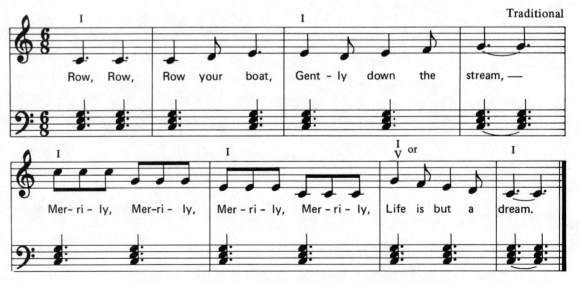

Fig. 12-6 *Row, Row, Row Your Boat* (**Cassette song 23-B**).

ments like the animals they see (to appropriate music). They could have a "sing-out" around a "campfire."

TECHNIQUES USED IN DIRECTING

The techniques used in the dramatization just discussed meet the needs of children. The teacher met these needs by

- Recognizing the need for a different activity
- Using one child's idea
- Using dramatic play
- Using the words of a well-known song to fit the situation
- Locating the "swaying" music (the resource) quickly
- Reinforcing the swaying motion of the child who is taking part and urging but not forcing the hesitant child to dance and/or act
- Creating songs (about colors)

- Using the *pentatonic scale* (black keys of the piano that play five notes per scale) to show the rising and falling motion of music

- Making suggestions to the children and encouraging creativity on their part

Further Techniques for Directing Musical Dramatizations

The most important influence is a positive attitude that the experience is worthwhile. The teacher needs to move freely. She cannot worry about the thoughts of other adults in the room.

Sometimes, one child starts to act silly. Often this silliness spreads throughout the group. (This is referred to as *behavioral contagion*.) If this occurs, the teacher may do any of several things:

- She can ignore the silly behavior, if it is possible. When the child sees he is not getting the teacher upset, the unwanted action may stop.

- She can stop her movements suddenly and wait for the children to quit their undesired behavior.

- She can cease the activity and try again another day.

Very often instruments are used in musical dramatizations. A ukelele is worked into the story; rhythm instruments are used for needed sounds. The teacher should strive for quality in musical dramatizations.

SUMMARY

Stories set to music are called musical dramatizations. Through dramatization, the children learn to be leaders and followers. Spontaneous creations stem from structured dramatizations. The enthusiasm and attitude of the teacher are most important; when she has a desire to succeed, creativity thrives.

SUGGESTED ACTIVITIES

- Visit a day care center or nursery school. See what musical dramatizations are available. Ask if they are used in the program. Record your findings.

- Invite an experienced teacher to speak to your class about musical dramatizations. Ask about techniques that are used.

- With your classmates, go on the "musical journey" to Yellowstone Park.
- Make several animal masks for your file.

REVIEW

A. Match each item in Column II with the correct item in Column I.

I	II
1. Strengthens behavior	a. Musical dramatization
2. Black keys on the piano	b. Pentatonic scales
3. Stories set to music	c. Dramatic play
4. Making a car from small chairs	d. Reinforces
5. Loves school routines	e. Behavioral contagion
6. Behavior that spreads quickly through a group	f. Preschooler

B. Indicate the best choice for each of the following.

1. Musical dramatizations

    a. Can be created by teachers and children.

    b. Are available in records.

    c. Are printed in music.

    d. All of the above.

2. Reasons for musical dramatizations are

    a. Musical skills are learned.

    b. They help reach goals of music program.

    c. The functions of music are used.

    d. All of the above.

3. Which of the following events would not lead to creation of a musical dramatization?

    a. TV specials.

    b. Children's movies.

    c. Punishing the children.

    d. Journeys by the children.

4. Musical dramatizations are done best

 a. On a planned program for mothers.
 b. With a large group of children.
 c. In the gym.
 d. With a small group of interested children.

5. The most important factor in using music with young children is

 a. Training in creative dramatics.
 b. Study of theory.
 c. Positive attitude.
 d. Recognizing behavioral contagion.

6. The main value of a musical dramatization such as a "Visit to My Little Friend" is

 a. It is not expensive.
 b. It does not further musical readiness.
 c. It does not motivate creative movement.
 d. It builds listening skills.

C. A story follows. Write musical activities that could be used for each of the numbered situations.

Story

The circus comes to town. (1) It gets underway with a big parade. (2) The first act features an elephant. (3) The horses gallop around the ring. (4) The trapeze artists swing on their trapezes. (5) The lions are in their cages. You can hear them roar. (6) The circus is long and the children get very sleepy before they get home.

D. Briefly answer each of the following.

1. Discuss goals which musical dramatizations help to meet.

2. Discuss skills which musical dramatizations help develop.

3. What are some functions that the musical dramatization helps achieve?

4. What types of group roles are developed by using musical dramatizations?

5. How would a musical dramatization become part of the school routine?

6. How can quality music be encouraged in musical dramatizations?

unit 13 singing games

OBJECTIVES

After studying this unit, the student should be able to

- List three reasons to teach singing games.

- Direct a new singing game.

- Discuss ways of teaching singing games to children of three age levels.

- List games that may be used in various ways and places.

Children everywhere play singing games. The time a teacher spends teaching a new singing game has value. Most children — once they know a game — play it again and again.

REASONS FOR TEACHING SINGING GAMES

Singing games are part of the cultural heritage of most children. Almost every teacher can think back to the time when she was a child and remember the singing games she played. It is usually a good memory, because she was part of a happy group.

Some singing games are played with just two people — usually a parent or teacher and a child. Most singing games are played in groups, however. Since one of the main aims of early education is to teach the child to get along in groups, this reason is an important one.

Another reason to teach singing games is that they can become an important part of the routine of the school or center. Some schedules call for a group game right after rest time. Others have group games when the children come in from outdoors. The children join the game when they get their wraps off. Then all proceed to a more quiet activity. Most teachers like to teach several games that the children can play when the weather is too bad to go outdoors. Almost every singing game can be played outdoors, as well as indoors.

Singing games are also played just for fun. For one minute, the child is the main person in the room as he acts out a part in the middle of the circle. In another minute, he feels that he belongs to the group as he does actions with all of the children.

DIRECTING SINGING GAMES

Groups should be small for singing games with younger children. It is better to have assistants or volunteers teach a few children at a time and join the class together after the game is learned.

Those who teach should know the game well. It is advisable that the game be played by the teachers and assistants before it is taught to the children.

The song is taught by rote. Often it is better to teach the song to the children before the actions are added to it. The actions

are added, or simple directions are given for playing the game. The less talking one can do, the better. If the teacher and assistants know the game well, the children will usually follow along with them.

Games are chosen for the age level and the nature of the children. Sometimes a group needs a game to quiet them. Often this is a game that releases energy; but at other times, it should be a quiet game.

SINGING GAMES FOR INFANTS AND TODDLERS

As an adult plays with an infant, singing games start. One of the first games is to sing as one wiggles the baby's toes. The following

is one of the chants of childhood referred to early in this text.

> *This little pig went to market (Wiggle big toe)*
> *This little pig stayed home (Wiggle second toe)*
> *This little pig ate roast beef (Wiggle third toe)*
> *This little pig ate none (Wiggle fourth toe)*
> *But this little pig cried, "Wee, wee, wee," all the way home (Shake little toe)*

The same action is followed in the singing game, *Airabella Bailey*. This is an example of a singing game handed down from mother to child, figure 13-2.

Fig. 13-1 Now is the time to play the game *Airabella Bailey* with the baby.

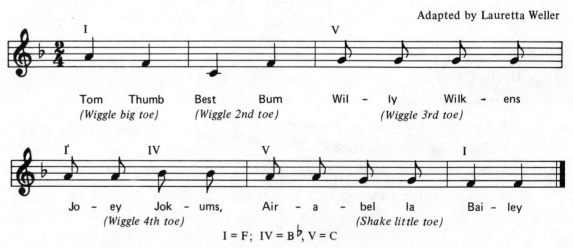

Fig. 13-2 *Airabella Bailey* (Cassette song 22-B).

A singing game that seems to go with toddlerhood is for the child to be bounced. The child loves to ride on an adult's ankle. The grown-up crosses his legs and moves his ankle up and down while the child squeals for "More!" The most common chant is

> *Ride a cock-horse*
> *To Bambury Cross*
> *To see a fine lady*
> *Upon a white horse.*
> *Rings on her fingers*
> *And bells on her toes*
> *She shall have music*
> *Wherever she GOES!!*
>
> *(On the last word the foot is given a big swing and the child falls off.)*

SINGING GAMES FOR PRESCHOOLERS

As a rule, preschoolers like games with an element of surprise or sudden action. That is why *Ring-around-the-Rosy* has stood the test of time. There are many ways to play this old game. A song very much like this is *Sally Go Round the Sun*, figure 13-3. The child jumps up when he says "Whoops" and then falls to the ground, laughing.

Three- and four-year-olds usually have to have help to get into a circle for a game. The teachers stand in the circle at first with a few children between them. A teacher can make

a big circle with her arms to show the children what they are going to do. Later she can just make the circle, and the children will know what to do.

Some younger nursery school children do better if they play games in which they do not hold hands or form a circle. *Up, Down, Whoops!* is such a game, figure 13-4. In this game, the music "tells" the child what to do as he listens to it.

The old game, *Did You Ever See A Lassie?*, figure 13-5, can be played while the children stand in a circle. They do not need to touch hands. Each child does his own action. The leader in this game has the chance to make up actions for other children to follow.

low. Sometimes the teacher will need to show the young leader some actions; other times the child is able to make up his own.

The game, *Let's Pretend*, can be played in a circle or any formation. It shows how a singing game can build a child's self-concept, figure 13-6. When a child comes back from the company picnic and says, "I got to climb up on a big tractor like my Dad drives," this game can be played. The words can be changed to fit any kind of job.

There are many singing games. A teacher should know many so that she can suggest the right game for the right time. Then the children will not become tired of the "same old game."

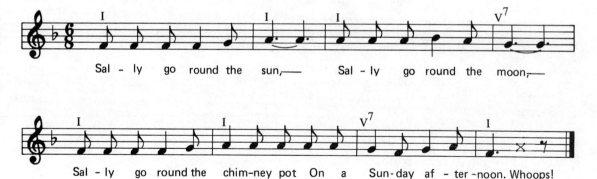

Fig. 13-3 *Sally Go Round the Sun* (Cassette song 22-K).

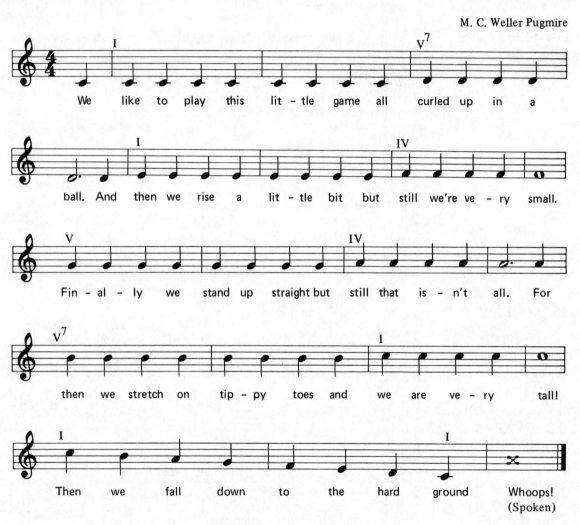

Fig. 13-4 *Up, Down, Whoops!* **(Cassette song 21-B).**

Fig. 13-5 *Did You Ever See a Lassie?*

GAMES FOR YOUNG SCHOOL CHILDREN

Children in kindergarten and the primary grades can have more structure to their singing games. However, if a child has not had a chance to be a part of a group, it is easier to teach him how to play the simpler games first. The teacher also checks to see that each child knows how to take a place in a circle game.

The game *Summer Is Coming*, figure 13-8, is played as a circle game. The children sing as they move around and around. The fives will move with bouncing steps. Some older fives and sixes will want to skip. The teacher picks one child. His name is sung in the proper place. The child comes to the center of the circle and *pantomimes* (acts out without any words or music) what he will be doing in the summer. The first child to guess becomes the one for whom the song is sung the next time.

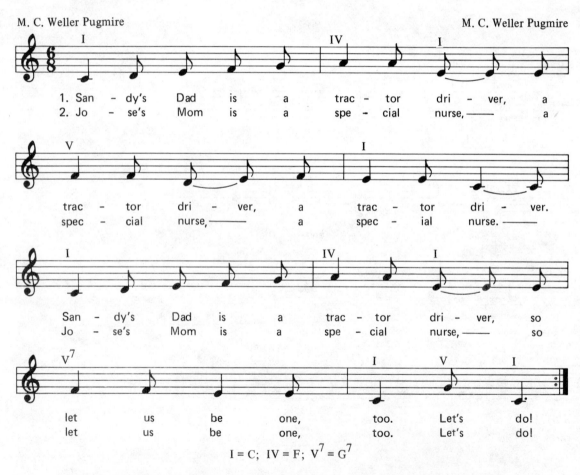

M. C. Weller Pugmire

M. C. Weller Pugmire

1. San – dy's Dad is a trac – tor dri – ver, a
2. Jo – se's Mom is a spe – cial nurse,——— a

trac – tor dri – ver, a trac – tor dri – ver.
spe – cial nurse,——— a spe – cial nurse.———

San – dy's Dad is a trac – tor dri – ver, so
Jo – se's Mom is a spe – cial nurse,——— so

let us be one, too. Let's do!
let us be one, too. Let's do!

I = C; IV = F; $V^7 = G^7$

Fig. 13-6 *Let's Pretend:* **Make up other verses to fit the jobs of the parents of the children!**

Fig. 13-7 Singing about his parent's job builds a child's self-concept.

M. C. Weller Pugmire   M. C. Weller Pugmire

1. Sum-mer is com-ing, Oh hip hoo -ray, the chil-dren will play in the
2. Christ-mas is com-ing, Oh hip hoo -ray, the chil-dren will have a good

sun.— They'll play with trucks, feed the ducks, mow the lawn, in
time.— They'll play with dolls, throw their balls, read their books, and

ma – ny a game they will run. So step in the cir - cle and
watch as the Christ-mas lights shine. So step in the cir - cle and

show to us, what you'll do on these sum - mer days.— Oh,
show to us, what you'll do on this Christ- mas day. — Oh,

(Name) we ask you, with-out an – y fuss, to show us how you will play.—
(Name) we ask you, with -out an – y fuss, to show us how you will play.—

*Adapted from "Family Home Evening Is Lot's of Fun")

Fig. 13-8 *Summer Is Coming* (Cassette song 22-L).

American Singing Game

1. Blue bird, blue bird, in and out the win - dow,
2. Take a little boy and tap him on the shoul - ders,
3. Blue bird, blue bird, in and out the win - dow,
4. Take a little girl and tap her on the shoul - ders,

Blue bird. blue bird, in and out the win - dow,
Take a little boy and tap him on the shoul - ders,
Blue bird, blue bird, in and out the win - dow,
Take a little girl and tap her on the shoul - ders,

Blue bird, blue bird, in and out the win - dow,
Take a little boy and tap him on the shoul - ders
Blue bird, blue bird, in and out the win - dow,
Take a little girl and tap her on the shoul - ders,

O John - ny, I am tired.
O John - ny, I am tired.
O Jen - ny, I am tired.
O Jen - ny I am tired.

Fig. 13-9 Blue Bird.

Bluebird, figure 13-9, is an example of another favorite with children. Several girls are chosen to be "birds." The other children stay in place, join hands, and raise them to make the "window." The girls go in and out the windows. All sing. The girls "tap the little boys" on the shoulders as they sing the second verse. Then these boys take the girls' places and go in and out the "windows." The teachers should see that every child has a turn.

GAMES FROM LOCAL AREAS

Every area has games that are special to that locality. When a child moves to a new place, he is sometimes amazed that the children are playing the game he loves the "wrong" way. An example is the child from the South who plays *Okra, Beans, and Barley Grow*, figure 13-10. When he moves to the West, he finds they play *Oats, Peas, Beans, and Barley Grow*. The teacher should watch for this.

Hambone, figure 13-11, is an example of a singing game from a special area that has been handed down from parent to child. The song is chanted. The body is used as a rhythm instrument like this:

> *"Ham-" (Right hand hits chest)*
> *"bone-" (Left hand hits chest)*
> *"Ham-" (Right hand hits knee)*
> *"bone-" (Left hand hits knee)*
> *"Where (Right hand hits chest)*
> *"ya" (Left hand hits chest)*
> *"been" (Right hand hits knee; left hand hits knee*

Fig. 13-10 *Oats, Peas, Beans and Barley Grow.* "Okra, Beans and Barley Grow."

Fig. 13-11 *Hambone.*

Fig. 13-12 *Pick a Bale of Cotton.*

The chant goes on with the rhythm pattern continued. The young child does this quite slowly. The older child does it faster and faster. Usually the game ends with much laughter. The student will note that part of the chant is like the song, *Hush, Little Baby* in unit 9. There are many different ways to sing this chant.

Pick a Bale of Cotton, figure 13-12, is a singing game from the South that comes from the work the people had to do. Often this is the background for a singing game. In this game, the children "act it out" as they sing. It is done faster and faster until the child has to drop out of the game. If one thinks about it, the game seems silly because cotton could not be picked that fast! Yet, such a game may show children something about other parts of the country and the work of that area.

The teacher should collect, file, and use games from her local area. When she visits other areas, she should add to the file. (Refer to the filing system in unit 2. Number 86 is suggested.) To know singing games that are suitable to use with a group of children is a valuable teaching tool.

SOME PRACTICAL HELP

The following pointers will help teachers with singing games:

- A young child has a hard time waiting for his turn. Keep the groups small enough in games that require turns so that this does not happen. Children like singing games better if they do not have to wait too long.

- Sometimes a child will pull a circle one way or the other. The adult must not let this go on or it becomes an unwanted "game" in itself. If a child continues to do this, he should sit to the side during one game. Then he may join again. If several children do this, the group is not ready for circle games. Other games should be chosen.

- If no room seems to be available to play singing games indoors, the space should be checked again. Perhaps tables can be stacked. Perhaps a hallway can be used during one period of the day — especially a day of very bad weather.

- Every child does not need to take part every time singing games are played.

Many chances may arise for playing games with part of the group.

- A special signal (such as the ring of a certain bell) can call children to play singing games outdoors. Only those come who want to play. Many children love singing games and should have a chance to play them regularly.

- Records are often used to accompany children's games. Since this sometimes limits the play, it is better to teach the children to sing the songs so they do not have to depend on having the record and a phonograph.

SUMMARY

Singing games are an important part of the education of a young child. The teacher should learn many singing games and how to direct them. Simple singing games are played with the infant; the games become more varied and complex as the child grows older. Some singing games are special to local areas. The teacher should collect, file, and use these games as well as others.

SUGGESTED ACTIVITIES

- Choose a game from this unit. Teach it to a child or a group of children of the suggested age level. Then answer the following questions: Did the game seem to appeal to the child of this age? Did each child take part? How would you teach the game if you were to do it again?

- Each class member should choose a group singing game that is new to her/him. Teach this game to other class members as though they were volunteers or assistants who were going to teach the game to young children the next day.

- Find one new game from the local area or from another area which is familiar to you. Teach this game to children or class members. File it for later use.

REVIEW

A.   Briefly answer each of the following.

1. List four reasons for teaching singing games.

2. List several actions the teacher can suggest to a young child to do in a singing game such as *Did You Ever See A Lassie?*.

3. Describe two ways to help children learn to form a circle. If you know other ways, state these too.

B.   Indicate the best choice for each of the following.

1. When teaching a singing game

   a. You should try it out with the children.
   b. You should know it well before you teach it.
   c. Reading about it is enough.
   d. You should have the talented children do it first.

2. Sometimes singing games are played

   a. After rest time.
   b. When the children have to be inside because of bad weather.
   c. During outdoor play time.
   d. All of the above.

3. Preschoolers often prefer games

   a. That have a modern sound to them.
   b. That teach certain skills.
   c. That have an element of surprise or action.
   d. None of the above.

4. To help children form a circle for games, the teachers should
   a. Insist each child stands in a certain spot.
   b. Stand in a circle with a few children between them.
   c. Separate the boys and girls.
   d. Not allow the child to play who will not stay in place.

5. When teaching games to kindergarten and primary grade children, the adult should remember

   a. They can learn any singing game.
   b. They do not like singing games.
   c. They need to play the simpler games if they have had no group experience.
   d. They are still too young for games in which the circle moves around.

6. The singing game *Hambone*

   a. Can be played by the parent or teacher with a child.
   b. Is an example of a game from a special local area.
   c. Has many ways it can be sung.
   d. All of the above.

7. The singing game *Pick A Bale Of Cotton*

   a. Is an example of a game that came from the people's work.
   b. Is sung faster and faster.
   c. Helps only the children in the South to understand their country.
   d. Both a and b.

C. A teacher and her assistant are playing a circle singing game with ten children. Some of the children are not happy. What response or action could be made to the following statements by some of the children?

1. "I want to go play on the climber."

2. "I'm tired. When do I get my turn?"

3. (Child in the center of the circle) "What do I do now?"

4. "Teacher, he's pulling my hand."

unit 14 creativity

OBJECTIVES

After studying this unit, the student should be able to

- Discuss ways an adult may create a musical time for a special lesson.
- Name ways to foster musical creativity in children.
- List ideas to help write a song.

Much has been said about creativity and how people enjoy music. People listen to and appreciate music. They also create music.

The key word is TRY. When there is a need and neither music nor an instructional aid is available, the teacher may create her own! The young child will not care if the music and instruments are not the best. The fact that it was made for him is the main point.

Teachers who create have children who create. These teachers are "tuned in to" and record the melodies that children hum and the movements they use.

CREATIVITY IN TEACHING

Karla, Lyle Ann, and Mary Susan are three college students with volunteer and student teaching experience who needed songs for special reasons. Each used her creativity in a different way.

Karla learned in science that the young child finds out about the world through his five senses — sight, smell, taste, sound, and touch. She could not find a song that related to touch, and she knew that the sense of touch fascinated the young children. She wrote a song, figure 14-1, with encouragement from her supervising teacher. She was delighted by the response of the children; they used the song in many ways. A "touch book" was made by stapling together (It could be done by filing

Karla Ann Livesey   Karla Ann Livesey

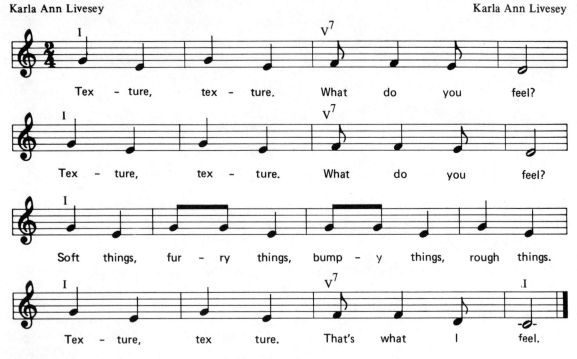

Fig. 14-1 *Texture.*

Sing joyously   Lyle Ann Virgin

Fig. 14-2 *Say Hello To Mrs. Circle.*

them in a ringed notebook.) pieces of cloth with different textures. The child chanted about the texture as he turned the pages of the touch book. Sometimes each child was given a page from the notebook (or an object with texture). He would sing about his object when the teacher pointed to him. For example, he would sing:

Thus, from a new song, came a new game.

Lyle Ann wanted to teach about shapes. Things in her classroom seemed humdrum. She wrote the tune *Say Hello to Mrs. Circle*, figure 14-2. Each child made Mrs. Circle, Mr. Square, and Mrs. Triangle. The school day seemed brighter as the children sang as they made their art projects.

Mary Susan knew that her group needed a song about machines; she wrote it, figure 14-4. It took effort to write the song and improve it in places. The children loved it and sang it for their parents. The pleasure of the children as they sang, "Rrrr," was well worth the time it took Mary Susan to write it.

A NEW VERSION OF AN OLD IDEA

One child-care student loved the old song *Over in the Meadow*, figure 14-5. Although

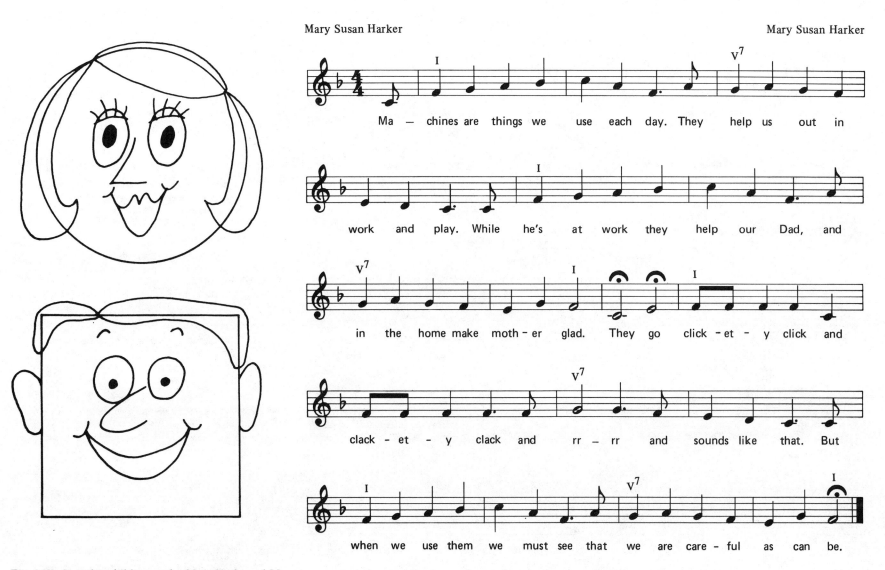

Mary Susan Harker   Mary Susan Harker

Ma — chines are things we use each day. They help us out in

work and play. While he's at work they help our Dad, and

in the home make moth – er glad. They go click – et – y click and

clack – et – y clack and rr – rr and sounds like that. But

when we use them we must see that we are care – ful as can be.

Fig. 14-3 Let the children make Mrs. Circle and Mr. Square.

Fig. 14-4 *Machines.*

OVER IN THE MEADOW

Over in the meadow in the sand in the sun,
Lived an old mother turtle and her little turtle one.
"Dig" said the mother
"I dig" said the one.
So he dug and was glad in the sand in the sun.

Over in the meadow where the tall grass grew,
Lived an old mother red fox and her little foxes two.
"Run" said the mother
"We run" said the two.
So they ran and were glad where the tall grass grew.

Over in the meadow in a nest in a tree,
Lived an old mother robin and her little robins three.
"Sing" said the mother
"We sing" said the three.
So they sang and were glad in the nest in the tree.

Over in the meadow in a tall sycamore,
Lived an old mother chipmunk and her little chipmunks four.
"Play" said the mother.
"We play" said the four.
So they played and were glad in the tall sycamore.

Over in the meadow in a brand new hive,
Lived an old mother queen bee and her honey bees five.
"Buzz" said the mother
"We buzz" said the five.
So they buzzed and were glad in the brand new hive.

Over in the meadow in a dam built of sticks,
Lived an old mother beaver and her little beavers six.
"Build" said the mother
"We build" said the six.
So they built and were glad in the dam built of sticks.

Over in the meadow in the green, wet bogs
Lived an old mother frog and her seven pollywogs.
"Swim" said the mother
"We swim" said the wogs.
So they swam and were glad in the green, wet bogs.

Over in the meadow as the day grew late,
Lived an old mother owl and her little owls eight.
"Wink" said the mother
"We wink" said the eight.
So they winked and were glad as the day grew late.

Over in the meadow in a web on a pine,
Lived an old mother spider and her little spiders nine.
"Spin" said the mother
"We spin" said the nine.
So they spun and were glad in the web on the pine.

Over in the meadow in a warm, dry den,
Lived an old mother rabbit and her little rabbits ten.
"Hop" said the mother
"We hop" said the ten.
So they hopped and were glad in the warm, dry den.

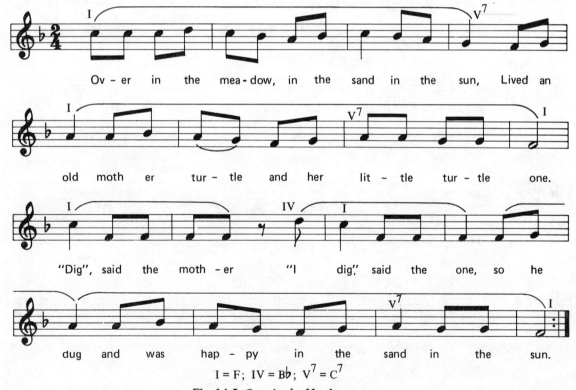

Fig. 14-5 *Over in the Meadow.*

Fig. 14-6 Line drawings for flip cards: instructional aid to be used with *Over in the Meadow*, pages 135 through 139.

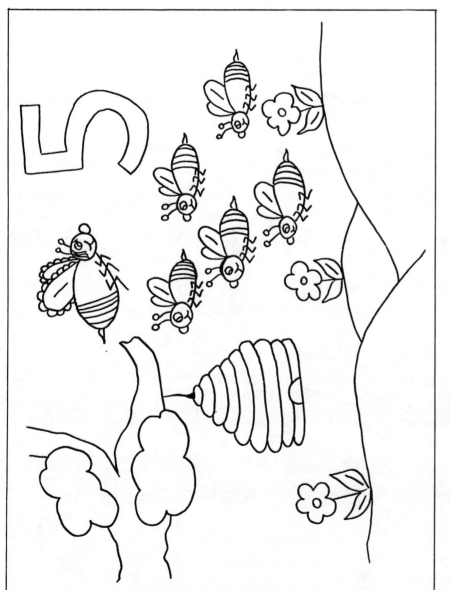

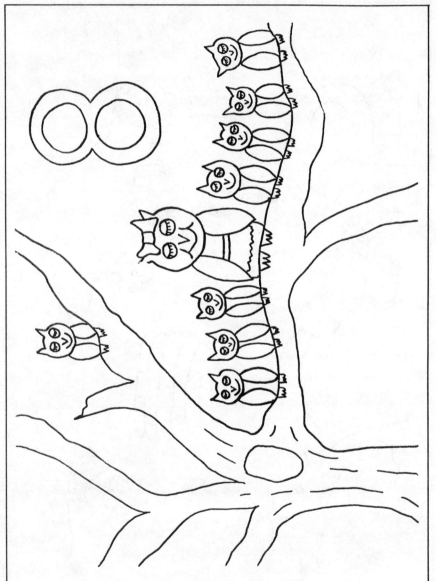

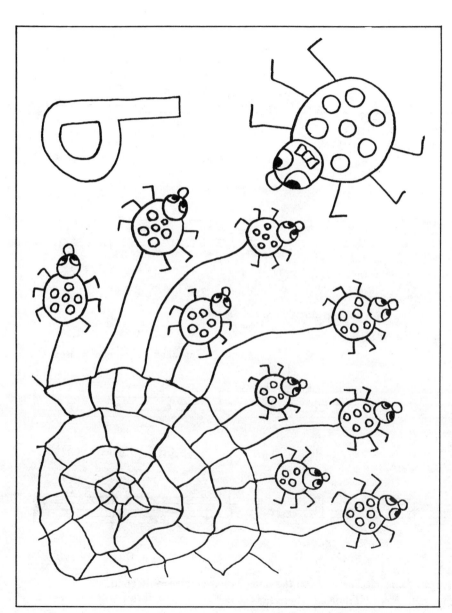

Debra Eames (Jubal)
Grand Junction, Colo.

139

she did not think of herself as a creative person, she made a flip card story to teach the song, figure 14-6. The children liked it. So did other student teachers. An assistant teacher made a flannelboard story from it and used it to teach number concepts from one to ten. Another teacher made cardboard figures, mounted them on popsicle sticks, and used them in the sandbox to teach about animals and their homes. Another teacher used the story to stimulate creative dramatics with songs as well as actions. These activities came about because one person was brave enough to try to make a new instructional aid for an old song.

Fig. 14-7 Children make up melodies as they play. How special if the song can be recorded!

Recorded by M. C. Weller Pugmire

1. We saw one but - ter fly fly - ing all a - round——
(Robin 2. I saw a lit - tle snake slid - ing on the ground, A
sang)

Fly - ing all a - round and land - ing on the ground.
Ti - ny lit - tle snake, Oh! That is what I found.

Fig. 14-8 *Merrill's Song.*

Adapted from singing by Angie Madsen

What's that Go - ing by? Go - ing by?

It's a truck. It's a truck. R — R — Roar, R — R — Roar by.

Fig. 14-9 *Angie's Song:* **Recorded from the singing of a three-year-old child. Most children are "born musicians."**

CREATIVITY AMONG CHILDREN

Children make up melodies as they work and play. Some of these are lovely; some are catchy. Quite a few people are able to hear a child's melody and write it down in musical notation. Others can sing the child's song over and over until they can record it on tape and transpose it into music. (Some teachers tape the child's voice as he sings it.)

As Merrill was walking with his teacher through a day camp, he sang this song over and over, figure 14-8. The teacher recorded it. When she presented it to the other children, Robin said, "Oh, I can make up a verse!"

> *"I saw a little snake sliding on the ground,*
> *A tiny little snake —*
> *Oh that is what I found."*

More verses were added. The field trip to the day camp became meaningful to all of the children, and Merrill's self-concept was improved.

FOSTERING MUSICAL CREATIVITY

There is no standard way to teach a person how to develop creativity, but a few ideas may help:

- Respect ideas and efforts. The idea of even the newest child-care assistant is valuable. Give the child with the "off-key" voice who wants to add his song to the puppet show a chance, as well as the child with the clear "on pitch" voice.

- Seek ways to fill the needs of each child. Do not fear failure; if you fail, the young child will not care. If you succeed, it will be a fine experience.

- Realize how creative efforts can improve the self-concepts of the teacher, the parent, and the child. *Angie's Song,* figure 14-9, is an example of a song recorded from the singing of a child who was not yet three years old. Both the parents and the child beam when they see the song written on a chart.

- Rapport (good feelings among those who work together) between the teachers and the children is necessary if creative efforts are to gain in quality. When one person helps another with suggestions for improvement, music becomes better.

WRITING NEW SONGS

Many teachers would like to try to write songs to meet a child's special need. The question asked most often is, "Do you just pick the tune out of the air?"

There are many books on *music theory* (facts, rules, and ideas about music) that should help one *compose* (write) music. However, the following brief guides should help the beginning writer of children's songs:

- Everyone should be able to express himself with music, just as he does with words. The text has stressed the fact that children are "born musicians." They hum and sing their own music; thus a person should feel free to record any musical thoughts the child has — either on musical staff paper or on tape. It may not be great music, but it may fill a special need and should be respected.

- Repeating words over and over in your mind sometimes gives an idea for the melody and rhythm of a song.

- If you think of just one phrase, remember it can be repeated using different words. Sometimes the ending of a repeated phrase can be changed just a little to make the song sound complete. Be encouraged when you have created one good musical phrase. Others will follow.

- Good music usually has a climax just as good writing does. This is often achieved by making the climax of the music on the highest notes.

- A song usually ends on the keynote or first note of the scale on which the song is based.
- Write the idea you want to express in a simple poem. Decide the mood of the idea — happy, sad. Think of songs you know with that mood. Often your new words can be changed slightly to fit the old tune. Doing this often leads to writing an original tune for a song.

SUMMARY

The keyword for fostering creativity in early childhood education is "Try." Songs and instructional aids can be created by beginning students. Self-concept of teachers, parents, and children is improved when creative efforts are respected. When there is a good rapport among those involved in the school or center, musical creativity is encouraged and improves in quality.

SUGGESTED ACTIVITIES

- Learn the *Texture* song. Make a touch book. Find a child and let him sing about the textures as he turns the pages of the book. Write a brief report of the results.

- Teach a child *Say Hello to Mrs. Circle*. Give him materials to make Mrs. Circle, Mr. Square, and Mrs. Triangle. Keep these for your file if possible. File in 84D: Math or 89: Instructional Aids.

- Make the flip-card music aid for *Over in the Meadow* or try an idea of your own that comes from studying this song and illustrations.

- Look around you. Find a child or a classmate with a special need. Create some music item for this person. Some suggestions are listed:

  a. A flip-card illustration for a well-known song. (See unit 17 for instructions for making.) Use the person's name in the words to the song.
  b. New words to an old song.
  c. A new song.

- Create different versions of the *Texture* song to teach about the other four senses. Make a booklet to go with each.

REVIEW

A. Match each item in Column II with the correct item in Column I.

<table>
<tr><td align="center">I</td><td align="center">II</td></tr>
<tr><td>1. Song that stimulated art activity</td><td>a. "Texture"</td></tr>
<tr><td>2. Key word for creativity</td><td>b. "Say Hello to Mrs. Circle"</td></tr>
<tr><td>3. Improved when person creates music</td><td>c. TRY</td></tr>
<tr><td>4. Song created to teach about sense of touch</td><td>d. "Merrill's Song"</td></tr>
<tr><td>5. Song created by a child</td><td>e. Self-concept</td></tr>
<tr><td>6. Good feelings among those who work together</td><td>f. Rapport</td></tr>
<tr><td>7. Facts, rules, and ideas about music that should help one compose music</td><td>g. Music theory</td></tr>
</table>

B. Indicate the best choice for each of the following.

1. The original song *Texture*

   a. Was written by a music major.
   b. Inspired a new game for the children.
   c. Has been judged to be musically correct.
   d. Refers to the texture of music tones.

2. The original song *Say Hello to Mrs. Circle*

   a. Is related to music, art, and math.
   b. Is a game to be played in a circle.
   c. Teaches manners.
   d. Teaches the child to speak into the telephone with a musical tone.

3. The song *Over in the Meadow*

   a. Was written by a student studying child care.
   b. Is a traditional song.
   c. Is too hard for young children to sing.
   d. Is an Easter song.

4. To record an original song sung by a child,

   a. Write it as music to be sung by others.
   b. Sing it with the child so you can write it or record it later.
   c. Make a recording of it.
   d. All of the above.

5. To develop creativity in music

   a. Be aware of needs that can be met by music.
   b. Just start writing notes on a musical staff.
   c. Do not fear failure.
   d. Both a and c.

6. The early childhood center where creativity is fostered has personnel who

   a. Respect ideas of others.
   b. Develop rapport among workers.
   c. Are interested in building self-concept.
   d. All of the above.

Section 5 Media and Materials

unit 15 musical instruments

OBJECTIVES

After studying this unit, the student should be able to

- List four ways rhythm instruments are used.
- Identify basic rhythm instruments.
- Discuss commercial instruments and homemade instruments.
- Discuss the use and abuse of the piano.

People make many sounds with their bodies. They slap their knees, click their tongues, clap their hands, and stamp their feet. They use their bodies to extend the sound of instruments.

PLAYING INSTRUMENTS

The young baby likes to make sounds. A mother (or another person caring for the child) finds instruments for him. A bell with a true, clear ring is one such instrument. The adult swings the bell over the baby so the child may discover the sound of the bell. Later, the bell is tied within his reach so the baby may ring it. . The child's safety must be kept in mind whenever any toy is created for a young child's use.

The most often used instruments in early education centers are rhythm band instruments: rhythm sticks, wood blocks, tambourines, triangles, jingle sticks, and drums. The child uses these instruments to find out about sounds. He discovers that one instrument makes a sharp sound while another makes a ring. He learns that an instrument can make music, not just noise. Secondly, he uses the instrument to *accompany* (play along with other music) his singing or humming and learns that the sound of the instrument must not be louder than his singing. Thirdly, he learns to pick out the rhythm patterns. Eventually, he uses instruments in complex ways.

COMMERCIAL INSTRUMENTS AND HOMEMADE INSTRUMENTS

Although the quality of commercial instruments cannot be matched by those made at home or in school, it is fun (and inexpensive) for the children to make their own rhythm instruments. Each child becomes aware of the sound of the instrument as he makes it. While the instruments usually last only a short time, the child takes pride in what he has made.

Playing Commercial Rhythm Instruments

The teacher should know the names of the rhythm instruments and how to play them correctly. When one rhythm stick is struck on another, they make a sharp, clicking sound. Some rhythm sticks are notched, and when one

Fig. 15-1 Stephanie enjoys the shaker she made and makes her own rhythm.

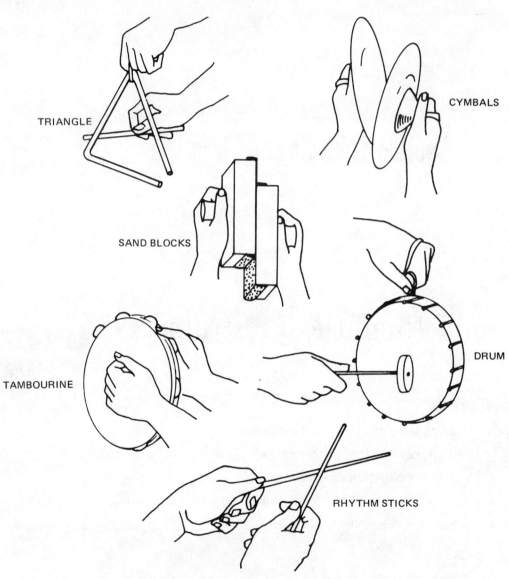

TRIANGLE

CYMBALS

SAND BLOCKS

TAMBOURINE

DRUM

RHYTHM STICKS

Fig. 15-2 Some common commercial rhythm instruments.

stick is rubbed over the other, a "click-click" sound is made.

The young child makes more music with a covered tambourine than with a hollow one; therefore, a good tambourine is well worth the money it costs. A light beat can be made by striking the cover (head) of the tambourine with the flat palm of the hand or fingers. A heavy beat can be made by hitting it with the knuckles. Another type of sound is made by shaking the tiny cymbals which are around the frame of the tambourine.

Listed below are instructions for playing various rhythm instruments:

- Triangle — Strike it on its side with a metal or wooden striking stick. Hang it from a cord loop in order to get the full sound; it makes the listener tingle.

- Tone Block — Strike it with a wooden mallet, between the two slots in the barrel.

- Sand Blocks — Rub these together with a swishing movement.

- Jingle Sticks — These are also called clogs. A jingle stick is hit against the palm of the hand for a single beat. It can also be shaken.

- Maracas — Play these by shaking them easily.

- Cymbals — Bring down one cymbal and slide it across the other, or bring the two

cymbals directly together to produce a dull sound.

- Finger Castanets — Wear one on the index finger and one on the thumb. Play them by bringing one finger against the other with short taps.

It does not seem necessary to give instructions for playing such widely used rhythm instru-

ments as drums, jingle bells, tom-toms, and gongs.

Homemade Instruments

There are many ways to make rhythm instruments. The teacher's imagination and awareness of sound are two factors that guide these projects. They help the child become

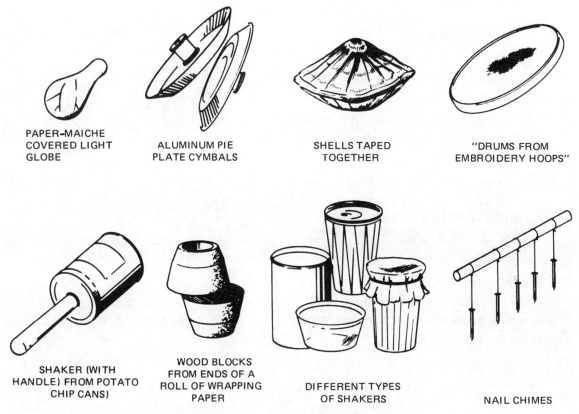

PAPER-MAICHE COVERED LIGHT GLOBE

ALUMINUM PIE PLATE CYMBALS

SHELLS TAPED TOGETHER

"DRUMS FROM EMBROIDERY HOOPS"

SHAKER (WITH HANDLE) FROM POTATO CHIP CANS)

WOOD BLOCKS FROM ENDS OF A ROLL OF WRAPPING PAPER

DIFFERENT TYPES OF SHAKERS

NAIL CHIMES

Fig. 15-3 Some samples of homemade rhythm instruments.

creative. Some ideas are given here but readers are encouraged to think up new instruments for themselves!

- Drums can be made from various materials:

  1. Oatmeal box — Tape it shut. Paint it to make it look better.

  2. Waste basket — Tie part of a rubberized sheet over the open end of a waste basket. Different sizes make different sounds.

  3. Embroidery hoops — Stretch a piece of cloth which has a tight weave between the two hoops.

  4. Old wooden salad bowl — Cover the top with oil cloth. Attach with thumb tacks.

  5. Flower pot — Tightly stretch a piece of heavy wet paper across top and bind it down with elastics and tape. Paper will shrink as it dries to make a tight surface.

- Beaters or drumsticks can be made from pieces of dowel, sticks, broom handles, pencils, wooden spoons. Even shoe horns give a different sound.

- Shakers can be made in several ways:

  1. Paper plates — Fold in half. Put popcorn kernels or small rocks inside. Staple shut.

  2. Paper cups — Put a bell or beans inside. Tape two cups together.

  3. Plastic soap bottle — Cut off the neck. Put small rocks inside. Cover neck and tape shut.

  4. Coconut shell — Put rice inside. Tape the opening, then paint the shell.

  5. Light bulb — Cover a light bulb with papier-mache. When dry, hit the bulb on the table. The glass breaks inside to make a splendid shaker. Paint and shellac it as this is a fine instrument to keep.

  6. Tennis ball can or potato chip can — Put small stones inside. Cut a small hole in the lid. Attach a stick for a handle.

- Wooden instruments are made from

  1. Wooden spoons — Strike them together!

  2. Wood blocks — Attach heavy sandpaper to one side. These are "swished" together.

  3. Narrow board — Nail short strips of wood across it. Rub another stick across this for a special sound.

Fig. 15-4 Lucky is the child who can be near the water and discover the rhythms to be found there.

- Special instruments may be made from

   1. Bones — One father, who was a rancher, cut bones so that they could be used to make different kinds of instruments. Fun!

   2. Shells — Lucky is the child who can look for shells to make rhythm instruments. That child will be aware of the sounds the water makes, too.

   3. Gourds and other plants — Some types of gourds can be dried and shellacked to make exciting sounds. Other plants can be used, too.

GUIDING CHILDREN'S INSTRUMENT PLAYING

As the child nears three years of age, he picks up the rhythm instruments on the music table and shows interest in their sounds. Sometimes, this stage is compared to the scribble stage in art. The child needs to be able to make any kind of sound he wants, before he progresses to other more structured activities.

The four-year-old likes to march and beat time in a parade, although the rhythm is seldom perfect. The older fours and fives can advance to more structured activities. While teaching young children, the author found that presenting one instrument at a time works well and helps the children become aware of specific sounds and rhythms.

SONGS ABOUT RHYTHM INSTRUMENTS

Every child can have a set of rhythm sticks because these are easy to make. The children should be given time to make any sounds they like. Then, the song, *Sticks Go Click-Click*, figure 15-5, is taught by rote. The children clap on the strong beats as they sing. The teacher then tells her group that she will be the music leader and when she holds up her hands, everyone will stop playing. In this way, children learn to follow a music leader.

Every child can also have a drum since large coffee or shortening cans with plastic lids work well and can be brought from home. Teach *Drum*, figure 15-6. Eventually, each child will want to decorate his drum, and the music activity leads to an art activity.

The children may have to share instruments for the next songs. Those who do not have an instrument can clap their hands on the accented beats. The instruments are spread among the group. The song may be sung over and over until each child has a chance to use an instrument. (The instruments are spaced around the circle and passed to the right.) First, use *The Triangle* song, figure 15-7; next, *Wood Block*, figure 15-8; then, *Tambourine*, figure 15-9.

The above scheme for teaching children through song to use instruments takes several days. Then, the group is ready to use two instruments at the same session. The song, *Drums and Sticks*, figure 15-10, can be used. The music leader points to the drums to play "boom" and to the sticks to play on the "click." The children love this!

THE USE AND ABUSE OF THE PIANO

The main instrument in many classrooms is the piano. It should be used as often as

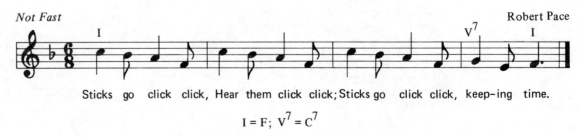

Not Fast   Robert Pace

Sticks go click click, Hear them click click; Sticks go click click, keep-ing time.

I = F; $V^7 = C^7$

Fig. 15-5 *Rhythm Sticks* (Cassette song 25-I).

Vigorously   Robert Pace

Drum, drum, rum – ty tum! Beat the drum a rum –ty – tum!

Drum, drum, rum – ty – tum! Rum – ty – tum, the drum!

$I = F; V^7 = C^7$ **Fig. 15-6** *Drum* (Cassette song 25-J).

Happily   by Robert Pace

Ring, ring, ring ting - a – ling! Ring, ring, ring ting – a – ling!

Ring, ring, ring ting – a – ling! I'll make the tri – an – gle sing ting –a– ling!

Fig. 15-7 *The Triangle* (Cassette song 25-K).

With a Swing   Robert Pace

Block, block, block of wood, You'd talk if you could,

Talk, talk, talk – a – talk! Talk, talk, wood block!

$I = F; V^7 = C^7$

Fig. 15-8 *Wood Block* (Cassette song 25-L).

possible. The piano promotes the love of music. If no teacher or assistant plays the piano, contact volunteers. Often, older students in a school enjoy the chance to play for a young audience.

The piano should be kept tuned. The young child should be taught to treat the piano with care. Instead of pounding on it, he should be shown how to play it gently.

The words, "Gently, gently," are often used as a guide.

Soon after reaching the age of four, children like to play *duets* (make music with another person), using the black keys of the piano. Each of two children plays one black key at a time, using a gentle touch. No matter what keys are played, the sound will not be offensive. Each child feels he is doing something very special and develops a greater interest in the piano.

OTHER TYPES OF INSTRUMENTS

Melody bells, resonator bells, and the Autoharp are also used in early education. These instruments increase the child's awareness of the variety of sounds. They also help children learn about elements of music. The

Tap, tap and shake, Tap, tap and shake! Two kinds of sounds the tam-bou-rines make.

$I = F; V^7 = C^7$

Fig. 15-9 *Tambourine* (Cassette song 25-M).

Boom! Chick, chick, chick! Boom! Chick, chick, chick! Boom! Chick, chick, chick! Drums and sticks,

Boom! Chick, chick, chick! Boom! Chick, chick, chick! Boom! Chick, chick, chick! Booms and chicks!

$I = F; V^7 = C^7$

Fig. 15-10 *Drums and Sticks* (Cassette song 25-N).

use of these instruments is discussed later in the units on melody and harmony.

In some schools, the music program features a different instrument each week. Someone may come to school to play an instrument — often, a parent or grandparent. Sometimes the children are allowed to experiment carefully with it.

SUMMARY

The very young child plays a variety of instruments that make different sounds; both commercial and homemade rhythm instruments are used. Special songs may be used to introduce each instrument. Musicians visit the classroom to broaden the child's experience.

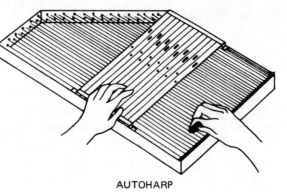

AUTOHARP

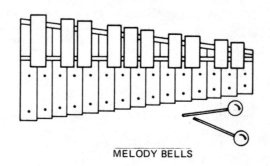

MELODY BELLS

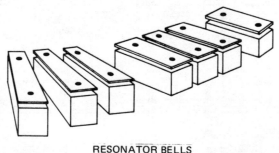

RESONATOR BELLS

Fig. 15-11 The words to use are "Gently, gently," when the child discovers the piano.

Fig. 15-12 Melody bells, resonator bells, and Autoharp are also used in early education.

Fig. 15-13 Sometimes the children can experiment with an instrument. Often this leads to excellent dramatic play.

SUGGESTED ACTIVITIES

- List four ways to use rhythm instruments with young children.

- Try to get a set of commercial rhythm band instruments. Explore the sounds they make.

- Make three or more of the rhythm instruments that are described in the text. Create one of your own from materials around your home.

- Teach a song about rhythm instruments to your fellow students or to a group of young children, following the instructions in the text. Discuss the results with your classmates.

REVIEW

A. Describe the sound made by each of the following rhythm instruments by using words such as clicking, ringing or tingling, swishing, booming, or others if appropriate.

1. Rhythm sticks
2. Jingle sticks
3. Sand blocks
4. Tone blocks
5. Tambourine
6. Drum
7. Wrist bells

8. Maracas
9. Triangles
10. Finger castanets
11. Sleigh bells
12. Wood blocks
13. Tom-toms
14. Cymbals

B. Fill in the blanks in the following steps used to teach about instruments through the use of songs.

1. Teach the song by _____ .

2. Children then _____ on the strong beats as they sing.

3. Teacher tells the children she will be music _____ that day.

4. When she holds her hands up and apart, every child _____ playing. She demonstrates this.

5. She gives each child a _____ .

6. The children are given _____ to make any sound they wish.

7. Then she holds her hands up, gets attention, and starts to _____ .

8. The children _____ and _____ .

C. The children bring the following items from home. Name and describe five rhythm instruments you could help the children make.

Bottle caps	Paint-stirring sticks
Nails, large	Paper towel tubes
Aluminum pie plates	Cottage cheese cartons
Wood spools	Jingle bells
2 strainers	Marbles
Split peas	2 cookie cutters (alike)
Pieces of wood	2 wooden ends from roll of wrapping paper

D. Briefly answer each of the following.

1. How can a mother (or her substitute) help a baby discover sounds?

2. Where do you hold a tambourine?

3. Why is it important to let each child make the sounds he wishes when he begins to play rhythm instruments?

4. Briefly discuss the value of commercial and homemade rhythm instruments.

5. Describe one way to teach the child to treat the piano with respect.

6. How can children play duets at a very young age?

7. Name three ways other instruments can be used in early education.

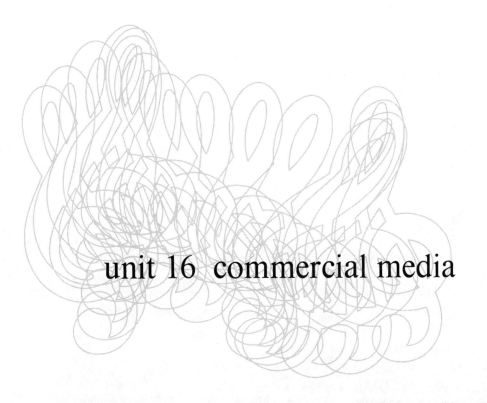

unit 16 commercial media

OBJECTIVES

After studying this unit, the student should be able to

- Name six sources from which to obtain commercial music materials.
- Briefly describe several types of music materials.
- List practical ideas gained from studying catalogs.
- Discuss the use of basic music programs.

There are many commercial materials available to help use music in early music education. This text stresses materials that the teacher can make. However, often money is allocated for commercial materials. The teacher should know what is available in order to make the most of the opportunity to buy materials.

Many fine ideas can be gained from commercial music companies. Often these companies help schools and centers build good music programs as they sell their materials.

WHERE TO FIND MATERIALS

Catalogs are probably the best place to find out about commercial music materials. Addresses of places to send for materials can be found in teachers' magazines. Most of the companies listed on the acknowledgment page of this book have catalogs that show a variety of materials. A library, especially one that serves a college that teaches music or education, has source books of media that are used to teach music. An example is a book that tells how to use a cassette and a filmstrip to teach a concept.

Curriculum centers — sometimes called educational media centers or a similar name — display materials that can be borrowed and used. These are usually found in general education or music colleges, but sometimes there is one in a local school district. A telephone call to the local public school office may disclose where these centers are located.

Music or school supply stores have commercial music materials although there are only a few that carry large stocks. The sales people at these stores have often studied catalogs or attended trade shows and can give suggestions to teachers.

Conventions are good places to find out about materials. Often there are displays put on by commercial companies that present many fine ideas. The teacher should visit such conventions if she has a chance.

Professional organizations can ask commercial companies to demonstrate their products at meetings. Sales representatives of companies will sometimes do this. Authors and teachers who use a certain product will often talk to groups of students and other teachers who want to improve their music programs.

TYPES OF MATERIALS

One usually thinks of phonographs, tape recorders, rhythm instruments, and similar items as being commercial equipment. However, teachers and assistants should study the entire wide range of such hardware. There are many types from which to choose. Often teachers do not realize that music hardware is available for selection that fits the special needs of their own program.

Records and sheet music are generally known to be available. As catalogs are studied, it becomes obvious that a wide variety of music books is also available for the young child. Fine records may be purchased to suit almost any need. A teacher can look through catalogs to find records to help reach almost any

Fig. 16-1 There is a wide variety of music books available for the young child.

Fig. 16-2 Records are available to meet special needs.

MUSIC AIDS

musical goal. For example, the teacher who feels she is weak in creative movement activities can usually find records to help her — most of which were tested in the classroom. Although some are better, of course, than others, most are very good. Other aids for teaching music are printed keyboards, music flash cards, *music staff liners* (holders for five pieces of chalk to draw a staff on the chalkboard), and music games.

KITS AND PROGRAMS

Some companies have developed kits and charts to teach music. This type of aid can often be seen in a curriculum center.

The *Threshold to Music* program is an example of a commercial program that has had great influence in early music education. This program uses a series of experience charts — based on the work of Zoltan Kodaly, a great

MUSIC AIDS

1. **No. 3900 FUNDAMENTALS OF MUSIC BOOK**........$1.50
   New 32 page book with emphasis on illustration. Teaches how to write music symbols and to understand theory. For private or class lessons, vocal or instrumental students.
2. **No. 3901 FUNDAMENTALS OF MUSIC FLASH CARDS (Teacher Set)**.......................$1.75
   Large 6" x 9" flash cards for teaching essential facts of music. Sixty-eight illustrations. 3 foot keyboard (42 keys) and instructions.
3. **No. 3902 FUNDAMENTALS OF MUSIC FLASH CARDS (Pupil Set)**.......................$1.50
   Contains 60—2" x 3" cards with directions. Self teaching and checking.
4. **No. 3905 CHORDS AND INVERSIONS (Teacher's Set)**..$2.75
   For drilling in recognition of chords and inversions, 207 chords are shown on 52 cards, 7" x 11". Instructions furnished.
5. **3906 CHORDS AND INVERSIONS (Pupil's Set)**......$1.50
   Self teaching and checking. 52 cards, each 2½" x 2½", with 207 chords. Instructions furnished.

6. **No. 3907 NOTES AND KEYBOARD**.................$1.15
   Contains a three foot keyboard and 25 flash cards that teach the names of 50 notes and their respective positions on the keyboard.
7. **No. 3908 SCHOOL DESK KEYBOARD**.....(set of 12) $1.50
   A 6" x 15" reproduction of two octaves (26 keys) of the piano keyboard.
8. **No. 3909 NOTE FINDER**..........................$1.25
   Movable slide covers 3 octaves in both treble and bass clefs. The name of each note position is indicated on the reverse side. A must for every teacher. Ideal for every beginner. On heavy board, 7" x 11".
9. **No. 3910 MUSIC RANGER**.........................$2.75
   Visually teaches the structure of SCALES, CHORDS, and INVERSIONS, etc. Eight double-sided cards with 27 inch keyboard.
10. **No. 3911 MUSIC BINGO**..........................$3.00
    Teaches names, descriptions and uses of music symbols in a game for 2-10 players.
11. **No. 3932 MUSIC STAFF LINER**...................$0.65
    Made of hardwood and built to high quality standards.
12. **No. 3912 METRONOME**...........................$14.00
    Attractive hand wound metronome records intervals from 1/5 to 2 seconds. Ideal for study of principle of the pendulum.

C

Fig. 16-3 There are many commercial music aids to help teach music.

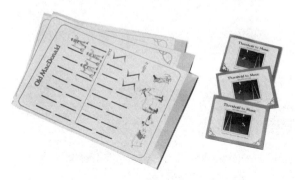

Fig. 16-4 The *Threshold to Music* program has greatly influenced early music education.

Hungarian composer who believes every child should read music just as he reads words. The charts are interesting to the child. The system uses much physical movement. It is based on sound principles of rhythm.

The child-care student may find such charts as these in a school or center where she teaches. She will have to decide for herself the worth of programs in reaching music goals. Such programs as *Threshold to Music* do not replace the musical activities that grow from children's play and interests. However, many educators seem to feel that a formal system should be used along with activities such as the ones described in this text. Students should become familiar with media such as the first charts of the *Threshold to Music* program, but continue to develop their own philosophies regarding early music education.

Fig. 16-5 An unusual rhythm instrument found in a music supply store created new interest in rhythm activities.

UNUSUAL MUSICAL INSTRUMENTS

A visit to a music supply store may give the teacher ideas. Often an unusual musical instrument can be seen. Stores use these to add interest to their displays. One teacher found an eighteen-inch red grooved board with big tambourine-type shakers on the side. She bought this for a small price. She was amazed at the interest this one new instrument created in rhythm activities.

The chromatic melody bells is an inexpensive instrument which the author found in a music supply store. This instrument can be easily moved, and children and teachers like to use it in many ways. Everyone should look for the unusual as standard items are bought.

THE BASIC MUSIC SERIES

Several companies that publish textbooks for elementary schools have developed a series of music texts. At first, there was a volume for each of the six grades. Then, kindergarten was added. Now, in several series, there are books for early childhood education. Much planning goes into these texts. They are excellent sources for ideas and songs to teach to children. Many times these companies exhibit at conventions where one can look at the texts. Some companies will send books to be looked at on a trial basis.

OTHER IDEAS FROM CATALOGS

There are some catalogs that give the teacher good ideas for the music program. These catalogs have fine pictures that may be used to stimulate activities. Ideas for bulletin boards that feature musical concepts are presented, as well as ideas and materials for storing music media.

SUMMARY

There are many places to find out about commercial music media. The teacher should be aware of the wide variety of hardware that is available. Music books, records, filmstrips, and cassette recordings help fill special needs. Kits and special music programs are important parts of music education in some schools. The child care student should be familiar with the basic music series that are available.

Ideas can be gained from catalogs. Care and storage of music materials should be considered when buying music media.

Fig. 16-6 The chromatic melody bells are used in many ways.

SUGGESTED ACTIVITIES

- Each member of the class should send for a different catalog or find a music resource book in the library and bring it to class for comparison. Make a list of some ideas gained that will help you to teach with music.

- Go to a day care center or school for young children. Make a list of all the commercial materials they have. Talk to the Head Teacher. Ask her what she will buy next. Record her reason for making these purchases. State your opinions.

- Obtain the first charts of the *Threshold to Music* program. If the charts are not available, get the teacher's manual. With class members, go through the charts. Discuss their value and place in early music education.

- Locate the curriculum centers in your area. If possible, visit one. Make arrangements to use the materials that are there so that you will be more familiar with commercial music media.

- Each class member should look at an early childhood, kindergarten, or grade one volume from a basic music series. Look for the strengths of the text. Compare findings that class members describe from books in the various series.

REVIEW

A. Briefly answer each of the following.

1. Name six sources of information about commercial music materials.

2. List at least one type of commercial material that can be found at each source.

3. Suggest ideas you might gain from studying catalogs that show commercial music media.

unit 17 materials made by teacher and children

OBJECTIVES

After studying this unit, the student should be able to

- Make three objects that stimulate children to sing.
- Create an aid to help with "choosing-time."
- Make (or describe) three aids to help build a foundation for music.

Most teachers of young children enjoy making *instructional aids* (objects to improve teaching). When deciding to make instructional aids, the teacher considers the time and money that will be spent. If the instructional aid takes a great deal of the teacher's time, she may not make it. Sometimes, the item can be bought for less than it costs to make it. However, when the teacher knows that something she makes really meets a special need of her group, the time and money may not seem most important.

COMMON INSTRUCTIONAL AIDS

Pictures are probably the most popular of all the aids. Students should build their files of pictures to use when they are teaching. The discussion of the file system in unit 2 is helpful in determining a system of filing. The pictures should be mounted on sturdy paper or poster board. An inexpensive material for mounting pictures is the plastic used to cover dry cleaning. The plastic is cut into pieces just smaller than the pictures. The mounting paper, plastic, and picture are stacked on a hard surface and then pressed with a warm iron. The plastic melts between the picture and the mounting paper, making a lasting bond. Pictures may be mounted using different types of glue, also.

The flannelboard is a good aid. Figures that show the objects described in a song are made. A good material to use is *pellon* (a nonwoven cloth used for interfacing when sewing. The best type is fairly heavy; yet one can see through it.) The pellon is placed over a picture of an object and the figure is traced. The pellon is then cut into the shape of the object or a border is left around it to make it sturdier to handle. The figures are colored, then placed on the flannelboard as the words to the song are sung.

Figures may also be cut from old pattern books, obtainable at stores where sewing supplies are sold. These and other figures can be backed with velour paper, flannel, felt, or pieces of lightweight sandpaper to make them stick on the flannelboard.

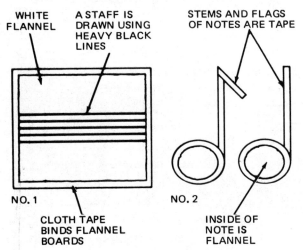

WHITE FLANNEL

A STAFF IS DRAWN USING HEAVY BLACK LINES

STEMS AND FLAGS OF NOTES ARE TAPE

NO. 1

CLOTH TAPE BINDS FLANNEL BOARDS

NO. 2

INSIDE OF NOTE IS FLANNEL

Fig. 17-1 Two types of musical flannelboards can be made. The note flannelboard can be made on a wall, window, or sturdy piece of cardboard.

A very useful flannelboard can be made from a 12" x 18" piece of corrugated cardboard. Two pieces of flannel of different colors are cut to the exact size of the board. These are attached with glue. The edges are bound with cloth tape. The finished flannelboard is light but sturdy. The different colors of the sides can show two parts of a song or activity.

A music staff flannelboard is made by drawing a staff across a piece of white flannel or felt, figure 17-1. Staffs and notes can be cut from black felt. This may be used with the song, *Do, Re, Mi*. The figures for the song are cut out and pasted on black felt notes. A child places these notes on the music flannelboard, or eight children may step up to place notes of the scale, figure 17-2, on the flannelboard. The music flannelboard may be used to teach other facts about music, too.

The student should learn to use the *opaque projector*, a machine available in most colleges and vocational schools. A visual aid is placed in the machine, the machine is turned on and focused, and a larger picture is shown and can be traced. The figures in this book can be made larger this way.

A "flip card" booklet may be made to teach the words of a song. Pieces of poster board of the desired size are held together with rings (sold at stationery stores). The front of the first card serves as a cover for the booklet. The first card (the cover) is flipped over. (It becomes the last card, then.) The words of the first phrase of the song are printed on the back of this first card (#1). The picture described in the first phrase of the song is shown on the front of the second card (#2). The second card is then flipped completely over. The words of the second phrase of the song are printed on the back of the second card (#2). The picture to illustrate the second phrase is on the front of the third card (#3). This is continued for as many phrases as desired as shown in figure 17-3. While the children look at the picture on the front card, the teacher glances at the words of the song printed on the back card, without losing eye contact with the children. The children will understand difficult words better when they can see the illustrations.

Real objects are interesting instructional aids. An umbrella will help the children learn the meaning of the word, "bumbershoot," used in the song, *Great Big Words*, figure 17-4. A real or plastic daffodil may be used, too. This is vocabulary development; music is related to all parts of the child's learning.

"Chalk talks" are another aid a teacher may use. She places a small chalkboard on her lap and, as she sings, quickly draws pictures that illustrate the song. Even the teacher with little drawing ability can learn several basic sketches, such as the facial expressions shown

Fig. 17-2 These pictures are placed on black felt notes. They are used on the musical flannelboard to illustrate "Do, Re, Mi."

Fig. 17-3 Flip-card instructional aid.

Fig. 17-4 *Great Big Words* (Cassette song 25-H): Three-dimensional instructional aids can be used with this song to help in vocabulary development.

in figure 17-5. Some teachers use stick figures for chalk talks. Others feel that stick figures are not proper examples for children to follow. The author suggests that students practice until they feel comfortable with the chalk and chalkboard.

Puppets fascinate many children. A child who does not want to sing for a teacher will sometimes sing for a puppet. A puppet to lead the singing may be made from a long glove of stretchy material that fits the thumb and the index and middle fingers of the hand, figure 17-6. The dress of the puppet is long to hold the puppet on the hand. The head can be bought or made from a styrofoam ball. The head is placed on the index finger — over the glove. This leaves the thumb and middle finger in a position to move much better than with traditional hand puppets. The puppet leads the singing, teaches the words of a new song, and asks the children (or a reluctant child) to sing.

Fig. 17-5 A teacher can learn to draw basic facial expressions.

AIDS TO STIMULATE SINGING

One of the main goals of music is stimulating children's responses. A musical thermometer is sometimes used to encourage children to sing, figure 17-7. Sometimes the "temperature" on the thermometer goes up if the children sing loudly; sometimes it rises if they sing softly. It rises when children sing with excellent expression, clear words, and

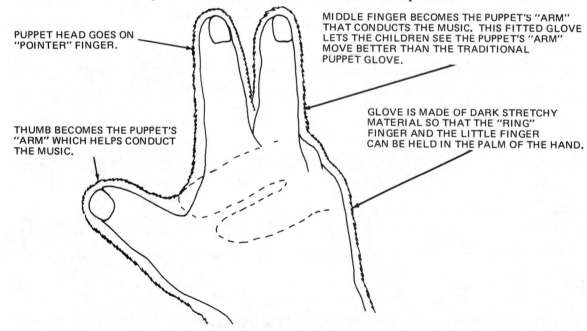

PUPPET HEAD GOES ON "POINTER" FINGER.

MIDDLE FINGER BECOMES THE PUPPET'S "ARM" THAT CONDUCTS THE MUSIC. THIS FITTED GLOVE LETS THE CHILDREN SEE THE PUPPET'S "ARM" MOVE BETTER THAN THE TRADITIONAL PUPPET GLOVE.

THUMB BECOMES THE PUPPET'S "ARM" WHICH HELPS CONDUCT THE MUSIC.

GLOVE IS MADE OF DARK STRETCHY MATERIAL SO THAT THE "RING" FINGER AND THE LITTLE FINGER CAN BE HELD IN THE PALM OF THE HAND.

Fig. 17-6 A music puppet which leads the singing has a special glove for its body.

full attention. A child who has done well during the music can be chosen to "raise the red" on the thermometer, thereby reinforcing his desirable behavior.

Many young children do not open their mouths wide enough to really allow the sound to come out; they mumble. Two empty salt boxes can become "Open-mouth Opal" and "Closed-mouth Clara," figure 17-8. Most salt boxes have a plastic shaker; paper is used to cover the top of the box except for the metal spout. Hair is made with yarn; hats can be made if desired. The following poem may be used with the salt box puppets:

> *Closed-mouth Clara lets no sound come out.*
> *Open-mouth Opal sings, but she doesn't shout.*

Boys and girls should not be encouraged to compete during music activities except in certain special circumstances. When the boys decide that singing is "girl's stuff," the boy and girl faces, figure 17-9, may be used. When the boys sing better, a boy is chosen to hold the boy-face. (At this point, however, the teacher should ask herself whether she is using songs that appeal to boys as well as girls.)

When the teacher holds up the "girl-face," the girls sing. When she holds up the "boy-face," the boys sing.

Another type of instructional aid is made on a piece of cardboard that is very sturdy. Attach a paper kite to a string. Put two holes in the cardboard and run the string through them, tying it in the back with a knot to make a loop. The children sing their favorite songs. When they sing very well, the teacher moves the kite up in the "sky" by moving the knot on the back. If they do not sing as well, she pulls the kite back down, figure 17-10. This encourages participation! (Other similar aids

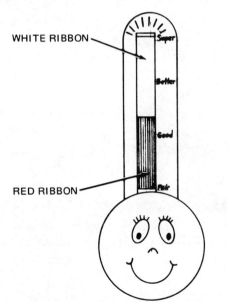

Fig. 17-7 The musical thermometer is a favorite instructional aid with the children.

Fig. 17-8 "Closed-Mouth Clara" and "Open-Mouth Opal" help the children sing better.

Fig. 17-9 Boy and girl faces are mounted on paint-stirring sticks. These encourage singing.

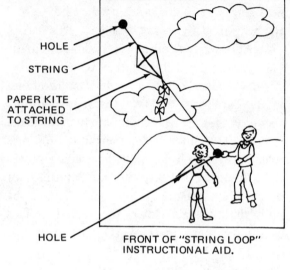

HOLE

STRING

PAPER KITE
ATTACHED
TO STRING

HOLE

FRONT OF "STRING LOOP"
INSTRUCTIONAL AID.

HOLE

STRINGS

KNOT

HOLE

BACK OF "STRING LOOP"
INSTRUCTIONAL AID.

Fig. 17-10 Kite Instructional Aid.

are a flag that is pulled up and down a flagpole, a bird that "flies" in and out of a tree, etc.)

AIDS FOR CHOOSING-TIME

A variety of instructional aids may be used for "choosing-time," when the teacher wants to review songs or music activities. She remembers, too, that the young child loves the songs he knows. Some ideas for choosing-time aids are listed

- A stuffed animal is placed in a box with several small hats of different kinds. (The small hats can be bought at hobby stores.) A child chooses a hat to put on the

stuffed animal. The children sing the song on the paper in the hat the child chooses.

- A small flower pot is filled with styro-foam. Flowers on stiff stems are placed in the pot. Each has the name of a song on it. One child chooses a flower; then the song is sung.

- Paper fish are made with songs printed on them. A paper clip is attached to each fish. The teacher makes a small fishing pole with a magnet for a hook. The children "fish" for songs to sing.

Fig. 17-11 Different hats containing musical titles are chosen by the child for the stuffed animal.

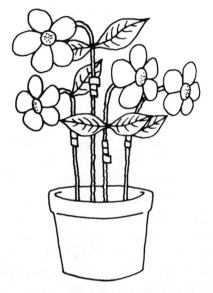

Fig. 17-12 **The child chooses a flower. The name of the song the group will sing is on the stem.**

AIDS MADE BY THE CHILDREN

The teacher looks for items made or brought to school by the children that can be kept for instructional aids. The child has to approve this, however, because he may want to take all of his projects home. Children's drawings make appealing visual aids. If it is possible to use them, they should be mounted following the suggestions given at the beginning of the unit.

A child sometimes brings items from home that can become instructional aids. An example of this is one of the plastic faces with a smile on it. Sometimes these say, "Have a happy day." Such an item could be used to interest the group in singing the song *Smiles* from unit 3.

Objects made by the children are useful, also. An example is a clay nest such as children often make. It could suggest singing *Up, Up in the Sky* from unit 4. Airplanes made at the woodworking table may suggest songs about airplanes, or perhaps the children will make up a song!

OTHER TEACHER-MADE MATERIALS

The teacher may create instructional aids to help meet a major goal of the music program — to build a foundation for further music education:

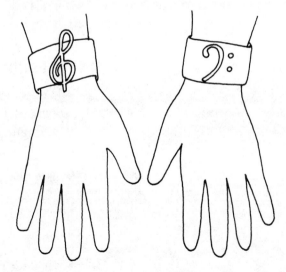

Fig. 17-14 **The child becomes familiar with musical symbols by having them near him.**

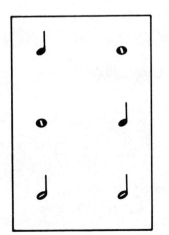

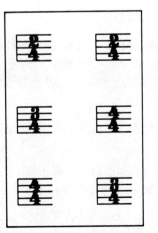

Fig. 17-13 **Examples of games in which musical symbols are matched by drawing lines between them.**

- "Matching" games about music in which musical symbols are placed in two columns on a piece of poster board 4" x 5 1/2", figure 17-13. This poster board is then covered with plastic. (One half of a blank overhead transparency will do and costs only a few cents.) The poster board and plastic are taped together with masking tape. The child matches the symbols by drawing lines between the two columns with a crayon or wax pencil. After the teacher looks at his work, she writes his name on the back and has him "erase" the lines he has drawn so that another child can use the game card.

- Letters of the alphabet and numerals are often cut from sandpaper to help the children become familiar with them by using the sense of touch. This can be done with the musical symbols, too. Notes and other musical symbols can be cut out, mounted on poster board, and given to the children to trace with their finger tips.

- Bass clef ($\mathbf{9}\colon$) and treble clef ($\oint$) signs can be made from black pipe cleaners. These can be sewn to a bracelet of white elastic on which the lines of the musical staff have been drawn, figure 17-14. The children can wear them in the classroom or even wear them home.

These are only a few of many musical instructional aids that can help the child learn about the elements of music. The student should try to add to this list.

SUMMARY

Most teachers of young children enjoy making teaching aids, but they should consider the time and money the projects require. Pictures, flannelboards and figures, flip card booklets, real objects, chalk talk materials, and puppets are standard aids. Other aids, such as the musical thermometer and salt box "singers" are used to stimulate singing. The teacher can also look for music aids made by the children. She can develop ideas that will help her reach the goal of building a foundation for musical experiences.

SUGGESTED ACTIVITIES

- Collect and mount several pictures to help teach music. Individual members of the class should make a different instructional aid described in the unit. Each one should use this aid with the class. Discuss its effectiveness in helping to teach music.

- Use the musical thermometer with a group of children. Discuss the results.

- Keep "Closed-mouth Clara" and "Open-mouth Opal" in your classroom. When students start "mumbling" in their singing, use these two aids.

- Invite a music teacher of young children to discuss the aids she uses to help in her teaching. Following her discussion, make some of the aids she suggests. File your aids or appropriately label a container for them.

- Make several of the instructional aids described in this unit. Keep a record of the cost and the time spent.

- Practice drawing facial expressions, using the guides given in figure 17-5.

REVIEW

A. Briefly describe an instructional aid of the type suggested that could be used with each of the following songs.

1. *Five Little Kittens* (flip card story)

2. *Santa Claus is Coming to Town* (puppet)

3. *Jingle Bells* (3 dimensional)

4. *Twinkle, Twinkle Little Star* (something to encourage nonsingers)

5. *Glory, Glory Hallelujah* (something to encourage the boys to sing)

6. *Over in the Meadow* (flannelboard)

7. *Cotton Needs Picking* (3-dimensional)

8. *Eensy Weensy Spider* (child-made visual)

B. Describe an aid to help with choosing-time. (other than those given in the text)

1. Name an object (such as the pot of flowers named in the text) that would contain several items and be very familiar to children.

2. Tell how the names of the songs would be attached to the objects in order to be chosen by a child.

C. Indicate the best choice for each of the following.

1. An instructional aid refers to

a. Any item that helps the teacher reach her goal better.

b. A volunteer mother.

c. A phonograph or tape recorder.

d. Something the child can hear.

2. The most valuable pictures for children are

   a. Bought from commercial companies.
   b. In color.
   c. Simple and/or tell a story.
   d. Very large.

3. Flip card booklets

   a. Are a good way to present the words of a song.
   b. Have the illustration on the front card and the words on the back card.
   c. Let the teacher have eye-to-eye contact.
   d. All of the above.

4. Which statements tell about the musical thermometer?

   a. It tells if the temperature in the room is best for singing.
   b. It gives encouragement for the children to do the musical activity better.
   c. It can help every member of the group to sing.
   d. "Raising" it can be a reward for a child.

5. Matching games

   a. Can be used to help the child learn about music symbols.
   b. Should be saved for language arts activities.
   c. Are too difficult for children in early childhood education.
   d. Are expensive but worthwhile.

6. Instructional aids made by the children

   a. Are not good because they are unrealistic.
   b. Should be kept only with the child's permission.
   c. Will not help reach the goals of the music program.
   d. None of the above.

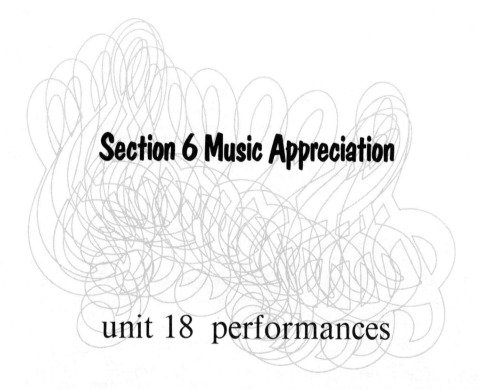

Section 6 Music Appreciation

unit 18 performances

OBJECTIVES

After studying this unit, the student should be able to

- Discuss the advantages and disadvantages of planned performances.
- List three ways to encourage musical performances.
- Name five criteria for selecting performers for the children.

When the children sing the songs they have learned very well, it tempts teachers to say, "Let's put on a program!" Why? Will a program help each child? Will it really involve the parents? Will the time spent in practice be used wisely? Every teacher of young children should consider these questions concerning musical performances by children and for children.

THE QUESTION OF PERFORMANCES BY CHILDREN

In many early centers — either school or day care — putting on programs is a big thing. There are some occasions when the time and effort this takes is worthwhile; there are many times when it is not.

Some disadvantages of planned performances are listed:

- They can take the children away from activities that further the goals of early childhood education more effectively. An example is using the time when the child usually plays or does art activities.

- They tend to become teachers' programs instead of children's programs.

- Though some children like a planned program, many others do not. A program tends to halt the progress of such children.

- Making costumes and props often takes time and money that could be spent more wisely on other projects.

Some factors favoring planned programs are listed:

- Sometimes they strengthen the fine traditions of a local area, because traditional music is taught and used.

- At times, parents can become involved in effective ways.

- Sometimes a program is a means of helping the children work together more effectively.

WHEN CHILDREN PERFORM

The picture in figure 18-1, which was taken during a performance in a school, shows

Fig. 18-1 Pictured above is an actual performance by children that came from the play and work of the class.

several positive things that should be considered when children perform.

- The program came from the curriculum. The children learned Christmas songs and wanted their parents to come and share the beauty of the carols.

- Every child took part. The children helped plan what each would do. Some danced; some sang; others played instruments.

- The program was centered around the children. A child leads the singing. The parents were asked to sing with the children. (The teachers helped the child leader, of course.)

Fig. 18-2 A folding screen and an old microphone stand spur the children on to a musical "performance." These types of activities come from the delightful play of children.

- The costumes were simple. The children planned what they would wear. It can be seen in the picture that Joseph's coat is made from towels.

These children worked together; they were pleased with their efforts. They will remember the special songs they learned. It was a more effective experience than a big, structured production could have been.

MUSICAL PERFORMANCES AMONG YOUNG CHILDREN

In the delightful play of early childhood, there are often musical performances going on. There are some things the teacher can do to encourage this.

Fig. 18-3 Perhaps no other piece of equipment encourages a child-performance as does an overturned "rocking boat."

Many centers have a rocking boat. Perhaps no other piece of equipment encourages child performances as well. When the rocking boat is turned over, there is something about climbing up the stairs that inspires the child to sing or play a rhythm instrument. If his teacher and classmates become part of the dramatic play and give him attention and clap for him, he does even better — thus, building his self-concept.

Children sometimes build a stage from large blocks, or long boards can be placed on rungs of aluminum climbers. A sturdy wooden box can be used outdoors to make an "open-air theatre." A word of encouragement from a teacher or aide stimulates this type of activity. Some other suggestions that can help in-class performances are listed:

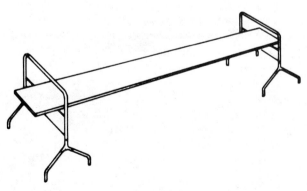

Fig. 18-4 A long board placed on the rungs of aluminum climbers becomes a "stage."

- Playing an accompaniment for the child on the Autoharp or piano. When the teacher does this for one child, others want her accompaniment, too.

- Finding a needed prop for a performer.

- Helping the children make tickets and programs for a performance they have planned in dramatic play.

The list seems endless when the skill of teaching music to young children is used effec-

Fig. 18-5 Even though an older brother might play a note that distresses him, he can often help the children because they are interested in him and what he has to say.

tively. It is a wise teacher who sees the opportunity to help a child with music, and knows how to encourage him to do the preparation and performance as part of his play activities.

PERFORMANCES AMONG CHILDREN IN SCHOOL

In more formal classrooms, performances among the children can also be encouraged. The children can build a stage in the music corner. If this would interfere with regular class activities, perhaps some place that is not being used in the school could be found. Often, halls are not used as much as they could be. The children might plan how a stage could be made that could be moved when necessary. One suggestion is to get a large box from an appliance store that could be made into a stage.

PERFORMANCES FOR THE CHILDREN IN SCHOOL

It has been suggested that musicians should be brought to the school to perform for the children. There are criteria to consider when inviting visitors.

- Members of a child's family almost always interest the children. It is good to bring older brothers and sisters to the school. It does not matter that the performance may have flaws. In fact, if an older brother shows that a bad note distresses him, the children understand. He may be better able to explain the instrument to the children because he is closer than the adult to their level.

• The performance should be short; it will hold the children's attention better than a long program.

• The children should be able to talk to the performer. They may want to ask how his instrument works or how he is able to sing in a way that sounds so fine.

• Different types of performers should be sought. Some schools try to introduce a new instrument or dancer or type of singer every week.

• If possible, the children should be able to participate. This is best at the end of the visit. Perhaps the child can hum while the violinist plays a simple melody or clap his hands while the country-western singer sings.

STRENGTHENING LOCAL TRADITIONS

A very good reason for having performances is to make the fine traditions of the local community a part of the children's lives. It has been shown that people placed under great stress have been able to endure it better if they have meaningful songs to think about instead of their troubles. These special songs can and should be part of the regular curriculum. If programs are to be held, however, it is wise to consider the possibility of using the special music of the area.

This is also a time when children's wrong ideas can be found and corrected. In one musical performance about cowboys and pioneers, a teacher found that the children had two mistaken ideas: they sang, "Home, home on the range, where the deer and the antelope play," wondering how a deer and an antelope could play on a kitchen stove; and as the

Fig. 18-6 A child's drawing of a father singing for the children.

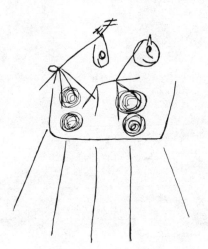

Fig. 18-7 A child's drawing of "Home, home on the range, where the deer and the antelope play," shows the animals on a kitchen range.

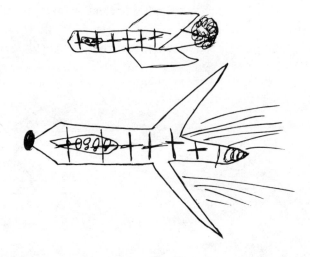

Fig. 18-8 The subject of the performance was the pioneers. This is how one child drew his interpretation of "crossing the plains."

teacher sang about the pioneers crossing the plains, a little boy drew a picture of airplanes with crosses on them.

Teachers need to watch for these wrong ideas and correct them where possible. Music can be used to help young children grow in their understanding of time and space. Sometimes while planning and preparing a simple program, teachers have a chance to learn what a child is thinking.

SUMMARY

There are reasons both for and against having planned performances by children. Simple programs that come from the curriculum are usually better than big, structured performances. Programs do give a chance to strengthen local traditions; this may mean a lot to the child as he grows older. Musicians who come to perform for the children should be selected by certain criteria. Seeing and hearing musical performers is a good way for children to learn about different types of music and instruments.

SUGGESTED ACTIVITIES

- Talk to nursery school, kindergarten, and primary grade teachers. Find out what they think about planned programs. Report to the class.

- Ask the teachers if they have musical performers come to their classes. What criteria do they use to choose them? Report on this, also.

- Ask the teachers about mistaken ideas their children may have formed from songs. As you report these to the class, talk about ways to help children gain correct ideas from songs.

- List the musical performers you know who might be asked to perform for children. Then decide which ones would meet the criteria outlined in this unit.

- Choose a holiday or a tradition such as a local celebration that is held every year. With class members, plan a program that might come from the play and the activities of the children around this theme.

REVIEW

A. Briefly answer each of the following.

1. List four reasons against having planned performances by the children.

2. List three reasons why children should take part in planned performances.

3. Name four factors that should influence a musical performance by the children.

4. List ways to encourage musical performances among the children.

5. Name criteria for selecting performers for the children.

B. Read the following paragraph and answer the questions which relate to it.

A junior college was operating a school day-care center for children during the summer. Some of the children were three and six, but most were four and five. Tim, who was a shy five-year-old, loved to sing the songs the teachers and assistants taught him. One particular day he was more excited than usual, because he had seen a TV show about folk songs and had recognized many of them. An assistant suggested that he "put on a show" during playtime. Tim found some friends to help him build a stage under the trees. They used large blocks and wooden boxes. Tim started planning songs to use. He asked the teacher if they could practice them during singing time. He wanted Joy, a six-year-old, to lead them. He wanted some of the children to play the rhythm sticks. Another child, Lupi, suggested that the smaller children could act out *Five Little Kittens*. The plans went on; the activity took about three days. It was decided that the audience would be made up of the teacher, the assistants, and all the dolls! At the last minute, Tim's mother stopped by to watch. It was the first time she had come to the school, except to let Tim out of the car. The children put on a good performance; they were happy about it.

1. List five values for individuals that might come from this performance.

2. List musical skills that were developed through this performance.

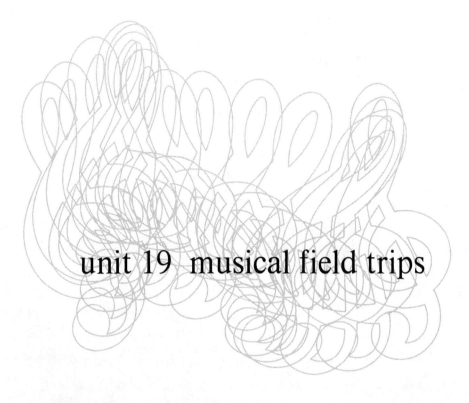

unit 19 musical field trips

OBJECTIVES

After studying this unit, the student should be able to

- Name four reasons for taking musical field trips.
- Name six places to go on musical field trips.
- List three techniques for guiding children on a field trip.

A famous symphony orchestra is coming to town. The teachers are excited. "Let's take the children to the performance," they say. Why? Young children are not yet ready to sit through a long concert. They will lose interest and disturb others.

Roy's brother is playing a drum solo with a high school jazz group. He cannot take the big set of drums from the music department of the high school, but the children can go there to hear the group play. Should the children go? Yes! Not only will they be interested in Roy's brother, but he will know some of them and know how to talk to them about the music. After the field trip, the children will make and play drums.

REASONS FOR TRIPS

There may be many reasons for taking musical field trips. Some of the main reasons are listed:

- When performers cannot come to the school or center, then the class can go to them.

- If they meet the special musical goals of the group, trips are worthwhile.

- Trips are enjoyable for children if they are interesting and well planned. Each child tends to learn a lot and appreciates the music.

- Follow-through activities have value. This includes dramatic play among the younger children and musical language arts activities at every age.

ARRANGING THE FIELD TRIP

Preparing for a musical field trip is the same as for any other field trip.

- The teacher should go to the place before taking the children.

- Any necessary arrangements should be made, such as group reservations and transportation.

- Permission slips should be signed by parents or guardians.

- The children should be told about the trip before they go.

- Every safety precaution must be taken.

- If anyone is to talk to the children on the trip, he should be asked to talk on the children's level.

PLACES TO GO

There are many places and occasions that are suitable for musical field trips. Some suggestions are listed:

- Local schools — especially those within walking distance.

- Homes which have a musical instrument that is hard to move.

- Performances that are on the young child's level, such as a short musical play for children.

- A monument or place that is important to the area. The children can sing songs concerning the event that happened there or the message the shrine depicts.

- Music stores. Some have salesclerks who can play special instruments; some have sound systems that produce special effects for listening.

- A dance studio where the children would have a larger area for movement activities than is available in the school.

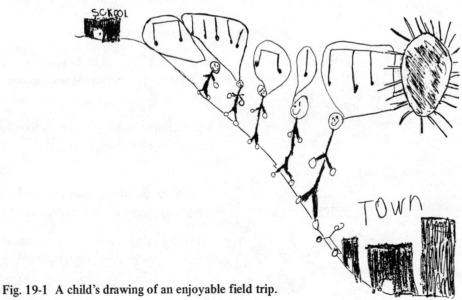

Fig. 19-1 A child's drawing of an enjoyable field trip.

Fig. 19-2 A trip can be taken to see a monument. The children sing songs they have learned about events that happened there.

Fig. 19-3 The children visit an injured child and her dog.

• The home of a child who has been unable to come to school because of injuries or long illness. The children can learn the joy of singing to a shut-in.

A Musical Visit

Kris was injured in a car accident and could not come back to school for some time. She missed the children in her class, and they planned to visit her. The teacher arranged everything for the short trip to Kris' home. When the group arrived, Kris was waiting with her beautiful dog by her side. The children sang these words, which they made up to *Hello Everybody*, figure 19-4.

> *"Hello, Kris, how are you?*
> *How are you? How are you?*
> *Hello, dear Kris, we're glad to see you,*
> *Yes, indeed, our darling."*
>
> *"We like your dog, yes indeed,*
> *Yes indeed, Yes indeed,*
> *We like your dog, yes indeed,*
> *Yes, indeed, dear Kris."*

Kris was pleased. She asked her mother to play their electronic organ for the children. The group was especially interested in the music the mother's feet made when she used the foot keyboard. Kris' mother pointed out that the same notes are on the foot keyboard as on the familiar hand keyboard.

The children brought a collection of rhythm instruments they had made to show to Kris and played them for her. They asked her to make some instruments to play for the group when she returned to school.

Back at school, the children ask to learn more songs about dogs; they want to sing them for Kris when she returns. Some children make a "pedal keyboard" with butcher paper, using black felt pens. They play "electronic organ" and entertain the dolls in the play hospital. The children draw pictures

Traditional

Hel - lo Ev' - ry bo - dy, Yes, in - de - ed.

Yes, in - de - ed. Yes, in - de - ed. Hel - lo ev' - ry bo - dy.

Yes, in - de - ed. Yes, in - deed, my dar - ling.

Fig. 19-4 *Hello, Everybody*.

and take part in dictating a "thank you" note to Kris and her mother. The teacher sends the pictures and the note to Kris' home.

PLANNING FOR FIELD TRIPS

The following method helps prepare for any field trip. The teacher holds up a three-finger instructional aid, figure 19-5, which interests the children. She tells them of a special way for every child to have a good time and to learn all he can on the field trip by singing, *Field Trip Song*, figure 19-6. Then, she asks the children what each finger means. She teaches the song by rote.

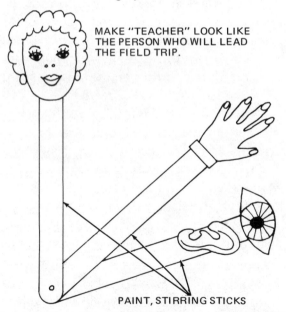

MAKE "TEACHER" LOOK LIKE THE PERSON WHO WILL LEAD THE FIELD TRIP.

PAINT, STIRRING STICKS

Fig. 19-5 "Three-finger" instructional aid.

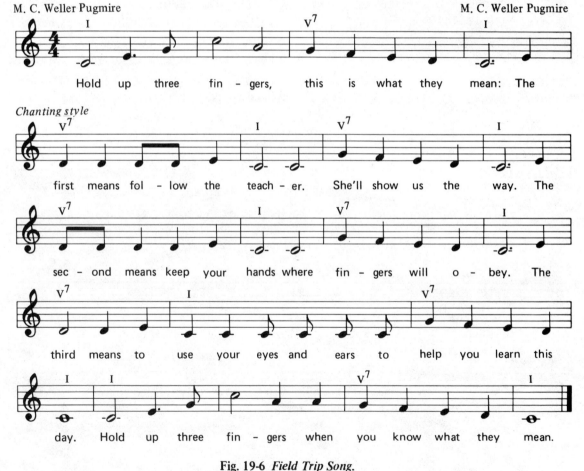

Fig. 19-6 *Field Trip Song.*

Fig. 19-7 The teacher and children practice with the "Three-finger" instructional aid. They sing the "Field Trip Song."

After a few practices and a field trip or two, the teacher will neither need to use the instructional aid nor sing the song. She can just hold up the three fingers and wait until each child does, too. This gets the group's attention so the field trip can start.

The goal of the trip should be stated in writing. Knowing exactly what she wants to do on a trip helps the teacher do it.

Children should be told about the trip at the right time. The right time depends on the age of the children and how the group reacts.

Three- and four-year-old children get so excited that they often do not enjoy the trip. If a child becomes ill the day of the trip and is not able to go, he is disappointed. It is often better to tell the children an hour or so before leaving and keep the trip short. Other children enjoy getting ready for the trip a few days ahead of time. They like to plan; often the plans help in reaching the music goals.

Teachers should learn songs that will help on the field trip: songs that keep hands busy with action, songs that help create a mood, songs to teach to the children. Teachers should also help the children make up songs and words to fit the trip.

SONGS FOR FIELD TRIPS

Singing, as one walks or rides along, may be among some of the best memories of childhood. Sometimes the child teaches songs to his family members as they travel together. Sometimes the children must wait — and keep their hands still. Singing lively songs like *Rig-A-Jig-Jig*, figure 19-8, helps them maintain a happy mood.

Action songs are very good for keeping hands busy. The song *Monkeys and the Crocodile*, figure 19-9, is a favorite. One hand is "the monkeys;" the other is "the crocodile."

The song *Quiet Thoughts* is excellent to use for the times children need to be quiet. The whole group sings the first verse; then, the

Fig. 19-8 *Rig-A-Jig-Jig* (Cassette song 24-B).

Fig. 19-9 *Monkeys and the Crocodile* **(Cassette song 25-G).**

teacher or assistant picks a child to tell the quiet thought he is thinking about. His thought is made to fit the music. Examples are given in verses two and three of figure 19-10. (Words can be made up for most of the melodies in this text to fit the particular field trip being taken.)

LEGAL IMPLICATIONS

When the children leave the school grounds on a trip, the school and teachers may be liable if an accident happens. (The child-care student will study about this in more detail in other college courses.) It should be pointed out, however, that a musical field trip is as safe as any other trip. In spite of the usual risks involved, the values gained make the trip very worthwhile.

SUMMARY

Musical field trips help teachers and children reach the goals of the music program. The children usually enjoy them and learn about music. When a worthwhile musical activity cannot be brought to the school, the teachers should consider taking the children on a field trip.

Arrangements should be made carefully. Travel techniques help make the trip more successful. Singing may be an important part of a field trip.

M. C. Weller Pugmire   M. C. Weller Pugmire

1. Qui - et thoughts,——— qui - et thoughts.———
2. Ma - ma hum - ming, ma - ma hum - ming.
3. Bree - zes blow - ing, bree - zes blow - ing.

Please tell me now what you're think - ing a - bout.
That is what Jai - mie is think - ing a - bout.
That is what Jal - ah is think - ing a - bout.

Qui - et thoughts,——— qui - et thoughts.———
Ma - ma hum - ming, ma - ma hum - ming.
Bree - zes blow - ing, bree - zes blow - ing.

Please share your qui - et thoughts with me.———
That is what Jai - mie shared with us.———
That is what Jal - ah shared with us.———

Fig. 19-10 *Quiet Thoughts* (Cassette song 24-C).

SUGGESTED ACTIVITIES

- Work in small groups. Each group makes a list of places for musical field trips. Compare lists.

- Members of the class who have had experience should tell techniques they know for arranging and taking field trips.

  Describe follow-through activities.

- Sing the songs in the unit. Do the music and actions to *Monkeys and the Crocodile* until you know them well enough to use them with children.

- If possible, go with a group of children on a musical field trip. State the goal. Make arrangements and guide follow-through activities. (If this is not possible, take your college class on a musical field trip. Plan and carry out each step as though children were present.)

- Make the "three-finger instructional aid." Place it in your file under 89: Instructional Aids.

REVIEW

A. List songs of the specified kinds that can be used when children are taking a field trip. Use songs from this text and others.

1. *Quiet Songs* (When the children need to be "settled down.")

2. *Action Songs* (When hands need to be busy.)

3. *Lively Songs* (When hands should be kept still but energy needs to be released.)

4. *Make-up Songs* (Music to be used from text songs; words are made up to fit the trip being taken.)

B. Indicate the best choice for each of the following.

1. Which are the best reasons for taking a field trip?

    a. It keeps the children busy.
    b. It helps reach the goals of the music program.
    c. Good dramatic play usually follows a trip.
    d. Both b and c.

2. Some things to do to arrange for a field trip are

    a. Check the place to make all necessary arrangements.
    b. Take all safety precautions.
    c. Have permission forms signed.
    d. Prepare the children.
    e. All of the above.

3. Some techniques that help a field trip go smoothly are

    a. Having a stated goal.
    b. Telling the children about it at the right time.
    c. Knowing appropriate songs to use.
    d. Both b and c.
    e. All of the above.

4. The *Field Trip Song* is

    a. A way to help children gain all they can from the field trip.
    b. A guide to doing actions for a song.
    c. A way to beat a young child's drum.
    d. Naming three places to go on a field trip.
    e. All of the above.

5. Types of songs for field trips are

    a. Quiet songs.
    b. Lively songs – no actions.
    c. Songs with "make-up" words.
    d. Action songs.
    e. All of the above.

C. The story about the visit to Kris' home brings out several facts that are good to remember. Indicate whether each of the following statements about the visit is true or false.

a. The trip was long.

b. The teacher had arranged it well.

c. The children sang words they had "rote-learned" to the tune *Hello Everybody*.

d. Kris' mother played the electronic organ. It was the right size to bring to school.

e. Kris' mother showed them that the foot keyboard has the same notes as the keyboard where the hands play.

f. Progress was made in reaching the goals of the music program.

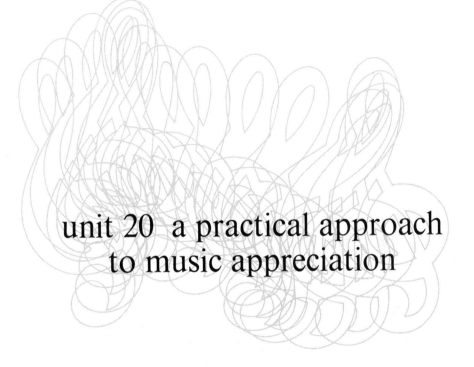

unit 20 a practical approach to music appreciation

OBJECTIVES

After studying this unit, the student should be able to

- Discuss the role of music appreciation in early education.
- List ideas that encourage music appreciation.
- Name steps to take to create a music appreciation activity.

It has been stressed throughout this text that the young child does not care how well his teacher sings or dances or plays an instrument. It is the fact that she loves music and lets music be a part of his life that means the most to the child.

Yet, there is much to be said for quality. There are reasons to learn to love the music that has stood the test of time. This learning can be a part of early music education, too

THE ROLE OF MUSIC APPRECIATION

In an earlier unit, music appreciation was defined as responding to music in a positive way. Often music appreciation is thought to be a liking for classical music or music from the composers who are considered great. Music appreciation is more than that. It is a positive attitude toward folk music. It is being able to have a respect for the very fine background music that is sometimes heard on TV shows and in good movies. It may be that the music that is loved from one generation to another is the music the child should learn. At least, music appreciation is a practical approach to music because the child will hear these songs and themes throughout his lifetime. They will become old friends.

ENCOURAGING MUSIC APPRECIATION

The music that one knows is the music that one loves. True, new music is learned all the time, but the familiar music becomes special. The teacher, then, can choose well-known classics that children can understand.

An example is the story of "Hansel and Gretel." This well-liked story is told to most young children. The teacher can play *Evening Prayer* by Humperdinck when she tells the story. Some storytellers do this better by waiting until the end of the story. Others can play the song right after they tell about the children praying. For some groups, playing just the first part is better because it is shorter, figure 20-1. Later the entire song can be played.

When performers come to visit the class, they can be asked to include short pieces of

Adapted by M. C. W. P.

Adapted from Humperdinck

When   at   night   to   bed   I   creep,

Four - teen   an - gels   guard   my   sleep

As   the   shep - herd   guards   his   sheep

They   o'er   me   their   watch   will   keep.

Fig. 20-1A *Evening Prayer* **(adapted by M.C. Weller Pugmire).**

Fig. 20-1B *Evening Prayer* by Humperdinck.

classical music that will hold the children's attention. An example is Greg's brother coming to play the piano. He can play the *Minute Waltz* by Chopin. Does it take just one minute? First the children listen to it. Then they watch the clock to see how long it takes. When they hear the music at a later time, they will appreciate it more.

MUSIC DURING REST TIME

It was suggested in an earlier unit that good music be played during rest time. The following are some of the suggestions that will help make this plan more effective:

- Choose suitable music. Check' with a librarian for suggestions.

Fig. 20-2 Greg's brother plays the piano for the children.

190

- PLAN FOR THIS PERIOD! Have the record or cassette ready before the children lie down.

- Generally, use familiar music that has been presented at another time.

- Prepare the children with a short story or some very interesting fact about the music.

- Listen to the music with the children.

- Hum the music while it is playing if it seems suitable.

- Follow the music with some comments such as, "The part at the end made me feel sleepy." Sometimes the children will want to add comments.

These suggestions are for the short rest periods often held in the middle of a nursery school or kindergarten session. Teachers working in centers where the children sleep for longer periods in the afternoon can change these to suit their program.

USING CLASSICAL MUSIC

As the teacher selects music, she can often find pieces by the great composers. There are sections in most of the basic series that have music by the great composers. *Allemande* by Beethoven, figure 20-3, is found in the early childhood volume of the New Dimensions in Music Series published by the American Book Company.[1] This selection is one of a group of pieces by great composers that are suitable for early music education.

Effective music appreciation activities can be created from great music that has been part of the teacher's life. An example is the student who is part of the chorus of the opera *La Boheme* by Puccini. After being in this production, she is surprised to hear themes from this opera played very often on TV and radio. She decides to share this musical knowledge with the young children with whom she works.

The *Tattoo* from the end of Act II is chosen. Some of the ideas she uses with a group of older nursery school and kindergarten children are listed:

- The meaning of the word "tattoo" is taught. This kind of tattoo is a beating on the drums while the trumpets and bugles play.

- The song, *Il bel tambur maggior* is used with English words that she makes up, figure 20-4. She tries to stay close to the original words, however.

- She plays the record so the children can hear the tattoo. It is such stirring music that marching follows. The prop box with band uniforms is brought out. The

[1] Berg, Choate, Kjelson and Troth, *Music for Early Childhood*, New York, American Book Co., 1970, p. 164.

Ludwig van Beethoven

Fig. 20-3 *Allemande.*

Fig. 20-4 *Parade March from "La Boheme."*

children make new hats to go with the uniforms.

- She encourages the children to listen — to hear that the song is sung in another language, Italian.   She tells the children that many people think that the Italian language is the most beautiful language for singing.

- Tony says his grandmother speaks Italian. He wants to get a copy of the Italian words to take home with him.   This is good for Tony because he does not talk very much to the class.

- The children are interested in the *musical score* (music for the singers and/or the orchestra).

- The teacher plays a lovely, quieter *aria* (a special, complex melody sung by a single voice in an opera) for the children during rest time. The children listen and like it. The teacher is rather surprised and then thinks that perhaps children should be introduced to opera at a young age.

MUSIC FROM TRAVELS

Bringing music to the children from places the teacher visits can work well. For example, the teacher shares with the children her excitement about visiting the schools in England. The children help the teacher look on the big,

simple globe to find England. They quickly learn English songs the teacher has brought back. The children there were singing the old favorite, *Where is Thumbkin?* However, the English children sang *"Tommy Thumb, Tommy Thumb,"* figure 20-5.

This idea works in another way, too. When a child goes on a trip, he brings back music.   One child was very happy to come back to school after going to a folk music festival in the South. He sang *Love Somebody* to the class, figure 20-6.   His parents were

Traditional   Recorded by M. C. Weller Pugmire

Where   is   thumb - kin?   Where   is   thumb - kin?
Tom - my   Thumb ——   Tom - my   Thumb ——

Here   I   am.   Here   I   am.   How   are   you   to - day, sir?
Where   are   you?   Where   are   you?   Here   am   I   to - day, sir?

Ve - ry   well,   I   thank   you.   Run   a - way,   Run   a - way.
How   are   you   to   day, sir?   Ve - ry   well,   Run   and   hide.

Fig. 20-5 *Where Is Thumbkin?* (**English** Version — "Tommy Thumb").

asked to visit the school. They came and sang some of the other songs they heard. This led to further music appreciation activities about the Southern folk music.

CREATING MUSIC APPRECIATION ACTIVITIES

This text does not give lists of music recommended for music appreciation. Sometimes these lists bewilder beginning students. Many times, the records or music is not available. The following steps outline practical ways for the beginning teacher to create music appreciation activities. Most of the steps have been illustrated by examples in this unit.

- Start with music you like that you believe will be heard through the years.

- Think about the ages and the needs of the children with whom you work. Use information you have gained from this text.

- Using this information, plan the activity. Keep it simple and short at first.

- One idea will lead to others. Take cues from the children. Remember you are building appreciation to last a lifetime. It is worth the time it takes in the school day.

Folk Song

Love some-bo-dy, Yes, I do! Love some-bo-dy, Yes, I do!

Love some-bo-dy, Yes, I do! Love some-bo-dy, but I won't say who.

Fig. 20-6 *Love Somebody.*

- Alter the plans if you need to do so. Do not be afraid to say that part of a plan did not work.

- Use different ideas, but stay with the plan until the music becomes well-known to the children.

- Enjoy the activity yourself. The children can sense that you appreciate the music.

- When one piece of music becomes part of the children's lives, start another appreciation activity. However, repeat the familiar music from time to time.

This approach works! It may be used by students with a very different type of music than *La Boheme*. There is much fine music; it is wise to begin by using music with which you feel comfortable, whether it is jazz or a symphony.

MORE IDEAS THAT HELP

Some students may feel that they are not familiar with any fine music. Many students have had poor experiences with music in school. In this text, Tchaikovsky's *Nutcracker Suite* has been used as an example; the record is available almost everywhere. The students should play the record, beginning with one of the sections that seems most familiar. Then they should use it!

- Seek help. This has been said before, but it is worth repeating. Most musicians wish that all children could enjoy music early in their lives. Many are willing to help the beginning teacher so that more young children have favorable music experiences.

- Try to learn more about all kinds of music. Take advantage of concerts, music demonstrations, and TV shows that teach about music.
- When you have an idea that works, share it with other teachers. In this way, your file will grow. Many children will be helped, too. Maybe a child will say, "I love to go to school 'cause I get to sing!"

SUMMARY

Music appreciation should be a part of early music education. The child should have the chance to become familiar with the music he will hear throughout his lifetime.

Fine music can be used with other classroom activities such as storytelling. It can be used effectively during rest time. Music by great composers can often be brought into the program.

A practical approach to appreciation activities is to use music with which the teacher is familiar. Music found while traveling is also good. The teacher should use her knowledge about children and music to create activities for children. However, she should seek help if it is needed. Above all, the teacher should strive to appreciate and enjoy music herself!

SUGGESTED ACTIVITIES

- Discuss the following topics in class:

  a. Definition of music appreciation
  b. Role of music appreciation in early education
  c. Types of music for a music appreciation program

- Visit a local library. Find the records and/or cassettes that are available for loan. If possible, borrow a suitable record and develop a music appreciation activity for the young child.

- Discuss the rest times you have observed in the schools and centers you have visited. Have any used music in a way that made it an interesting time for the children?

- Each class member should bring a record or music that would be good to use for music appreciation. Compile a list with suggestions from class members. File it under 87 — "Music Appreciation."

REVIEW

A. Briefly answer each of the following:

1. List ideas that encourage music appreciation in early education.

2. List seven suggestions to use to make rest time a music appreciation time.

3. Name two songs that were appreciated because they came from a teacher's and a child's travels. Name several songs you could use from trips you have taken. Do not overlook short trips.

B. Match each item in Column II with the correct item in Column I.

I	II
1. Music for singers and/or orchestra	a. Music appreciation
2. Composed by Beethoven. Suitable for young children.	b. "Allemande"
	c. "La Boheme"
3. Responding to music in a positive way	d. Tattoo
4. A special, complex melody for a single voice	e. Musical score
5. English version of "Where is Thumbkin?"	f. Aria
	g. "Tommy Thumb"
6. Opera written by Puccini	
7. Played by the drums and trumpets	

C. List eight practical ways to create music appreciation activities.

PART II
FUNDAMENTALS OF MUSIC

Section 7 Understanding the Mechanics of Music

unit 21 melody

OBJECTIVES

After studying this unit, the student should be able to

- Name the notes of a song and locate them on a piano.
- Construct scales in five keys.
- Identify five major key signatures.
- Teach children to play song bells.

Some people read music well and with ease; to others, the elements of music are a mystery. Many teachers wish that all young children could be taught the elements of music. Some children are able to learn about music and how to read music as they learn to read words and stories.

The simple elements of music are presented in this text. The approach taken is practical, and it works when properly applied. The student should begin this section with a positive attitude — even excitement — because music is the "language of the world." Each teacher should know as much as possible about music so she can help the children with whom she works.

MELODY

The tune of a song is the *melody*. These tunes are often sung by a mother to her child. The melodies of some of the best known classical music are based on old tunes.

Melodies can be very simple. *Twinkle, Twinkle, Little Star,* for example, has a simple melody; yet, orchestrations have been written for it. The melody is universal; almost every child knows it.

A good melody helps a child remember a song. When one listens to *Give, Said the Little Stream* (Cassette song 21-A, figure 2-7), one realizes how interesting the melody is! Many young children love it.

Every melody moves. It moves up and down; it moves across — that is, some notes in the melody are repeated. Play *Up, Down, Whoops!* (Cassette song 21-B, figure 13-4). Listen to the melody; then, play it again. Move your hand up and down to show how the melody moves: move it up as the melody moves up; move it down as the melody moves down. Leave your hand in the same place when the notes of the melody are repeated.

Move your hand with the melody of *Give, Said the Little Stream.* You must know the melody well to do this. This action shows how melodies move. Note that there are many *skips* or *intervals* (distances between notes) in this song.

Play *Give, Said the Little Stream* again. By now, you should know it well. Note that some parts of the melody are alike — that "Singing, singing all the day" is sung twice. Some parts of the melody, such as "Give, oh give," are similar. Most parts of the melody are contrasting. The student should be aware that some parts of the melodies are exactly alike, some are similar, and some are contrasting. Listen for these and learn more about the melody.

READING THE NOTES OF THE MELODY

To understand more about melody, one should be able to read the *melodic line* (the notes of the tune). Play *Now is the Time,* (Cassette song 21-C, figure 1-2). The way the first part of this song would be played on the piano is shown in figure 21-2. (This is not a practical way to read music!)

Notation (the way of showing musical sounds by using symbols) is the easy way to read music. Most of these symbols have been used in this text, but they may be reviewed by studying figure 21-3. The first *phrase* [a

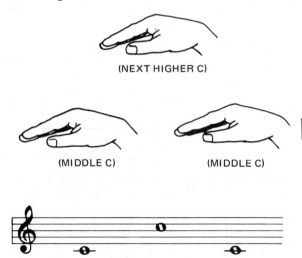

Fig. 21-1 The hand may be moved as shown to indicate the highness or lowness of tones (pitch).

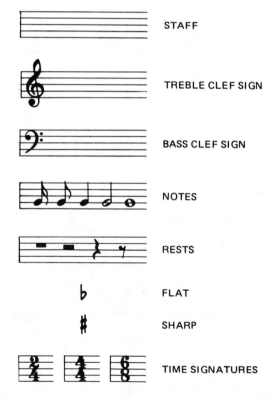

Fig. 21-2 This is the way *Now Is the Time* would look if it were written on the piano.

STAFF

TREBLE CLEF SIGN

BASS CLEF SIGN

NOTES

RESTS

FLAT

SHARP

TIME SIGNATURES

Fig. 21-3 Review of musical symbols used in this text.

natural division of the melodic line and usually lyrics (words)] of *Now is the Time* could be sung as shown:

> "*C, D, E, F, G, A, B, C,*"

The letters are the names of the notes. They look like this when placed on the staff:

The names of the spaces in the treble clef spell "FACE:"

The names of the lines are E, G, B, D, F. Many music teachers help their students remember this by the sentence, "Every good boy does fine," or "Every good boy deserves fudge!"

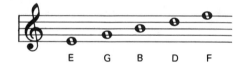

The music for *Now is the Time* is shown.

Figure 21-4 illustrates how to play this first line on the piano.

THE GRAND STAFF

The notes of the grand staff are shown in figure 21-5. In this unit, only the notes of the treble clef are stressed. The notes of the bass clef will be presented in the unit on harmony.

Notice that the notes between the two staffs have letter names, too. These are used

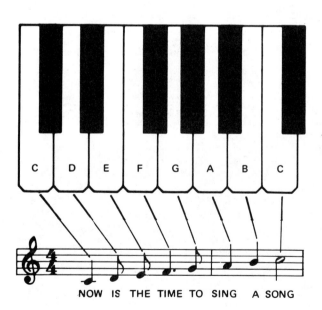

Fig. 21-4 Notes on the piano to be played for *Now Is the Time*.

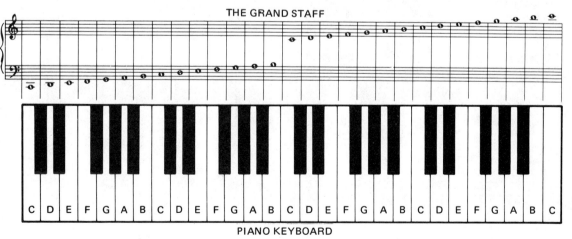

Fig. 21-5 The Grand Staff.

very often in music for the young child because they lie within the range of his voice. Study figure 21-6 to learn the names of these notes and their location on the piano. Play them on the piano.

The black notes on the piano keyboard are usually called sharps or flats. When a note has a *sharp sign* (#) by it, it means to play the note to the right (usually a black key). Therefore, C# is the black key on the keyboard to the right of middle C. When a note has a flat sign (♭) by it, it means to play the note to the left of it, (usually a black key). Therefore, D♭ is the black key on the keyboard to the left of

the D. A study of figure 21-7 should help the student to understand this. It shows, also, that the black notes have two names. The black key between C and D on the piano can be either C# or D♭ White notes can be sharps or flats, too. This happens very rarely in children's music, however.

SCALES

All melodies are made from scales or parts from scales. The first phrase of "Now is the Time" is an *ascending scale* (a scale that goes up). The second phrase is a *descending scale* (a scale that goes down). To compare, sing the first phrase of *Joy to the World.* Notice that it is a descending scale.

JOY TO THE WORLD, THE LORD IS COME

The scale used in *Now is the Time* is a major scale. Scales are made up of half steps and whole steps. This can be seen on the keyboard of a piano, figure 21-8. From one key to the next (white to black, black to white, and in some places, white to white) is a half step. A whole step is twice the distance of a half step, and, therefore, a key lies between (white to white with black between, black to black with white between, or in some

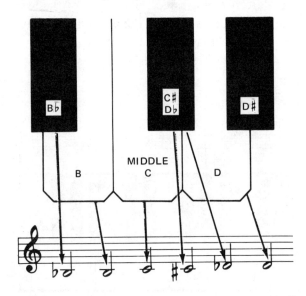

Fig. 21-6 The notes B, C (Middle C), C#, D, and D# are used a great deal in music for young children.

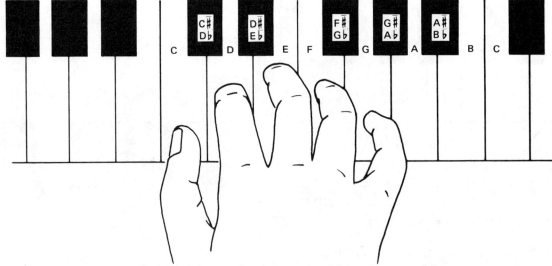

Fig. 21-7 Each black key on the piano can be either a sharp or a flat note.

places white to black with white between). The same scale formation of half steps and whole steps may be shown with a picture of a ladder, figure 21-9. The notes of a scale can be numbered; sometimes they are given syllable names.

LETTER NAME	C	D	E	F	G	A	B	C
NUMBER	1	2	3	4	5	6	7	8
SYLLABLE NAME	DO	RE	MI	FA	SOL	LA	TI	DO

These *music syllables* are called *solfeggio.* This vocal technique is not used very often in early music education although children often know the syllable names for the musical tones because the song, *Do, Re, Mi* is on many children's records.

MUSICAL SIGNATURES

The C scale just shown has no sharps or flats. C is called the key note, "do," or 1. The steps and half steps are in the places shown on the keyboard in figure 21-8 and the ladder in figure 21-9.

In the F scale, however, to make the half steps come in the right places — between notes 3 and 4 and notes 7 and 8 — the fourth note B has to be lowered one-half step to a B♭.

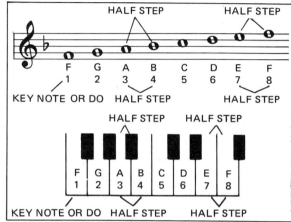

In order to make the music simpler to read, the flat is put on the staff at the first of each line of music, after the clef sign. The

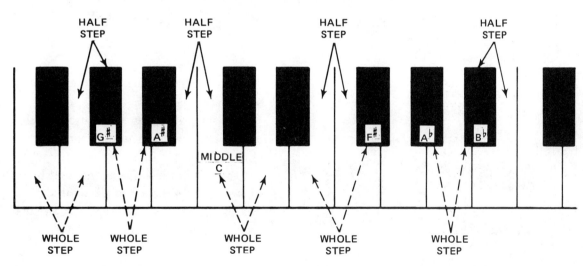

Fig. 21-8 Steps and half steps on the piano.

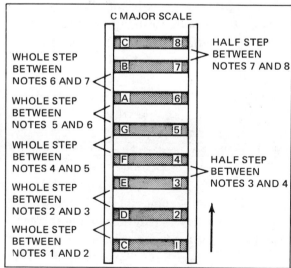

Fig. 21-9 A ladder illustrates the steps and half steps of a major scale.

user knows this means that all through the song, the B note is lowered or played as a B♭. This notation is called the *key signature* and shows which notes of the scale are to be made into sharps or flats. Throughout this text, there are more songs with one flat than with any other key signature.

Other Key Signatures

To find the keynote for a key signature that has flats, count down four lines and spaces from the last flat. (Start to count on the line or space that has the flat.) Thus a key signature with one flat is the key of F. The scale starts on F.

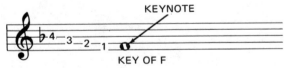

Note "1" or "do" comes on F.

Another key signature found in this text that has flats is the key of E♭.

Since B, E, and A have flats, the half steps come in the right places (between 3 and 4, and 7 and 8). When flats are used in the key signature, the B♭ is always written first (to the left) regardless of its position in the scale.

The same system of notation is used with sharps. Many children's songs are based on the G scale, which has one sharp. The F or number 7 note has to be raised to F♯ to make the

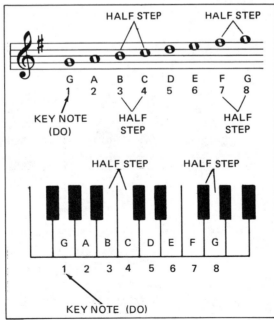

half steps come in the right places. The key signature shows that all through a song, the F note is raised (made into a sharp).

Play *You Tell Me Your Dream* (Cassette song 21-D, figure 7-7). As you look at this music, you will note there is a *natural sign* (♮). This cancels the F♯ that is required by the key signature. The white F key is played. The symbols for sharps, flats, and naturals that are not called for in the key signature are called *accidentals*.

Another key signature used in this text that has sharps is the key of D. Since F and C

are made into sharps, the half steps come in the right places.

The name of a key signature that has sharps is found by going up one line or space from the last sharp. In a key signature where the last sharp is in the C space, the next line is D. This song is in the key of D. Note "1" or "do" is on D. The whole steps and the half steps can be figured from the keynote. When sharps appear in the key signature, the F♯ is always written first (to the left) regardless of its location in the scale pattern.

Only five key signatures are used in this text: C, F, E♭, G, and D. However, any key signature or scale can be constructed using the method described. The rest of the key signatures and scales are shown in the Appendix.

PLAYING SONGBELLS

One can become more aware of melody by playing bells. There are several kinds of bells. It would be helpful to the student to have a set of melody bells or resonator bells to use.

Play *Sleep, Baby, Sleep* (Cassette song 21-E, figure 4-2). Every time the words "Sleep,

baby, sleep" are used, play 3, 2, 2, 1 on the bells. It is fun to teach this to a child!

Swiss-type melody songbells can be bought for a reasonable price at most toy or music stores. While the tone quality of the bells is not exceptional, both the student and the child can learn a lot about melody by using them. Most often these bells are in the key of F. Each bell has a number on it to match one of the eight tones of the scale. Almost any song in this text in the key of F can be played on these bells.

If a child is able to read the numbers one through eight, an adult can help him learn to

to play the bells. The adult calls out the number; the child gives each numbered bell a sharp shake. He soon is able to play ascending and descending scales and intervals (skips) easily.

Playing Bells by Color Matching

Some teachers help young children play bells by color matching. This can be done with the Swiss-type melody bells. Each bell is a different color. Notes are drawn on big staffs. Each note is made of the color that matches the bell to be played, figure 21-11. For very young children, bells cut out of

C = Orange   O   F = Green   Gn
D = Blue   B   G = Yellow Y
E = Gray   G

Fig. 21-10 Swiss melody bells are enjoyed by teacher and children.

Fig. 21-11 "Color Coding" for *Shake Your Hands Up High*. When making the musical notes on a chart, use the colors of the bells in the set being used.

paper that matches the color of the bell to be played may be used successfully. The bell cutouts need not be placed on a staff; they are used only to give direction and relative position.

MAKING MELODY INSTRUMENTS

Instruments may be made to show a child the tones in the scale. Some of these instruments are not difficult to make, and making them helps the teacher learn more about scale tones, too. Eight glasses with tall, straight sides are used. The first glass is filled almost to the top with water. A little less water is put in each of the following glasses. (The more water there is in the glass, the lower the tones.) It is quite easy to tune the glasses of water to the key of C: C is played on the piano; the glass is filled until it makes the same sound; the same is done for D, E, F, G, A, B, and C. The three higher tones are harder to match, but many songs can be played with five glasses tuned to C, D, E, F, and G. *Shake Your Hands Up High* (Cassette song 21-F, figure 9-6) can be played on these. Striking the glasses with the handle of a spoon or fork above the water line produces a good tone. Bottles — such as vinegar, apple juice, and others with similar shapes — with a lid or a cap can be used in the same way.

Another type of melody instrument is made from electrical conduit, which can be

C   D   E   F   G

Fig. 21-12 Water glasses containing water can be tuned to the first five notes of the scale. Other glasses can be filled to obtain the upper three notes although it is more difficult. It is fun to try; let the children help!

bought at a hardware store.[1] Standard 1/2-inch diameter, thin-wall electrical conduit cut to the following lengths (in inches) gives the sounds of the C-major scale: When this instrument is used, the player holds the tube in one hand about one-fourth of the way down from the top, and strikes it with a pencil with

$12\frac{1}{2}$	$11\frac{3}{4}$	$11\frac{1}{16}$	$10\frac{5}{8}$	$10\frac{1}{8}$	$9\frac{7}{16}$	$8\frac{29}{32}$	$8\frac{5}{8}$
C	D	E	F	G	A	B	C

[1] Slind, Lloyd H. and Davis, D. Evans, *Bringing Music to Children*; New York, Harper and Row, 1964.

the other hand. Almost any simple song in the key of C can be played on these "tuneful tubes."

SUMMARY

The tune of the song is the melody. A student can learn to read the notes of the melodies used in this text by following suggestions in this unit. Only five key signatures are used in this text although the key signature for any major scale can be figured out.

Playing bells tuned to the notes of a scale helps the teacher become more aware of melody. Instruments can be made on which simple melodies can be played.

SUGGESTED ACTIVITIES (for the Beginning Student)

- Sit at a piano keyboard. Give the names of all the keys. Tell where the half steps and whole steps are. If you do not have a piano available, use a piano keyboard made from paper or white cardboard.

- Write the names of the notes of the melody above the staff of each of ten songs. Do this lightly in pencil so it can be erased after you learn the names of the notes. Find the names of the notes by using information from the text and illustration 21-5.

- Choose 10 songs from the text. Write the name of each key signature by the song. Play the scale on the piano that has the same name as the key signature. *Give, Said the Little Stream* is used here for an example.

KEY OF D   PLAY THIS!

SUGGESTED ACTIVITIES (for the Musically Trained Student)

- Study this chapter as a review. Create one idea to teach young children about melody. Share this idea with your classmates.

- Make one of the melody instruments — or a similar one — discussed in this chapter. Use it with a young child.

SUGGESTED ACTIVITIES (for All Students)

- Have each class member sing or hum a melody that he likes very much. Talk about these melodies. What makes them appealing? Compare ideas in order to learn more about melody.

- Each class member should talk to one or more children and find out their favorite songs. Compare findings. What can you tell about melodies from this activity?

REVIEW

A.   Match each item in Column II with the correct item in Column I.

I	II

I

1. Melodic line
2. Musical intervals
3. Keynote
4. Notation
5. Phrase
6. F, A, C, E
7. E, G, B, D, F
8. Ascending scale
9. Musical syllables
10. Descending scale
11. Lyrics

II

a. the names of the lines on the treble clef.

b. a natural division of the melodic line.

c. the notes of the tune.

d. first note of a scale.

e. way of showing musical sounds by using symbols.

f. distances between tones in the melody.

g. the names of the spaces on the treble clef.

h. a scale that goes down.

i. a scale that goes up.

j. words that are sung to the melody.

k. do, re, mi

B.   Indicate the best choice for each of the following.

1. Melody is
    a. The tune of a song.
    b. Found in almost all music.
    c. Learned by a young child from his mother and other sources.
    d. All of the above.

2. A good melody
    a. Must be part of every song.
    b. Helps the child remember a song.
    c. Is liked by every person.
    d. Must have parts that are hard to sing.

3. A melody
    a. Moves up.   c. Is repeated.
    b. Moves down.   d. All of these.

4. A melody usually has parts that are
    a. Too high for the young singer.
    b. Too low for the young singer.
    c. Alike, similar, and contrasting.
    d. Complex

5. A scale
    a. Is made of whole steps and half steps.
    b. Can be used in a melody.
    c. Is a basic part of music.
    d. All of the above.

6. Notes in a scale can be illustrated by using
    a. Numbers (1 through 8).
    b. Letter names (C, D, E, etc.).
    c. The syllables do, re, mi, etc.
    d. All of the above.

7. In a major scale, the half steps come between
    a. Notes 2 - 3 and 7 - 8.   c. Notes 2 - 3 and 6 - 7.
    b. Notes 3 - 4 and 7 - 8.   d. None of these.

8. Regarding melody instruments made of electrical conduit,
    a. The longer tubes have the higher sound.
    b. The longer tubes have the lower sound.
    c. The length of the tube makes no difference.
    d. None of the above.

C. Draw ladders, similar to the one shown in figure 21-9, for major scales
    in the Keys of F, E♭, G, and D. Write in the names of the notes of the
    scale. Mark the number of each note. Indicate the location of the half
    steps and whole steps.

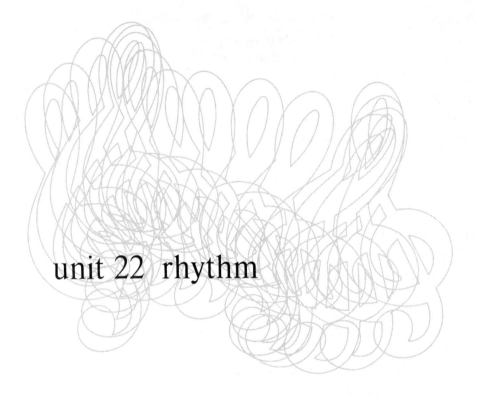

unit 22 rhythm

OBJECTIVES

After studying this unit, the student should be able to

• Explain the values of notes and rests.

• Tell what time signatures mean.

• Illustrate rhythm patterns.

• Play the melodies in this text with correct rhythm.

Rhythm is sometimes called the "feel" of the music. The underlying steady pulse of the music is called the beat. Rhythm is the part of music that people respond to with lyrics, movement, and by playing instruments.

It is fun to learn about rhythm. Once the facts are learned, the student can see there is little mystery to this element of music. Almost all music can be understood after learning some basic rules about rhythm.

THE VALUE OF NOTES

Most often, the *quarter note* (♩) gets one count. In the song *Let's Go Walking* (Cassette song 22-A, figure 11-2), notice the quarter notes in the melody. Play the song. Clap to get the feeling of the beat. The *half note* (♩)

Fig. 22-1 Learning about music can be fun — for the young child and the teacher, too.

at the end of the first line of music gets twice the number of counts as the quarter note. In this song, it gets two counts. The *whole note* (o) at the end of the second line gets four times as many counts as the quarter note. In this song, that is four beats, figure 22-2.

The singing game song *Airabella Bailey* (Cassette song 22-B, figure 13-2) has *eighth notes* (♪) and *sixteenth notes* (♬). Two eighth notes are equal to one quarter note; four sixteenth notes are equal to one quarter note, figure 22-3.

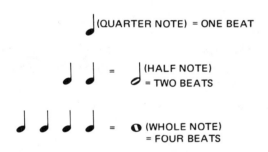

Fig. 22-2 Notes found in *Let's Go Walking*.

Fig. 22-3 Some notes found in *Airabella Bailey*.

THE TIME SIGNATURE

There are two numbers in a time signature:

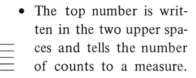

- The top number is written in the two upper spaces and tells the number of counts to a measure.

- The bottom number is written in the two lower spaces and identifies the note that receives one count.

The time signature is placed at the beginning of the music after the sharps or flats if there are any.

The time signature is written at the beginning of the song only, unless it is changed later in the music. This tells the musician to have the time signature in his mind before he plays or sings the song.

The *measure* (a grouping of rhythmical notes) is marked on either side by a bar line. The last measure in a piece of music is followed by a double bar line, figure 22-4.

Four time signatures have been used for songs in this text:

$\frac{4}{4}$, $\frac{2}{4}$, $\frac{3}{4}$, and $\frac{6}{8}$

Examples of each of these follow.

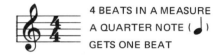

4 BEATS IN A MEASURE
A QUARTER NOTE (♩)
GETS ONE BEAT

Let's Go Walking is written in $\frac{4}{4}$ time. Play the song and count the beats in each measure. Note that the strongest feeling comes on the first count. This is called the *accent beat* (the note or notes in each measure which have the most *pulse*, or force).

2 BEATS TO A MEASURE
A QUARTER NOTE (♩)
GETS ONE BEAT

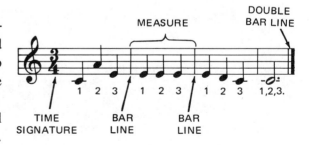

Fig. 22-4 The last measure in a piece of music is followed by a double bar line.

Airabella Bailey is written in $\frac{2}{4}$ time. Count the beats in each measure as the song is played. Again notice that the strongest pulse is on the accent beat or the first count.

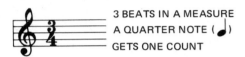

3 BEATS IN A MEASURE
A QUARTER NOTE (♩)
GETS ONE COUNT

Fly, My Pretty Balloon (Cassette song 22-C, figure 2-3) is written in $\frac{3}{4}$ time. Count the beats in each measure and note the feeling of swaying as the music plays. Sometimes the count is done: pulse-two-three; pulse-two-three; or strong, weak, weak; strong, weak, weak. This helps some students feel the accent in the music.

More About Note Values

The fourth time signature used in this text gives different values to notes.

6 BEATS TO A MEASURE
AN EIGHTH NOTE (♪)
GETS ONE COUNT

Play *The Fan* (Cassette song 22-D, figure 11-6). As the song is played the first time, look at the music. Since an eighth note gets

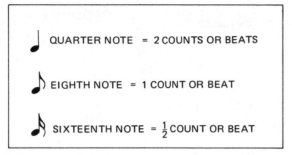

♩ QUARTER NOTE = 2 COUNTS OR BEATS

♪ EIGHTH NOTE = 1 COUNT OR BEAT

♬ SIXTEENTH NOTE = $\frac{1}{2}$ COUNT OR BEAT

Fig. 22-5 Values received by notes in a song with a $\frac{6}{8}$ time signature.

one count, all other notes have corresponding values. This is shown in figure 22-5. Two accent beats in each measure — beats one and four — can be heard in *The Fan:* pulse, two, three; pulse, five, six — or strong, weak, weak; strong, weak, weak.

BACK AND **FORTH, GOES** THE **FAN**

The symbol used to mark an accent is >. This is usually placed above the staff and over the note of music that is to be accented.

DOTTED NOTES

A dot following a note adds to that note half the value of the note, figure 22-6. Play *Fly My Pretty Balloon* again. This time sing the words in the next column with the notes.

BEATS IN $\frac{2}{4}$, $\frac{3}{4}$, AND $\frac{4}{4}$ TIME	$\frac{6}{8}$ TIME
♩. = ♩ + ♩ 3 BEATS	$4\frac{1}{2}$ BEATS
♩. = ♩ + ♪ $1\frac{1}{2}$ BEATS	3 BEATS
♪. = ♪ + ♬ $\frac{3}{4}$ BEAT	$1\frac{1}{2}$ BEATS

Fig. 22-6 Values received by dotted notes.

Dotted notes, dotted notes
Regular notes lead to dotted notes
Dotted notes, dotted notes
A dotted note comes at the end.

Play *The Fan* on the cassette and watch the music as you listen. Remember, this music is in $\frac{6}{8}$ time: a dotted quarter note receives 3 counts; a dotted eighth, 1 1/2 counts. Note values are compared to money values in figure 22-7. This should help the student gain a better understanding of note values.

RESTS

Rests have different values just as notes do. Sometimes the importance of rests is not taught to the child. The silence, symbolized by the rests, does not seem as important as the music indicated by the notes. Yet, as rhythm is felt and recorded in music, rests become very important, figure 22-8.

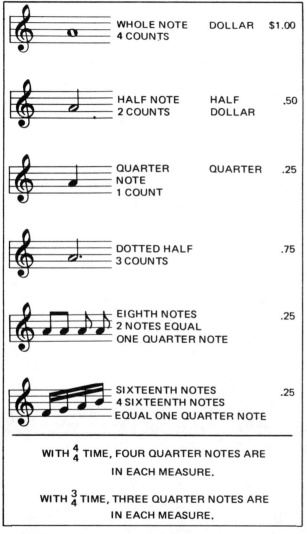

Fig. 22-7 Note values compared to money values.

[1]Allen Hackworth, *Guitar Pleasure: A Study Course*, Rexburg, Idaho, 1975.

Play *Snapdragons* (Cassette song 22-E, figure 10-5). Look at the music as you play. Point to the rests in the music. Now play *The Sparkling Christmas Tree* (Cassette song 22-F, figure 8-3). Look at the music as you play the song. Play it again and dance as you hear the music. Try stamping in the places where the rests occur in the melody. The song is more effective with the rests than it would be without them.

Fig. 22-8 Rests.

TIES

A *tie* is a curved line connecting two notes of the same pitch ( ). The pitch is held without stopping — for the value count of both notes. Play *I'm Going to Leave Old Texas Now* (Cassette song 22-G, figure 4-7). Look at the music as you play the cassette, and notice the three ties.

A *slur* is a curved line connecting two notes of different pitches. It means that one word is to be sung on the pitches of the two notes.

Play *I'm Goin' to Leave Old Texas Now* again, but sing these words:

La, la la *TIE, SLUR* la la la.
La, la la *TIE,* la, la, la, la *TIE.*

REPEAT SIGNS

Many songs have repeat signs so that the music will not have to be printed again. The symbol (:||) means sing or play again from the previous repeat (||:). If there is no previous repeat sign, return to the beginning. Play *Wheels* (Cassette Song 22-H, figure 3-6). Note the repeat sign.

SONGS THAT DEMONSTRATE VARIOUS METERS

The *meter signature* (another name for a *time signature*) tells what kind of rhythm

213

Fig. 22-9 *Popcorn Popping On The Apricot Tree* **(Cassette song 22-I).**

patterns can be written into each measure. This is called the meter of the music.

Popcorn Popping on the Apricot Tree (Cassette song 22-I, figure 22-9), written in $\frac{4}{4}$ time, is an all-time favorite with children. They like the humor and the sound of the words, and the rhythm is very "catchy." As you play the song, look at the music and notice all the dotted eighth notes and sixteenth notes. This makes the music very interesting.

Cotton Needs Picking (Cassette song 22-J, figure 1-4) has a $\frac{2}{4}$ meter. This song has a rhythm that seems to help people get their work done.

Play *Sally Go Round the Sun* (Cassette song 22-K, figure 13-3). The $\frac{6}{8}$ meter of this game-song gives a feeling of the rhythm of the child going around and around.

Play *Summer Is Coming* (Cassette song 22-L, figure 13-8). Clap on the accented beats of each measure. There are two. The $\frac{6}{8}$ meter of this game song is "bouncy" and gives most children a feeling of having a good time.

WAYS TO ILLUSTRATE RHYTHM PATTERNS

There are patterns of rhythm everywhere. This fact has been brought up throughout the text. Now these patterns can be illustrated with the use of notes. The teacher says the

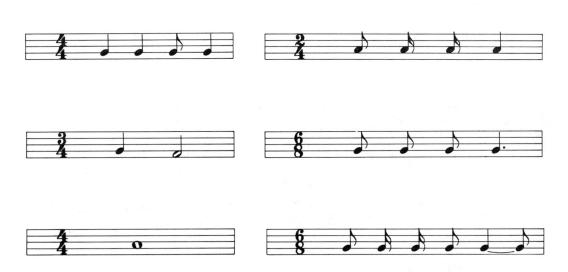

Fig. 22-10 Samples of exercises for the student to practice on the music flannelboard.

children's names, claps their rhythm patterns, and writes the notes:

> *Jack Smith – Clap, Clap –*
> *Lizabeth Lopez – Clap, clap clap,*
> *clap clap –*
> *Carolyn Moe – Clapty clap,*
> *Clap (Hold) –*

The music flannelboard and symbols described in unit 17 are a good means of helping the student learn about rhythm patterns and note values. The student becomes more sure of herself as she makes up exercises for the flannelboard and practices using them, figure 22-10.

Moving to music also helps the student learn about rhythm. This was discussed in unit 11. Now this music can be studied to show how these rhythms are written and played.

Play *Do As I'm Doing* (Cassette song 22-M, figure 11-4), then sing "Walk As I'm Walking." Note that it says "In strict rhythm" at the top of the music. Sing and clap with the cassette. Note that there are no dotted notes in this music.

Play *We Can Run, We Can Play* (Cassette song 22-N, figure 22-11). Note that it says "With good accent" at the top of the music. The $\frac{4}{4}$ meter of the song is played and sung in such a way that the child wants to run or hop to the rhythm.

PLAYING THE MELODIES IN THIS TEXT

The reader has been given basic information to help in playing the melodies in the first twenty units of this text. Study and practice are essential to gaining skill; there is no other way for the beginning student to advance.

Once learned, playing an instrument is a priceless tool for teaching. When the student is able to play the melodies in this text, she should be able to play almost any melody written for children.

It helps to follow the listed steps for playing each melody:

- Give the name of the key signature and decide which notes have flats or sharps.

- Read the time signature and decide how many beats to a measure and the type of note that gets one count.

- Look over the music for any special notation — such as ties or repeats.

- Begin to play. Count the beats in each measure.

- Do not hesitate to ask for help, because experienced musicians usually will help a beginning student.

SUMMARY

Rhythm is the element of music that people respond to most freely. There are four time signatures used in this text. The top number tells how many counts in a measure. The bottom number tells what type of note gets one count. After the student studies unit 21 and this unit, she should be able to play the melodies in the text correctly. This, of course, requires practice.

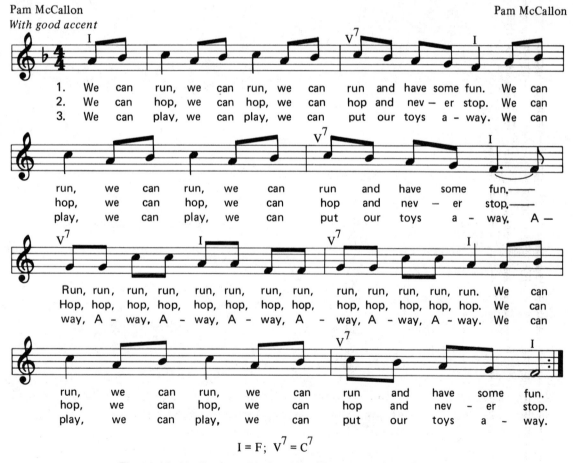

Pam McCallon   Pam McCallon

With good accent

1. We can run, we can run, we can run and have some fun. We can
2. We can hop, we can hop, we can hop and nev - er stop. We can
3. We can play, we can play, we can put our toys a - way. We can

run, we can run, we can run and have some fun.——
hop, we can hop, we can hop and nev - er stop.——
play, we can play, we can put our toys a - way. A —

Run, run, run, run, run, run, run, run, run, run, run, run, run. We can
Hop, hop, hop, hop, hop, hop, hop, hop, hop, hop, hop, hop, hop. We can
way, A - way, A - way, A - way, A - way, A - way, A - way. We can

run, we can run, we can run and have some fun.
hop, we can hop, we can hop and nev - er stop.
play, we can play, we can put our toys a - way.

I = F; V^7 = C^7

Fig. 22-11 *We Can Run; We Can Play* (Cassette song 22-N).

SUGGESTED ACTIVITIES FOR THE BEGINNING STUDENT

- Follow all suggestions in the text. Set a goal for the amount of time that you will practice each day. Be realistic when setting it; then, stick to your goal. Learn to play all the melodies. Listen to the cassette to see if you are playing them correctly.

   a. If you do not have a piano, locate one you can use. Leaders of churches, organizations that own meeting halls, and schools often let a teacher practice on their piano during hours when the building is not being used.

   b. Ask for help if there is something you do not understand.

SUGGESTED ACTIVITIES FOR THE MUSICALLY TRAINED STUDENT

- Study this chapter as a review. Create one or more ideas to teach children about rhythm. Share this idea with your classmates.

- Present one of the more complex rhythms — such as calypso or Latin American — to your classmates. Illustrate how it sounds by playing it on a rhythm instrument or piano. Show how it looks when it is written in music.

SUGGESTED ACTIVITIES FOR ALL STUDENTS

- Do the activities in the text that illustrate rhythm patterns. Each student should also develop one additional way to demonstrate the values of notes and rests.

- With your class, sing the songs used in this unit. Singing and clapping together in a group often helps individuals learn more easily.

REVIEW

A. Indicate the best choice for each of the following.

1. If a piece of music has more than one set of staves, the time signature comes

    a. After the sharps or flats at the beginning of the music.
    b. After the sharps and flats on each line (staff) of music.
    c. Either on the first staff or every staff depending on the publisher.
    d. At the beginning and end of each staff.

2. With a $\frac{4}{4}$ time signature

    a. There are four beats to a measure.
    b. A quarter note gets one count.
    c. It takes 4 quarter notes to make one count.
    d. Both a and b.
    e. Both a and c.

3. With a $\frac{2}{4}$ time signature

    a. There are two beats to the measure.
    b. There are four beats to the measure.
    c. A quarter note gets one count.
    d. Both a and c.
    e. Both b and c.

4. With a $\frac{3}{4}$ time signature

    a. Every third note gets one count; there are 4 beats in a measure.
    b. There are three beats to the measure; a whole note gets one count.
    c. There are three beats to a measure; a quarter note gets one count.
    d. There are four beats to a measure; a third note gets one count.
    e. None of the above.

5. With a ⁶⁄₈ time signature

   a. There are six beats to the measure.
   b. An eighth note gets one count.
   c. A quarter note gets two counts.
   d. There are two accent beats in each measure.
   e. All of the above.

6. Concerning rests in music, they

   a. Are as important as the notes.
   b. Give the singer relaxation.
   c. Add interest to the music.
   d. Are not used very often in music for children.
   e. Both a and b.
   f. Both a and c.

7. With a ⁴⁄₄ time signature, which measures are correct?

   a. Four quarter notes.
   b. A quarter note and a whole note.
   c. A whole note.
   d. Two eighth notes, a quarter note, and a half note.
   e. All except b.
   f. All except d.

8. With a ⁶⁄₈ time signature, which measures would be correct?

   a. Six eighth notes.
   b. Two dotted quarter notes.
   c. Eight sixth notes.
   d. Two sixteenth notes, two eighth notes and a dotted quarter note.
   e. All except c.
   f. All except d.

B. Match each item in Column II with the correct item in Column I.

<table>
<tr><td>I</td><td>II</td></tr>
</table>

I

1. Measure
2. Accent beat
3. >
4. Tie
5. Slur
6. Meter signature
7. :‖
8. ‖: :‖

II

a.

b.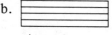

c.

d. go back to the first and repeat the music again.

e. symbol for an accent beat.

f. the note or notes in each measure which have extra emphasis.

g. play the music between these signs again.

h. another name for time signature.

unit 23 harmony

OBJECTIVES

After studying this unit, the student should be able to

- Define harmony and discuss its place in early music education.
- Play notes in the bass clef of some of the songs in this text.
- Identify a minor and a pentatonic scale.

Melody, rhythm, and harmony are the basic elements of music. Some musicians divide these three elements into smaller parts. However, the student who is aware of melody, rhythm, and harmony is able to use music in teaching young children.

Harmony (two or more tones sounded at the same time) is not as important to the young child and his teacher as melody and rhythm. Yet, harmony is important as a foundation for later musical experiences.

HARMONY IN EARLY MUSIC EDUCATION

There is a readiness factor in music, just as there is in reading — a time when the child can be expected to do a musical task. During the third grade (or at the ages of eight and nine) children usually start singing *rounds*. (The second voice or group of voices starts singing, at the same pitch, what the first group has just sung!) The singing of rounds usually leads to the singing of parts, such as alto and soprano.

Five through seven-year-olds can learn to sing rounds and parts; however, their time is better spent on other musical activities that have more value for them. It is not recommended that they sing rounds.

The teacher builds an awareness of harmony in the children; it is harmony that gives support to the melody. When two musicians perform together for the class, the teacher explains that they are singing or playing their instruments "in harmony." She plays a melody and its harmony on the Autoharp or piano.

NOTES OF THE BASS CLEF

The notes of the bass clef are shown below. The sentence, "Good boys do fine always," helps the student remember the names of notes on the lines.

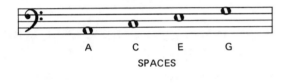

A   C   E   G

SPACES

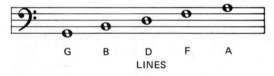

G   B   D   F   A

LINES

The notes above the bass clef are the following:

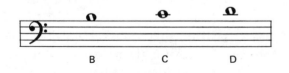

B   C   D

These notes are played on the same piano keys as the notes written below the treble clef, figure 23-1.

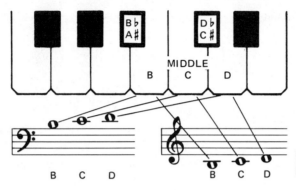

Fig. 23-1 Notes between the treble and bass clefs and their position on the piano.

PLAYING THE BASS CLEF NOTES

Play *Raggedy Ann* (Cassette song 23-A, figure 7-1). The song is written in the Key of C; there are no sharps or flats. The part that is played by the left hand is an ascending C scale. Figure 23-2 shows how it would be played on the piano. Each note in the bass clef is tied; the time signature means that each of the bass notes is held six counts. Practice playing the melody in the treble clef with the right hand. Use both hands to play both staffs, together. Listen to the cassette to see if you are playing the song correctly.

Play *Row, Row, Row Your Boat* (Cassette song 23-B, figure 12-6). It, too, is in the Key of C. The part played by the left hand is called a I chord in root position. Figure 23-3 shows how it is played on the piano. Find this chord on the piano. Play it all through the

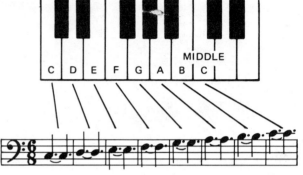

Fig. 23-2 This is the way that the bass clef notes of the song *Raggedy Ann* are played on the piano.

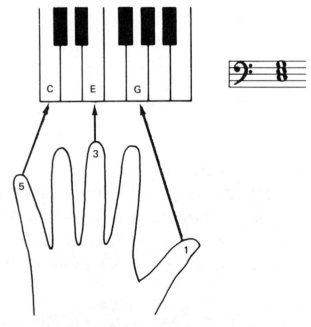

Fig. 23-3 This is the way the root chord (or I chord) of the C scale is played on the piano.

song as you play or sing the melody. Listen to the cassette to see if you are doing it correctly.

Now play *Follow Me* (Cassette song 23-C, figure 3-4). The I chord in root position can be played throughout this song, also.

MINOR SCALES

Many of the songs in the first twenty units of this book are based on the major scales. There is much music, however, that is based on minor scales. The sound of a minor scale is different from that of a major scale. Folk music, especially Jewish and Indian music, are often written in a minor key. Play *Happy Hanukkah Time* (Cassette song 23-D, figure 8-4). There is one flat in *Happy Hanukkah Time*. Notice, however, that this song has a different sound than the other songs in this

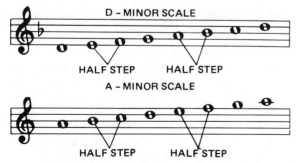

Fig. 23-4 D-Minor scale; A-Minor scale.

text written in the key of F. Note also that the song ends on a D note. It has been stated that a song usually ends on the first note, or keynote, of a scale. Two things — the sound and the final note — indicate that this song is in a minor key.

Note that the half steps come between notes 2 and 3, and notes 5 and 6 in the D-minor scale. (To review: In a major scale, the half steps come between notes 3 and 4 and between 7 and 8.)

Play *Ki, Yi, Yi* (Cassette song 23-E, figure 5-3). This chant is written in the key of A-minor and has an easy accompaniment. Find bass notes A and E on the piano, as shown in figure 23-5. Play these notes over and over in a steady rhythm. A young child likes to do this, too.

The minor scale that has been described is called a natural minor scale. Actually, there are other minor scales that are more often used. This text will not go into any more detail about them because the important skill is recognizing songs based on minor scales. This explains their different sound and builds a foundation for later studies of harmony.

THE PENTATONIC SCALE

In unit 13, a method is described by which children play duets on the piano. (To review: each of the two children play any black note; the result sounds all right.) These

duets are based on the pentatonic scale. This scale is one of many that are not used as often as the major scales. Music based on this scale often sounds as if it comes from the Orient, although many American children's songs are built on the pentatonic scale, also.

One pentatonic scale is shown:

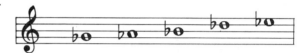

Note that there are only five tones. Play the scale on the piano.

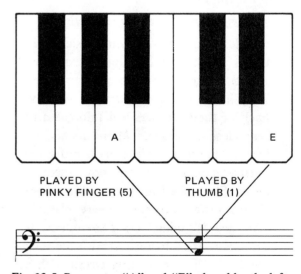

Fig. 23-5 Bass notes "A" and "E" played by the left hand for the song, *Ki, Yi, Yi.*

223

Songs based on the pentatonic scale also help teachers and young children gain an awareness of harmony. Play *Pretty Japanese Dolly* (Cassette song 23-F, figure 23-6). Sing it and play it on the piano. Just play every note on a black key. Once you have learned to do this, play the accompaniment by playing any black key or two black keys you want. Do this with the left hand and keep the hand moving — or ask a child to do it. The result is an interesting accompaniment. An example is played on the cassette.

M. C. Weller Pugmire   M. C. Weller Pugmire

Pret - ty Jap - an - ese dol - ly. I love you so.——

Pret - ty Jap - an - ese dol - ly. I love you so.——

Fig. 23-6 *Pretty Japanese Dolly* (**Cassette song 23-F**).

A STORY THAT TELLS ABOUT HARMONY

The following story helps children learn about harmony.

Neighbors Should Play Together[1]

It was a summer day in Music Town, U.S.A. All the little instruments had been shined up to go out to play together. They had a new song to learn to play. Each of their mothers had told them to stay close to home. Mama piano was busy in the house when she heard some terrible sounds that did not resemble music. She looked out the window where all the little instruments were playing. "No, no. It's mine," cried Saxophone as Trombone tried to run off with the song sheet. Violin was hitting Drum with a

[1]Story and illustrations by La Fawn G. Holt, Salt Lake City, Utah. Used with permission.

bow. Drum was ready to hit her back with the drumstick. What a way for friends to play! Mama Piano went out to see if she could help.

She began to play some pretty notes on her long keyboard. Soon every little instrument forgot to be angry and came over by the piano. Trombone offered the song back to Saxophone who very happily wanted to hear the music played by Mama Piano. She had little Drum beat the time, and soon everyone was playing together, each taking turns instead of fussing. You see, if we play together in harmony, we can make beautiful music.

Some teachers feel that objects like horns and drums should neither be given faces in a story, nor made to "come to life" because in

the early years, children often confuse reality with fantasy. However, this story has been told to hundreds of children, who loved it. They wanted to hear it again and again. It does explain some basic facts about harmony.

SUMMARY

Harmony is not as important in early music education as melody and rhythm. Yet the teacher of young children should think of it as a foundation for later studies in music.

The beginning student learns the notes of the bass clef and plays them on the piano, taking time to practice. The minor scale and pentatonic scale have different sounds than a major scale. Being aware of these sounds helps the student to build an awareness of harmony for herself and the children she will teach.

PATTERN IDEAS

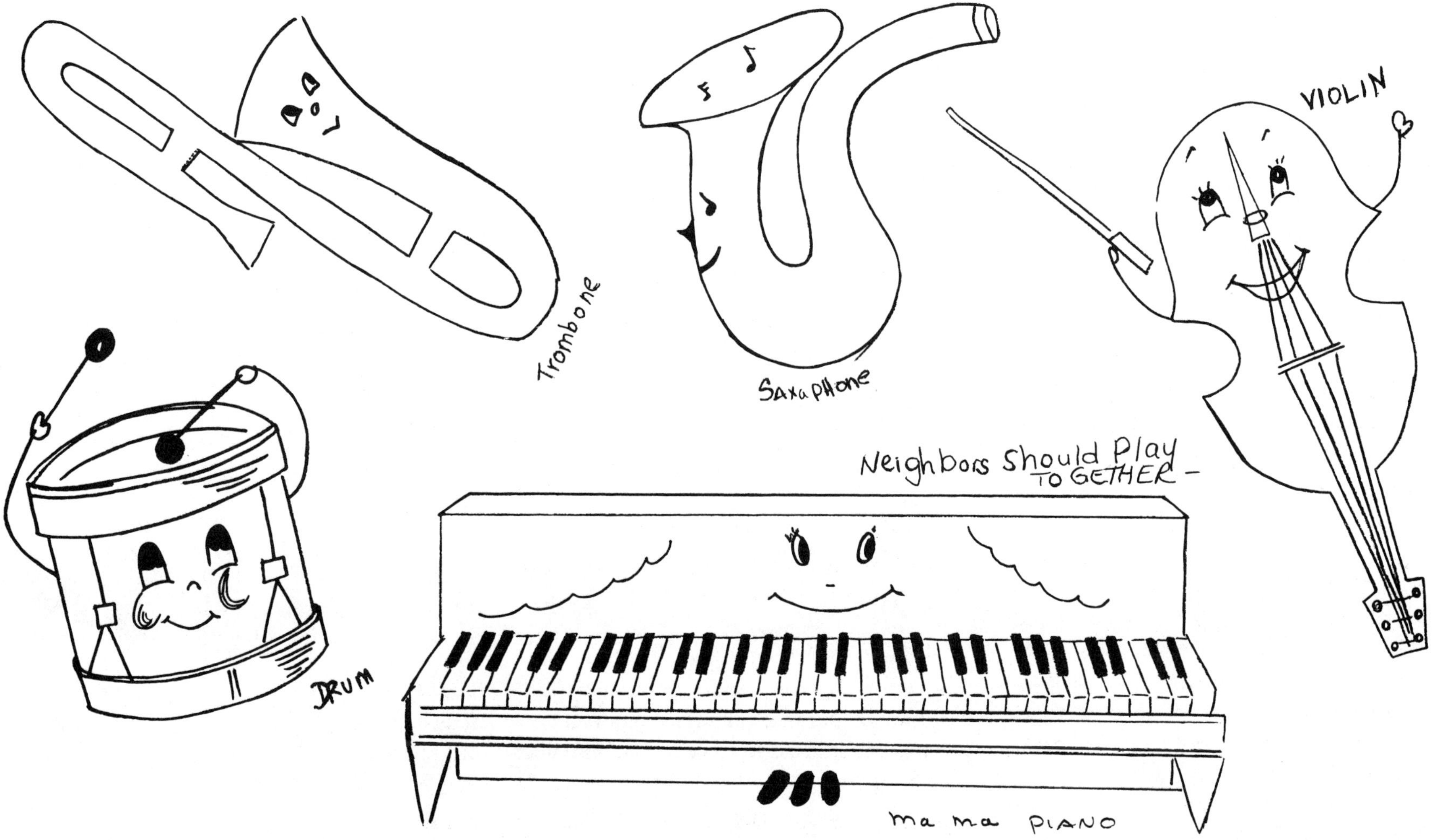

Fig. 23-7 Illustrations for the story, "Neighbors should play together." (Illustrator, LaFawn Holt)

SUGGESTED ACTIVITIES FOR THE BEGINNING STUDENT

- Prepare a written report for your instructor regarding

  a. Your practice periods and what you are doing in them.
  b. Whether or not you are reaching the goal you set for a certain amount of practice time.
  c. Any questions you may have.

- Follow suggestions in this unit in order to learn to play notes in the bass clef. Practice until you can play the music on both clefs of the songs mentioned in this unit.

SUGGESTED ACTIVITIES FOR THE MUSICALLY TRAINED STUDENT

- Lead your classmates in singing rounds. Some suggestions are listed:

  a. *Row, Row, Row Your Boat*
  b. *Three Blind Mice*
  c. *Are You Sleeping?*
  d. Others from your region

- Lead a discussion with your classmates about the value of teaching rounds — or the singing of parts — to young children.

- If you play an instrument, demonstrate the playing of harmony on it.

SUGGESTED ACTIVITIES FOR ALL STUDENTS

- To gain an awareness of harmony, class members should do this: Each puts a piece of waxed paper over a clean comb. On a signal, each person places the comb between his lips and starts to hum any song he wishes. This is not harmony!

  On a second signal, everyone should hum *Twinkle, Twinkle, Little Star*. Some can hum the alto (lower) part; others sing the melody. This is one form of harmony.

- Do the above activity with a small group of children. They will not be able to hum the alto part, but as they all hum the melody together, the teacher can say, "When we play together we have a feeling of unity," or she can say, "We sing in unison."

- Show a child how to play the I chord for *Row, Row, Row Your Boat*. Have him play this while you sing or play the melody. Record his reactions. Do the same with the song *Follow Me*.

- Talk to local teachers. Find out at what age rounds and singing of parts are taught. Report to the class the local teachers' opinions on this subject.

- Make a flannelboard study of "Neighbors Should Play Together." Tell it to a child or a group of children. Record their reactions. File the story under 81 C – Music Elements: Harmony.

REVIEW

A. Match each item in Column II with the correct item in Column I.

I	II
1. Harmony	a. The scale often used in Indian and Jewish folk music.
2. Pentatonic scale	b. The 1, 3, 5 notes of a scale that are played together.
3. Minor scale	c. Played on black keys of the piano.
4. A, C, E, G	d. Names of the notes on the lines of the bass clef.
5. G, B, D, F, A	e. Song based on a minor scale.
6. Rounds	f. Song based on the pentatonic scale.
7. *Pretty Japanese Dolly*	g. Two or more tones sounded together at the same time.
8. *Ki, Yi, Yi*	h. Usually taught at age 8 or 9.
9. Root chord	i. Names of the notes in the spaces of the bass clef.

B. Name the following notes from the bass clef.

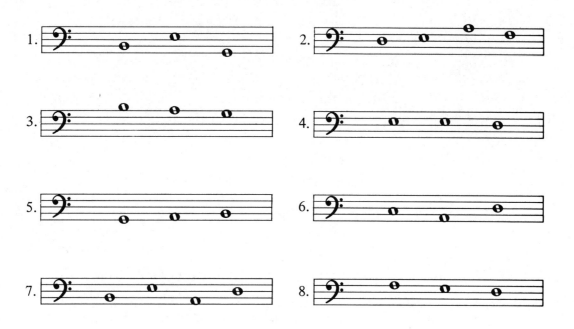

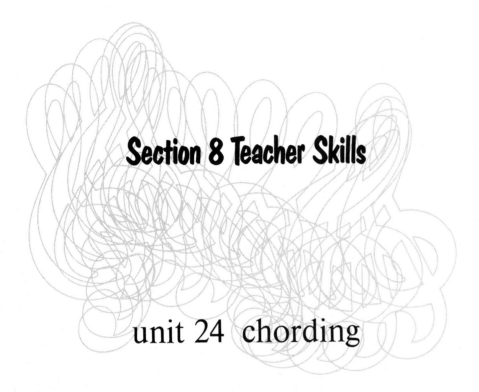

Section 8 Teacher Skills

unit 24 chording

OBJECTIVES

After studying this unit, the student should be able to

- Build and play I, IV, and V (V⁷) chords in five keys.

- Mark and play the chords of songs in the text.

- List three uses of the Autoharp in early childhood education.

Harmony was defined in the preceding unit as "two or more tones sounded at the same time." Very often the words, "usually in chords" are added to this definition. The teacher who can play chords has a skill that helps her use music more effectively with young children. Most children's songs can be accompanied by the use of the I, IV, and V (V⁷) chords.

CHOOSING ACCOMPANIMENT

Music for young children can be sung without accompaniment. Often the melody is played on the piano, using both hands, one *octave* apart (eight notes apart; an example is from low C to middle C), figure 24-1. A song can also be accompanied with chords, a method which gives the most support to children's singing.

BUILDING CHORDS

Chords are built in the following ways. If the bottom note is on a line, notes are added on the next two lines above.

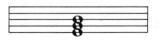

If the bottom note is on a space, the notes are added on the next two spaces above.

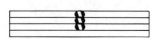

A chord built on the first note or keynote was shown in unit 23. (To review: this is called the I chord in *root position* when the root (keynote) of the chord is on the bottom and the other tones are on the next lines or the next spaces on the staff.) Study figure 24-2,

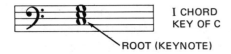

I CHORD
KEY OF C

ROOT (KEYNOTE)

which shows the I chords in root position of the keys used in the songs in this text.

I TO V CHORD PROGRESSION

In unit 23, *Row, Row, Row Your Boat* was played using only the I chord. Now play *Row, Row, Row Your Boat* (Cassette song 24-A, figure 24-1). Note that the second time through the song sounds better at the end. This is because a *V chord* (a chord built on the fifth tone of a scale) is used. A *chord progression* (the movement of chords, such as from the I chord to the V chord) makes the accompaniment sound better. Play *Rig-A-Jig-*

Traditional

Row, row, row your boat Gent-ly down the stream.——

Mer-ri-ly, Mer-ri-ly, Mer-ri-ly, Mer-ri-ly. Life is but a dream.——

Fig. 24-1 *Row, Row, Row Your Boat* (Cassette song 24-A): To accompany children's song, the notes of the melody can be played one octave apart.

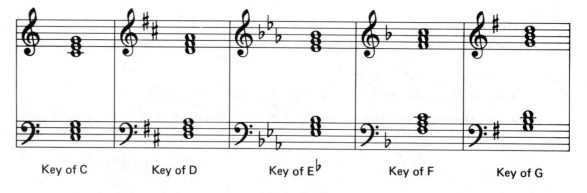

Key of C   Key of D   Key of E♭   Key of F   Key of G

Fig. 24-2 These are the I chords in root position of the keys used in this text.

Jig (Cassette song 24-B, figure 19-8) and *Quiet Thoughts* (Cassette song 24-C, figure 19-10). Look up the music, noting that both of these songs have chord progressions that go from I to V to I. As you play the cassette, try to listen for the sounds that "tell" you the chords should change.

Often, it is said that a person can play "by ear." This means that he can play the melody and chords without any music once he has heard the song. Few people can do this, although some can learn to play chord progressions by listening to the music and developing "an ear" for them.

THE V⁷ CHORD

Very often a fourth tone is added to a V chord. If the chord is built on lines, a note is added on the line above. If the chord is built on spaces, a note is added on the space above. This is called a V⁷ chord. It gives a richer sound and is used often in children's music.

V⁷ CHORD – KEY OF C

V⁷ CHORD – KEY OF D

I, IV, V, (V⁷) CHORD PROGRESSION

Play *Chords Progress* (Cassette song 24-D, figure 24-3). This song should help you develop "an ear" for chord progression from I to IV to V. Play it again. Study the chords in the bass clef of the music as you listen. Now play the chords on the piano. Sing or play the melody.

Almost every song in this text can be played with the I, IV, and V (or V⁷) chords. Play *My Grandpa* (Cassette song 24-E, figure 8-8). Many children's songs are like this. The chords move from I to IV to V⁷ to I. Look at the music. Mark the chords as they are marked in figure 24-4. Chords can be marked as follows:

I chord – named for the first note of scale. (Example: "C" in the key of C.)

IV chord – named for the fourth note of the scale. (Example: "F" in the key of C.)

V chord – named for the fifth note of the scale. (Example: "G" in the key of C.)

M. C. Weller Pugmire

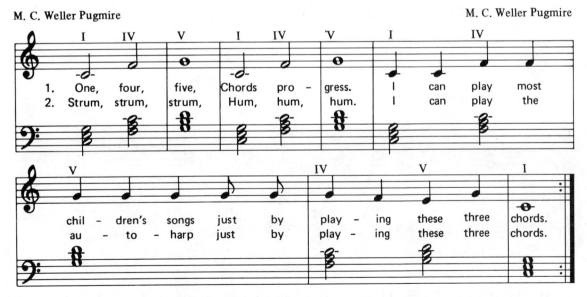

Fig. 24-3 *Chords Progress* (Cassette song 24-D).

> *V⁷ chord — named for the fifth note of the scale. A small 7 is added to indicate another note has been added to the chord. (Example: G^7 in the key of C.)*

Marking the chords for the songs in the text is a practical way to learn about chords. Figure 24-5 shows the I, IV, V⁷ chords for the five major scales used in this text.

A DIFFERENT WAY TO CHORD

There are many ways to play the chords on the piano. This is necessary because sometimes the music indicates that the two hands should play the same notes. As one practices, ways are found to play the same notes in different positions.

- To play the I to IV progression, leave the keynote (note 1) as it is. Move the second note up one-half step. Move the third note of the chord up one whole step. This is now a IV chord. Study figure 24-6. Notice that the same notes are played that are in the IV chord in root position, but the C note is played on the bottom of the chord instead of the top. This is called an *inverted chord* (a chord not in root position).

- To play the I to V progression, leave the third note or the fifth tone of the scale

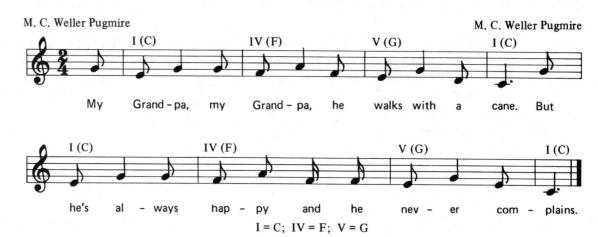

M. C. Weller Pugmire

M. C. Weller Pugmire

My Grand‑pa, my Grand‑pa, he walks with a cane. But

he's al‑ways hap‑py and he nev‑er com‑plains.

I = C; IV = F; V = G

Fig. 24-4 *My Grandpa* (Cassette song 24-E): **Chord markings in the text should be named as shown above. This is a practical way to learn about chords.**

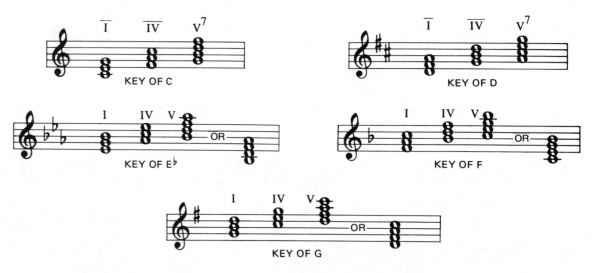

KEY OF C

KEY OF D

KEY OF E♭

KEY OF F

KEY OF G

Fig. 24-5 The I, IV, and V⁷ chords for the five major scales used in this text. Each of the bottom notes of these chords is called the "root note" or "keynote" of that chord.

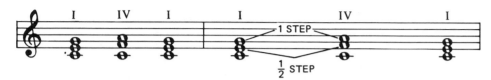

Fig. 24-6 The I to IV progression for Key of C. The IV chord is inverted.

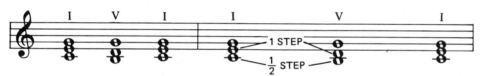

Fig. 24-7 The I to V progression for Key of C. The V chord is inverted.

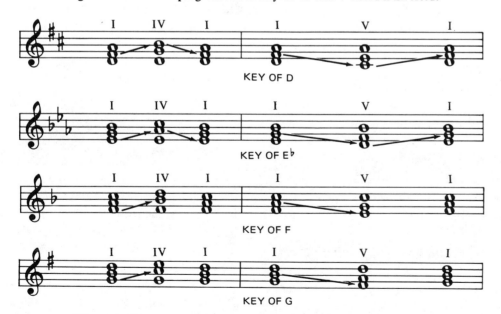

KEY OF D

KEY OF E♭

KEY OF F

KEY OF G

Fig. 24-8 Chord progressions for the other four keys used in the text.

as it is. Move the middle note down one whole step. Move the bottom note, or keynote, down one half-step. This is now a V chord. Study figure 24-7. The same notes are played as in the regular V chord of the C scale, but the B and D notes are played on the bottom instead of the top. Figure 24-8 shows these chord progressions for the other four keys used in this text.

• When playing a V^7 chord the fourth note of the chord is often played on the bottom instead of the top of the chord. Sometimes one of the other notes of the chord is left out — usually the third note, figure 24-9.

As the student gains more skill in chording, other ways to build chords may be developed. It is easier to play chords than to read about them. Play *President's Day* (Cassette song 24-F, figure 8-5) and *Great Big Words* (Cassette song 24-G, figure 17-4).

THE AUTOHARP

The Autoharp is an instrument on which chords are played by pressing bars down with buttons. Most schools have Autoharps, although teachers do not use them as much as they should. Actually, the Autoharp can be a very effective music aid. It gives support to children's singing. It helps children learn

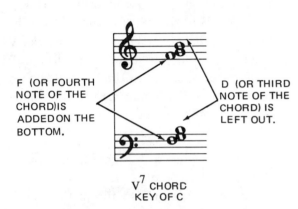

F (OR FOURTH NOTE OF THE CHORD) IS ADDED ON THE BOTTOM.

D (OR THIRD NOTE OF THE CHORD) IS LEFT OUT.

V⁷ CHORD
KEY OF C

Fig. 24-9 The fourth note of the V chord is added on the bottom. The third note of the chord is left out.

Fig. 24-10 The Autoharp can be used very enjoyably with young children.

about chords. It helps people acquire "an ear" for chord progressions. It even helps with reading readiness as children learn the letter names of the chords and the fact that this letter is a symbol for a chord with a certain sound.

Exploring The Autoharp

The student should be able to study and practice using an Autoharp with twelve bars. Although there are some differences in instruments from various companies, they are basically alike.

The Autoharp is held in front of the player. Press down firmly with the index finger of your left hand on the bar with the C-Major button. Cross over the top of your left hand and strum the strings on the main part of the Autoharp with your right hand. Do it first with your fingers. Then strum with your thumb. Finally use the felt strummer, or pick, that comes with the Autoharp. The felt pick is usually best to use as it makes the most pleasing sound. Make both long strokes and short strokes on the strings.

Now strum on the right side of the bars. Note the difference in sound. Try pressing the bars with the right hand and strumming on the main part of the Autoharp with the left hand.

Hold the Autoharp in your lap and strum. Then put it on a wooden table and strum. Notice the difference in sound.

Look at the letters on the Autoharp buttons. Find the C Major, F Major, and G⁷ buttons. These are the I, IV, and V⁷ chords in the key of C.

Playing The Autoharp

Sing the second verse of *Chords Progress* (Cassette song 24-D, figure 24-3). Strum one time for each of the first three notes. Press the C Major button, then the F Major button, then the G⁷ button. Play the cassette to see if you are doing it properly. Sing the song as you play the chords. At first, you will have to look at the music. Soon you will develop "an ear" for the chord progressions.

Now play *Chords Progress* using the following buttons:

> *F, B♭ and C⁷ (I, IV and V⁷ for Key of F)*
> *G, C and D⁷ (I, IV and V⁷ for Key of G)*

Some Autoharps have 15 bars for chords. The last three are usually F⁷, D and E♭. This enables the player to play the I, IV and V⁷ chords in the Key of D, that is D, G and A⁷. After you have learned to play the I, IV, and V chords on the Autoharp, with practice you will become able to accompany most of the songs used in the text.

More About The Autoharp

Some people play the Autoharp by holding it up against the body. The right buttons are then pressed "by touch." This is easier than learning where the keys are on a typewriter since there are fewer keys. With practice, one learns where the keys are.

There are many other techniques that one can learn for playing the Autoharp. However, the simple playing of the I, IV, and V^7 chords is a helpful skill for use in music programs for young children.

The Autoharp must be tuned from time to time. Instructions come with it that show how to do this.

Teaching The Child To Play

The child needs supervision to learn to play. He should be taught to respect the instrument and help take care of it.

A three-year-old can strum the Autoharp as the teacher or assistant presses the buttons on the bars. Fours have to be taught to press the buttons firmly, but they are able to do this and play one-chord songs. Fives can learn to play a I to V progression; the C and G^7 buttons are used as they are next to each other. Sixes and sevens can learn to play the I, IV,

and V^7 progressions if they have been through the simpler steps.

A listing of songs from this text using one chord (I), two chords (I and V or V^7), and three chords (I, IV, and V or V^7) has been placed in the Appendix. This should help the teacher as she plays. It should also help her teach the children to play.

OTHER CHORD INSTRUMENTS

Some teachers think the ukelele is the best instrument to accompany young children's singing. It is actually quite an easy instrument to play. Practice is needed in order to do it well, of course. The I, IV and V^7 chords can be used on the ukelele to accompany almost all children's songs.

In actual practice, it seems that very few teachers use the ukelele effectively. The beginning student seems more at ease with the Autoharp. Perhaps this is because the names of the chords are on the Autoharp and a rich, full chord can be obtained by pressing a bar. Musically talented people usually go on to play the guitar. Many early education teachers would rather be good guitarists than good pianists! If the student plays the guitar, it should certainly be used in the classroom.

The chords for playing the ukelele are included in the Appendix. Students who learn

to play the ukelele find their efforts to be worthwhile. A ukelele is easy to carry and the children love to sing as it is played.

Other chord instruments are used in some early childhood centers. Sometimes a small organ-type instrument is used. The chords are marked on these instruments. Again, the I, IV and V (V^7) chords are used most often.

Chord instruments are useful for use with young children. They should not replace a piano if one is available. The piano has many more uses and has better tone quality. Both piano and chord instruments should be used when possible. Each has its place in the music program.

SUMMARY

Children's singing is often accompanied with chords. The I, IV, and V (V^7) chords are most often used. The beginning student can build these chords and develop "an ear" for knowing when the chords progress.

The Autoharp is a chord instrument that can be used effectively in early music education. It is easy for both the teacher and child to play. The ukelele and guitar are also good to use, but none of these should replace a piano if one is available.

SUGGESTED ACTIVITIES

- Mark the names of the chords of the songs used in this text. This will take time, but will help you gain the skill of chording.

- Practice the I, IV, V^7 chords shown in figure 24-5 on the piano. Practice all chords with the right hand. Then play the same chords an octave lower with the left hand.

- Play the I to IV progressions and I to V progressions as they are shown in figures 24-6, 24-7, and 24-8.

- Follow the suggestions in the text for playing the Autoharp. Practice until you can accompany the songs in this text.

- Teach a young child to play the Autoharp. Let the child's age and ability guide which chords to use. Report your experiences and the results to the class.

- Discuss other chord instruments such as the ukelele and guitar. Invite a guitarist to play accompaniment for the class to sing. Interact with other class members concerning the value of ukelele and/or guitar accompaniments.

REVIEW

A. Indicate the best choice for each of the following.

1. Young children's music

   a. Can be sung with no accompaniment.
   b. Can be accompanied by playing the melody notes an octave apart.
   c. Can usually be accompanied using the I, IV, and V (V^7) chords.
   d. All of the above.
   e. Both a and c.

2. Playing music "by ear"

    a. Is not done in early childhood education.
    b. Means the person can play without music.
    c. Is a skill some people have.
    d. Can be developed to some degree by many people.
    e. All except a.

3. The V^7 chord

    a. Is not used very often.
    b. Is made by adding seven notes to a V chord.
    c. Makes the V chord have a richer sound.
    d. Is unnecessary for children's music.
    e. All except d.

4. The Autoharp

    a. Gives support to singing.
    b. Helps children learn about chords.
    c. Helps people develop "an ear" for chord progression.
    d. Can help a child get ready to read.
    e. All of the above.

5. When learning about the Autoharp, it is best to

    a. Try different ways of strumming.
    b. Wait until you find a professional teacher.
    c. Learn the name of every string.
    d. Realize there is one best way to play it.
    e. Both a and c.

B. Match each item in Column II with the correct item in Column I.

I   II

1. Octave   a.

2. Root position   b. Movement of chords (as from I to V)

3. Chord progression   c. Low C to middle C

4. I chord   d. Two or more tones sounded at the
                                     same time, usually as chords
5. IV chord

6. V chord   e.

7. Harmony   f. When the root of the chord is on the
                                     bottom
8. Inverted chord

                                  g.

                                  h. A chord not in root position

C. Write the chords in both the treble and bass clefs. Use whole notes.

I CHORD – KEY OF C

V CHORD – KEY OF G

IV CHORD – KEY OF E♭

I CHORD – KEY OF F

IV CHORD – KEY OF D

V⁷ CHORD – KEY OF C

V⁷ CHORD – KEY OF G

IV CHORD – KEY OF D

unit 25 gaining a musical vocabulary

OBJECTIVES

After studying this unit, the student should be able to

- Define and illustrate terms of musical expression.
- Identify musical symbols.
- Briefly discuss the skill of teaching music.

Terms and symbols used in music are interesting because they are so widely used. Every teacher who has taught a child to read knows that the child learns to read a word like "helicopter" more easily than a short word like "had." This is true of terms used in music. The child likes to say in a soft voice, "This song is sung pianissimo."

TERMS OF EXPRESSION

Several terms are used in children's music to indicate expression. Often a symbol is used in place of the term.

Term	Indication	Symbol
Piano	*Softly*	*p*
Pianissimo	*Very softly*	*pp*
Forte	*Loudly*	*f*
Fortissimo	*Very loudly*	*ff*
Crescendo (cres.)	*Gradually make louder*	<
Diminuendo	*Gradually make softer*	>

WAYS TO ILLUSTRATE EXPRESSION

Play *Master, the Tempest is Raging* (Cassette song 25-A, figure 25-1). This song is based on a Biblical story. Students like to sing it because it grows louder and louder, . . . then softer. Sing it with the cassette; make it

The winds and the waves shall o – bey his will; Peace,— be

still!—— Wheth – er the wrath of the storm – tossed sea or

de – mons or men or what – ev – er it be, No wa – ters can swal – low the

ship where lies the Mas – ter of o – cean and earth and skies. They

all shall sweet – ly o – bey my will. Peace, be still! Peace, be still! They

all shall sweet – ly o – bey my will. Peace, peace, be still!——

I = C; IV = F; V⁷ = G⁷

Fig. 25-1 *Master, The Tempest Is Raging* (Cassette song 25-A).

very soft — *pianissimo* — and then very loud — *fortissimo*. Then sing it softly, again, *piano*.

Play *The Cymbals* (Cassette song 25-B, figure 10-4). This is fun to sing — louder and louder (*f*) and at the end very loud (*ff*) with a "crash!"

Two pieces of heavy poster board (24" by 1 1/2") can be fastened together with a heavy brad. This can be used as a large crescendo or a diminuendo symbol, figure 25-2. As the children sing more loudly, the pieces of poster board can be opened wider. As they sing more softly, the pieces are closed together. A child can do this, too.

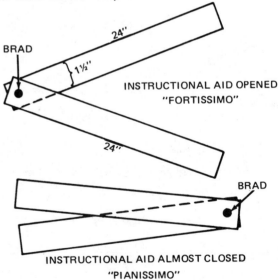

Fig. 25-2 A crescendo — diminuendo instructional aid. Children like to use this to show that the music grows louder or softer.

OTHER MUSICAL TERMS AND SYMBOLS

The children like to use the following terms when they sing:

- Animato   Animatedly
- Allegro   Lively, Quickly
- Dolce   Sweetly, Softly
- Presto   Very Quickly
- Moderato   At a Medium Speed
- Adagio   Slowly, Smoothly

Play *Mother, You're Special* (Cassette song 25-C, figure 8-6). Note that it is marked "Dolce." It is to be sung sweetly by a child to his mother. Many songs say, "Sing Sweetly" at the top. It extends the child's vocabulary to teach him the term, "Dolce." If the teacher finds any musical term she does not understand, she looks it up in a dictionary.

Play *Five Little Kittens* (Cassette song 25-D, figure 8-9). It is marked "Animato." See if you feel the kittens are jumping and playing as you listen to the cassette recording; sing with the cassette as you play the song again.

Play *Two To . . .* (Cassette song 25-E, figure 7-5). It, also, is marked "Animato." Put a lot of expression into this song; it should lead to good dramatic play!

Some symbols tell what to do in the song:

Fermata

This is called a "hold." It means the note is held a little longer than it would be without the sign.

Glissando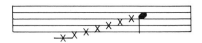

Sliding over several keys rapidly on the piano, or over the strings of other instruments.

 This symbol means that a word of this song is spoken instead of sung.

Play *Manners Can Be Fun* (Cassette song 25-F, figure 6-3). Study the music. Notice that it contains a fermata and a glissando. Play the song on the cassette. Point to the fermata and the glissando on the staff, at the time they are played.

Children love to play a glissando. (Practice first before teaching a child. Move the back of your thumb quickly over the piano keys from middle C either up or down to the next C.) Most schools have small toy xylophones. The child can make a glissando on this musical toy by rubbing the wooden mallet over the keys.

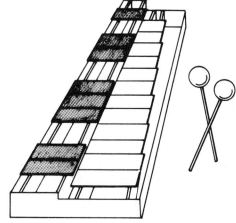

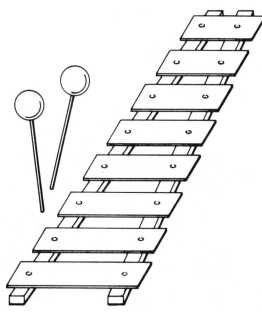

Fig. 25-3 Most schools and centers have a toy xylophone. A child can make a glissando on this. A set of resonator bells works well, too.

Play *Monkeys and the Crocodile* (Cassette song 25-G, figure 19-9). Study the music; notice the symbol on the last line that tells you the "oops!" is to be spoken. Words are often spoken in children's music, because they add interest to the songs.

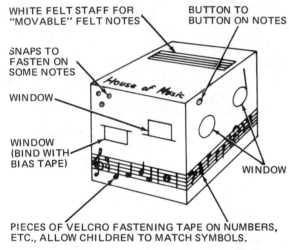

WHITE FELT STAFF FOR "MOVABLE" FELT NOTES

BUTTON TO BUTTON ON NOTES

SNAPS TO FASTEN ON SOME NOTES

WINDOW

WINDOW (BIND WITH BIAS TAPE)

WINDOW

PIECES OF VELCRO FASTENING TAPE ON NUMBERS, ETC., ALLOW CHILDREN TO MATCH SYMBOLS.

Fig. 25-4 **Rear view of Music House described in unit 1. The child plays matching games with the symbols of music.**

THE MUSIC HOUSE AND SYMBOLS

Many of the symbols used in this chapter can be added to the "Music House" described in unit 1. Make more of the symbols of music with black felt tip markers on the house itself. Then make matching symbols from heavy black felt or black pellon. Sew small pieces of velcro fastening material to the house and to the symbols. The children match the symbols and attach them. This gives the "Music House" added appeal.

Matching musical symbols is a reading-readiness type activity. It can usually be done by the child who is five years old and older. It is also a music-readiness activity. Children become familiar with the musical symbols.

GAINING THE SKILL TO USE MUSIC

This text presents a practical approach by which the student can gain the skills necessary to use music effectively with young children. The most important skill is a com-bination of a positive attitude and a willingness to try. Some might not call this a skill, but it really is. When the young child wants to sing and dance and play instruments, he needs a teacher who will encourage him. The teacher who uses the skills she learned as a student will develop more ideas of her own. She will enjoy teaching music and will pass that joy to the children.

SUMMARY

Although it is not absolutely necessary to know the terms of music, they are interesting for both the teacher and the child. Symbols are used a great deal. Becoming familiar with them helps build a readiness for further learning in music.

The greatest skill in using music to teach the young child is a positive attitude and a willingness to try musical activities. With this skill, the teacher can help the child realize the joy music brings.

SUGGESTED ACTIVITIES

- Look at songs 15-5 through 15-10 (Cassette songs 25-H through 25-M). These songs have markings like "Lightly" and "Happily." Have each class member make up symbols to take the place of these markings. Class members should compare symbols they make up. Then discuss the importance of the musical symbols that are so widely used.

- Visit local schools and early childhood centers and observe musical activities. Do the children use good expression in their singing? Do the teachers follow terms and symbols in the music? Report on this and note ways that better quality in music may be obtained.

- Make a cardboard symbol for crescendo and diminuendo. Use it with a child to sing one of the songs in the unit.

- Have a "regular" classroom teacher of young children (one who has a positive attitude toward teaching music) talk to the class. Record at least one idea from her talk that would help to improve your skill. Try it to see if it works for you.

- Add symbols to the "House of Music" that was made in unit 1. Use it with children. Keep the "House" for your own use or donate it to the center where you observe musical activities.

REVIEW

A.   Match each item in Column II with the correct item in Column I.

	I		II
1.	p	a.	Fermata (or hold)
2.	⌢	b.	Forte
3.	ff	c.	Crescendo
4.	pp	d.	Piano
5.	f	e.	Diminuendo
6.	▦	f.	Fortissimo
7.	<	g.	Word is spoken instead of sung
8.	>	h.	Pianissimo

B. Match each item in Column II with the correct item in Column I.

I	II
1. Piano	a. Very softly
2. Pianissimo	b. Gradually make softer
3. Forte	c. Softly
4. Fortissimo	d. Very loudly
5. Crescendo	e. Loudly
6. Diminuendo	f. Gradually make louder

C. Match each item in Column II with the correct item in Column I.

I	II
1. Animato	a. Medium speed
2. Adagio	b. Slowly, smoothly
3. Moderato	c. Lively, quickly
4. Dolce	d. Hold note a little longer
5. Allegro	e. Animatedly
6. Presto	f. Sweetly and softly
7. Fermata	g. Move fingers quickly over several keys
8. Glissando	h. Very quickly

Appendix A

Appendix B

UKELELE CHORDS

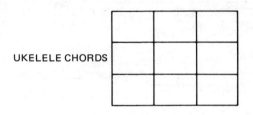

NOTES USED TO TUNE UKELELE

"MY   DOG   HAS   FLEAS"

C MAJOR

C OR I

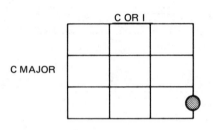

F OR IV

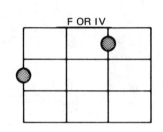

G^7 OR V^7

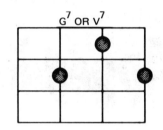

F MAJOR

F OR I

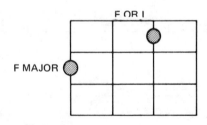

B OR IV

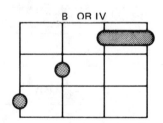

C^7 OR V^7

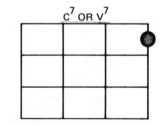

G MAJOR

G OR I

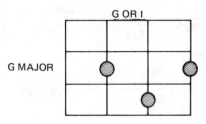

C OR IV

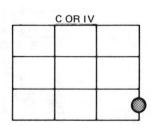

D^7 OR V^7

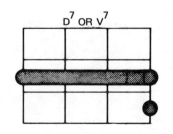

Appendix C

UNIT 21

Cassette song

21-A *Give, Said the Little Stream* (figure 2-7).
21-B *Up, Down, Whoops!* (figure 13-4).
21-C *Now Is the Time* (figure 1-2).
21-D *You Tell Me Your Dream* (figure 7-7).
21-E *Sleep, Baby, Sleep* (figure 4-1).
21-F *Shake Your Hands Up High* (figure 9-6).

UNIT 22

Cassette song

22-A *Let's Go Walking* (figure 11-2).
22-B *Airabella Bailey* (figure 13-2).
22-C *Fly, My Pretty Balloon* (figure 2-3).
22-D *The Fan* (figure 11-6).
22-E *Snapdragons* (figure 10-5).
22-F *The Sparkling Christmas Tree* (figure 8-3).
22-G *I'm Goin' To Leave Old Texas Now* (figure 4-7).
22-H *Wheels* (figure 3-6).
22-I *Popcorn Popping On the Apricot Tree* (figure 22-9).
22-J *Cotton Needs Picking* (figure 1-4).
22-K *Sally Go Round the Sun* (figure 13-3).
22-L *Summer is Coming* (figure 13-8).
22-M *Do As I'm Doing* (figure 11-4).
22-N *We Can Run; We Can Play* (figure 22-11).
22-O *Look at Chico's New Shoes* (figure 7-4).

UNIT 23

Cassette song

23-A *Raggedy Ann* (figure 7-1).
23-B *Row, Row, Row Your Boat* (figure 12-6).
23-C *Follow Me* (figure 3-4).
23-D *Happy Hanukkah Time* (figure 8-4).
23-E *Ki, Yi, Yi* (figure 5-3).
23-F *Pretty Japanese Dolly* (figure 23-6).

UNIT 24

Cassette song

24-A *Row, Row, Row Your Boat* (figure 24-1).
24-B *Rig-A-Jig-Jig* (figure 19-8).
24-C *Quiet Thoughts* (figure 19-10).
24-D *Chords Progress* (figure 24-3).
24-E *My Grandpa* (figure 24-4).
24-F *President's Day* (figure 8-5).
24-G *Add On* (figure 3-5).

UNIT 25

Cassette song

25-A *Master, The Tempest Is Raging* (figure 25-1).
25-B *Cymbals* (figure 10-4).
25-C *Mother, You're Special* (figure 8-6).
25-D *Five Little Kittens* (figure 8-9).
25-E *Two To . . .* (figure 7-5).
25-F *Manners Can Be Fun* (figure 6-3).
25-G *Monkeys and the Crocodile* (figure 19-9).
25-H *Great Big Words* (figure 17-4).
25-I *Rhythm Sticks* (figure 15-5).
25-J *Drum* (figure 15-6).
25-K *The Triangle* (figure 15-7).
25-L *Wood Block* (figure 15-8).
25-M *Tambourine* (figure 15-9).
25-N *Drums and Sticks* (figure 15-10).

APPLICATION SONGS

A *Kookaburra* (figure 9-7).
B *We'll Have a Happy Day Today* (figure 10-2).
C *Crunchy Lunch* (figure 3-7).
D *Kum Ba Yah* (figure 7-6).
E *For America, For Canada* (figure 5-4).
F *Field Trip Song* (figure 19-6).
G *Smiles* (figure 3-3).

Appendix D

One Chord Songs

			Suggested Curriculum Use
Fig. 1-2	Now Is The Time	1-2	Music*
Fig. 3-4	Follow Me	3-4	Transition
Fig. 9-7	Kookaburra	9-7	Language Arts; Art
Fig. 9-8	Missus Mac, Mac, Mackle	9-8	Music
Fig. 12-6	Row, Row, Row Your Boat	12-6	Transition
Fig. 13-12	Pick A Bale Of Cotton	13-12	Social Studies
Fig. 20-5	Where Is Thumbkin?	20-5	Music

Two Chord Songs

Fig. 1-4	Cotton Needs Picking	1-4	Social Studies
Fig. 1-7	Itisket, Itasket	1-7	Music
Fig. 2-1	Fun To Do	2-1	Music
Fig. 2-3	Fly, My Pretty Balloon	2-3	Science
Fig. 3-6	Wheels	3-6	Science
Fig. 4-1	Sleep, Baby, Sleep	4-1	Music
Fig. 4-7	I'm Goin' to Leave Old Texas Now	4-7	Social Studies
Fig. 4-8	Here's a Ball for Baby	4-8	Social Studies
Fig. 6-5	Here We Go 'Round the Mulberry Bush	6-5	Social Studies
Fig. 7-5	Two to . . .	7-5	Social Studies
Fig. 9-4	Hush, Little Baby	9-4	Social Studies
Fig. 9-6	Shake Your Hands Up High	9-6	Music
Fig. 10-2	We'll Have a Happy Day Today	10-2	Science
Fig. 10-4	Cymbals	10-4	Music
Fig. 11-6	The Fan	11-6	Art
Fig. 12-1	Monkey See, Monkey Do	12-1	Language Arts
Fig. 12-6	Row, Row, Row Your Boat	12-6	Transition
Fig. 13-3	Sally Go Round the Sun	13-3	Music
Fig. 13-5	Did You Ever See a Lassie?	13-5	Music
Fig. 13-10	Oats, Peas, Beans and Barley Grow	13-10	Science
Fig. 14-1	Texture	14-1	Science
Fig. 14-2	Say Hello To Mrs. Circle	14-2	Art; Math
Fig. 14-4	Machines	14-4	Science
Fig. 14-8	Merrill's Song	14-8	Science
Fig. 14-9	Angie's Song	14-9	Science
Fig. 15-5	Rhythm Sticks	15-5	Music

	Two Chord Songs		**Suggested Curriculum Use**
Fig. 15-6	Drum	15-6	Music
Fig. 15-8	Wood Block	15-8	Music
Fig. 15-9	Tambourine	15-9	Music
Fig. 15-10	Drums and Sticks	15-10	Music
Fig. 19-8	Rig-A-Jig-Jig	19-8	Transition
Fig. 19-10	Quiet Thoughts	19-10	Language Arts
Fig. 20-6	Love Somebody	20-6	Social Studies
Fig. 22-11	We Can Run; We Can Play	22-11	Clean-Up

	Three Chord Songs		
Fig. 1-2	Now Is The Time	1-2	Music
Fig. 2-6	If You're Happy	2-6	Music
Fig. 3-3	Smiles	3-3	Social Studies
Fig. 3-5	Add-On	3-5	Transition
Fig. 3-7	Crunchy Lunch	3-7	Health, Nutrition
Fig. 4-4	Up, Up in the Sky	4-4	Science
Fig. 5-1	Nobody Knows the Trouble I've Seen	5-1	Social Studies
Fig. 5-2	Home on the Range	5-2	Social Studies
Fig. 5-4	For America, For Canada	5-4	Social Studies
Fig. 6-3	Manners Can Be Fun	6-3	Social Studies
Fig. 7-3	When We're Helping	7-3	Social Studies
Fig. 7-4	Look at Chico's New Shoes	7-4	Music
Fig. 7-7	You Tell Me Your Dream	7-7	Language Arts
Fig. 8-3	The Sparkling Christmas Tree	8-3	Social Studies
Fig. 8-5	President's Day	8-5	Social Studies
Fig. 8-6	Mother, You're Special	8-6	Social Studies
Fig. 8-7	Grandma's Name	8-7	Social Studies
Fig. 8-8	My Grandpa	8-8	Social Studies
Fig. 8-9	Five Little Kittens	8-9	Math
Fig. 10-5	Snapdragons	10-5	Science
Fig. 11-2	Let's Go Walking	11-2	Science
Fig. 11-4	Do As I'm Doing	11-4	Transition
Fig. 13-2	Airabella Bailey	13-2	Music
Fig. 13-4	Up, Down, Whoops!	13-4	Music
Fig. 13-6	Let's Pretend	13-6	Social Studies

Three Chord Songs		**Suggested Curriculum Use**	
Fig. 13-8	Summer Is Coming	13-8	Science
Fig. 13-9	Blue Bird	13-9	Music
Fig. 13-11	Hambone	13-11	Social Studies
Fig. 14-5	Over in the Meadow	14-5	Math, Science
Fig. 15-7	The Triangle	15-7	Music
Fig. 17-4	Great Big Words	17-4	Language Arts
Fig. 19-4	Hello, Everybody	19-4	Language Arts
Fig. 19-6	Field Trip Song	19-6	Field Trips
Fig. 19-9	Monkeys and the Crocodile	19-9	Science
Fig. 20-1A	Evening Prayer	20-1A	Music
Fig. 20-4	Parade March from "La Boheme"	20-4	Music
Fig. 22-9	Popcorn Popping On The Apricot Tree	22-9	Language Arts
Fig. 24-3	Chords Progress	24-3	Music
Fig. 25-1	Master, The Tempest Is Raging	25-1	Music

*Of course, all songs could be used to teach music. The songs mentioned are particularly good for concept development.

Answers

PART I TEACHING WITH MUSIC

SECTION 1 GOALS AND FUNCTION OF MUSIC FOR THE YOUNG CHILD

Unit 1 Influences of Music

A. 1. d   2. b   3. c   4. a   5. c   6. c   7. d

B. 1. f   2. g   3. b   4. c   5. a   6. e   7. d   8. i   9. h

Unit 2 Objectives of the Music Program

A. 1. d   2. a   3. e   4. b   5. c   6. f   7. g

B. 1. c   2. a, b, c, d   3. c   4. b   5. c   6. d   7. b, c, d

C.
Happy   = *If You're Happy* (reinforces)
Sad   = *Give, Said the Little Stream* (changes)
Sleepy   = *Rock-a-Bye Baby* (reinforces)
Patriotic = *America* or *God Save the Queen* (reinforces)
Dejected   = *Cotton Needs Picking* (changes)
Bored   = *Little Wheel A-Turning* (changes)

D. 1. a. Listening   b. Singing   c. Movement   d. Playing instruments   e. Creating

2. Rhythm, melody, harmony

3. To make refiling easier

4. Periodical article or a suggestion for movement

Unit 3 Uses of Music in Early Childhood Programs

B. 1. b   2. c   3. a   4. e   5. d

C. 1. b   2. b   3. d   4. d   5. d   6. c

SECTION 2 INDIVIDUAL DIFFERENCES

Unit 4 Developmental Influence of Music

A. 1. b   3. a, c, d   5. a, b, c, d   7. b   9. b   11. a

2. d   4. c   6. c   8. c   10. a, b, c   12. a, b, d

B. 1. c   2. a   3. b   4. e   5. d   6. h   7. f   8. g

C.

	Rhythm and Movement	Singing
Infants	Some infants will rock their cribs back and forth.	Singing to the infant is part of an "enriched environment."
Toddler	He jiggles his whole body when he moves.	Likes traditional family songs like lullabies sung by Grandma.
Preschooler	Rhythm is part of his daily life.	Can usually carry a "tune."
Young School age	Very active. Needs movement activities that use his whole body.	He likes to look at music books to read the words he sings.

Unit 5 Preferences of Children and Teachers

A. 1. d   2. c   3. b   4. c   5. c   6. a   7. d   8. d

B. 1. c   2. a   3. b   4. e   5. f   6. d   7. i   8. g   9. h   10. j

SECTION 3 PLANNING AND CONDUCTING MUSIC EXPERIENCES

Unit 6 The Structured Music Period

C. 1. c   2. d   3. e   4. a   5. f   6. b   7. h   8. g

D. 1. a. The teacher knows she organizes her lesson better.
   b. She knows what concepts she is developing.
   c. She is building her file for future teaching.

2. a. The size of the group that is taught.
   b. The place it is taught.

3. a. An object such as a chart or toy.
   b. A person who can do something interesting.
   c. Songs or finger plays.

4. a. Seeing or hearing the result of what one has done.
   b. Being given something like the animal cutout or a special sign.
   c. Receiving praise from the teacher and/or knowing she is proud.

5. As little as possible and yet remain effective. Get the children to answer questions. Interact with them.

Unit 7 Spontaneous Music Experience

A. 1. b   2. a   3. e   4. c   5. d   6. g   7. f   8. h

B. 1. b   2. a   3. b   4. a   5. c   6. d   7. a, c, d   8. a

C. 1. Buy toys that have musical or interesting sounds. Examples are toy animals that make sounds, sturdy wind-up music toys, such as "play" cassettes and televisions, musical rattles, and/or push toys that make musical sounds. (Note safety features of such toys.)

   2. Play music such as soft Hawaiian music.
   Note: Other answer would be right, too. Check facts in the text.

D. 1. Sing a lullaby.

   2. Review or present the concept that music is printed so that people can sing or play it.

   3. Make a prop box for the children to play disc jockey.

   4. Give the children a chance to show how the ukeleles are alike. Have a listening time to see if the sounds are alike.

   5. Sing a song about spring or have a listening time about sounds of spring.

   6. Set out rhythm instruments so that children can play parade.

Unit 7 (continued)

E. 1. *Reasons for* spontaneous music period.

>   a. Child learns faster when he is interested.
>   b. Good for infants and toddlers.

>   *Reasons against*

>   c. Interest might not be shown all the time. Thus some children might miss needed lessons.

2. Any facts that might hurt the child or family.

3. a. Motivate dramatic play.
    b. Use the facts the child knows about music from his background.
    c. Help child gain new facts.

SECTION 4 MUSIC AREAS AND ACTIVITIES

Unit 8 The "Music Corner" and Related Areas

A. 1. d   2. c   3. d   4. b   5. b, c, d   6. b   7. a   8. b

B. 1. c   2. a   3. e   4. b   5. d   6. g   7. f

C. 2. a. Pictures become part of the wall after 2 to 3 days.
        b. Too many articles confuse the child.
        c. A routine time for changing area is beneficial.
        d. Spontaneous changes add interest.

3. Mobiles can be hung from the ceiling. Walls can have musical figures painted on them.

4. Textured materials encourage the child to explore by touching. This helps him become familiar with musical symbols.

5. Empty floor space should be available for movement and creating. Furnishings can be pushed together or stacked in order to make this space.

6. Outdoor activities are encouraged in early childhood education. Noise bothers no one. There are fewer limits to restrict movement.

Unit 9 Singing

A. 1. c   2. f   3. b   4. e   5. d   6. a   7. g

B. 1. c   2. a, b, c   3. d   4. a   5. b   6. a   7. d

C. 1. a. Breathe in the right places.
       b. Pay attention to dynamics
       c. Know the correct tempo.
       d. Use expression.

    2. a. Children get to listen to male voices.
       b. Good examples of tone quality.
       c. An orchestra plays the music.

    3. Action, folk and ethnic, self-concept, fun and fancy, and songs for the very young.

Unit 10 Listening

A. 1. c   2. f   3. d   4. e   5. a   6. b

B. 1. Personal Opinion

    2. *Reasons for* using rest time as listening period:

       a. There is a great deal of listening music available that is good for rest time.
       b. Music from former lessons can be reviewed.
       c. Listening skills can be strengthened if the period is well planned.

       Reasons against using rest time as listening period:

          Some groups of children do not like this type of listening period.

    3. Suggestions to help children listen as rest time begins:

       a. Teacher can relax and listen herself.
       b. Use special effects that appeal to the children.

    4. Personal Opinion

Unit 10 (continued)

5. Ways to use the phonograph effectively:

    a. Have a phonograph that the children can use.
    b. Have a good phonograph that only the staff uses.
    c. Teach each child to care for the phonograph and records.
    d. Keep phonographs in good repair.
    e. Return records to jackets.
    f. Replace worn out records.

Unit 11 Movement

A. 1.

pat	touch	point	push	flip	bend
pinch	snap	pull	rub	wiggle	make circles

    2.

kick	wiggle	point toes
stamp lightly	click heels together	shuffle
stamp heavily	heel and toe movements	

    3.

swing	make large circle movements	lift	shake
reach	wave	punch	

    4.

nod up and down	shake	tip to one side
nod back and forth		move in circles

B. (Use your own ideas, too!)

1. Walk to "Itisket, Itasket" (Unit 1)

2. Run to "Merrily We 'Run' Along" (Unit 12)

3. Jump to "Pick a Bale of Cotton" (Unit 13)

4. Hop to "Sticks Go Click-Click" (Unit 15)
    Note: Sing "Children go hop, hop. Watch them hop, hop."

5. Gallop to "Summer is Coming" (Unit 13)

6. Leap to "Snapdragons" (Unit 10)

7. Slide to "A-Hunting We Will Go" (Unit 9)
Note: Children sing: "A-sliding we will go."

8. Roll — Use your own ideas.

9. Skip to "Here We Skip Round the Mulberry Bush" (Unit 6)

C. 1. b   2. c   3. d   4. a   5. e   6. f

Unit 12 Musical Dramatizations

A. 1. d   2. b   3. a   4. c   5. f   6. e

B. 1. d   2. d   3. c   4. d   5. c   6. d

D. 1. All goals are furthered (Enjoyment of music, listening, encouraging responses, foundation for musical experiences, fostering creativity).

2. All skills are furthered (Listening, singing, playing instruments, movement, creating music).

3. All of the five functions of music are furthered. (Structured musical activity, spontaneous musical activity, working with children in groups, music in related areas, and parent involvement.)

4. Leadership roles; follower roles.

5. It could be either a planned or an unplanned activity. However, resources are available at all times for such experiences.

6. The teacher can aim to achieve this.

Unit 13 Singing Games

A. 1. a. Singing games are part of the heritage of childhood.
    b. Singing games help the child to get along in groups.
    c. Singing games can become an important part of the routine of the school or center.
    d. Singing games are fun.

Unit 13 (continued)

    2. a. Clapping to one side, then the other.
           b. Shaking hands high, then low.
           c. Jumping back and forth (slowly).
           d. Wiggling hands in front, then in back.
           e. List others!

    3. a. As the teacher tells the children to form a circle, she makes a big circle with her arms.
           b. Teachers and/or volunteers stand in the circle with only a few children between them.

B.   1. b   2. d   3. c   4. b   5. c   6. d   7. d

C.   Responses and actions to the children in the circle game:

    1. Not every child needs to play the games. Let the child play on the climber – especially if it is outdoors. If the situation is one where he needs to stay with the group, encourage him to do so. Finish the game; then play one that will hold the attention of more children, and one which they will enjoy.

    2. Young children have a hard time waiting for their turns. Keep the "turns" short.

    3. "Put your hands up high and then put them low." (Demonstrate.) "Maybe your actions can be just a little different from mine."

    4. "Johnny, we hold hands loosely in our games without pulling." (If Johnny continues to pull, he should sit to the side during one game. Then he may come back into the circle. A teacher can stand by him, but he should have limits set so that he knows he cannot spoil the game for others.)

Unit 14 Creativity

A.   1. b   2. c   3. e   4. a   5. d   6. f   7. g

B.   1. b   2. a   3. b   4. d   5. d   6. d

SECTION 5 MEDIA AND MATERIALS

Unit 15 Musical Instruments

B. 1. rote   3. leader   5. instrument   7. lead

2. clap   4. stops   6. sound   8. sing and play

C.

Instrument	Description
Nail Chimes	Suspend nails from board by tying string around board and around nailheads. Strike with the largest nail.
Strainer Shaker	Put marbles inside strainers. Tape together.
Soft Cymbals	Fasten the wooden spools to the aluminum pie plates. Softly clash them together.
Peas Ping	Put split peas inside cottage cheese cartons. Tape shut.
Wood Blocks	Decorate wooden ends from roll of wrapping paper. Hit together.

Note: There are many more. Share your ideas!

D. 1. She can watch for items that make sounds that she can use. She should always keep safety in mind.

2. Hold the tambourine in the space where there are no metal discs.

3. He needs to have this chance before he goes to more structured activities. This is compared to the "scribble stage" in art.

4. Commercial and homemade instruments are two different types of instruments. Each has its place in a music program.

5. When the young child starts to play or pound on the piano, the teacher says, "Gently, gently."

6. Each of the two children plays one black key at a time. The children sit beside each other and play at the same time. The resulting sound is not bad.

7. Other instruments can be used to

   a. Teach about music elements such as melody and harmony.
   b. Expand the child's awareness of sounds.
   c. Teach about the instruments of the orchestra and other musical groups.

Unit 16 Commercial Media

A. 1. a. Catalogs   d. Music supply stores
        b. Libraries   e. Conventions
        c. Curriculum centers   f. Demonstrations at professional meetings

    2. a. Catalogs — Variety of materials such as records, books, games and music aids
        b. Libraries — Filmstrips, cassettes, and records
        c. Curriculum centers — Kits and music programs
        d. Music supply stores — Unusual musical instruments
        e. Conventions — Basic Music Series
        f. Demonstrations — Instruments and ideas used by a person

        Note: There are, of course, many other materials at each source.

    3. a. Knowledge of the great variety of materials that are available
        b. Materials that will fill a special need, such as help with creative movement activities
        c. Ideas to stimulate the music program such as pictures of children dancing that are found in catalogs
        d. Ways to store and take care of music equipment

Unit 17 Materials Made by Teacher and Children

A. 1. Picture that tells about the words is on front card. Words are on the back of the previous card as shown in figure 17-3.

    2. Buy a Santa puppet head. Put over special glove that makes the puppet body.

    3. Bells.

    4. Musical thermometer.

    5. Boy-girl faces mounted on paint-stirring sticks.

    6. Flannelboard figures made from old picture books.

    7. An actual boll of cotton.

    8. Picture of a spider the child has made.

B.   Suggestions for instructional aids for choosing-time.

   1.   A bunch of balloons. The child chooses one. The names of the songs are taped on the balloons. This instructional aid can also be made from felt for the flannelboard. (There are many other examples.)

   2.   Christmas ornaments to be placed on a small Christmas tree. The names of the songs are taped on the ornaments. (There are many other examples.)

C.   1. a   2. c   3. d   4. b, c, and d   5. a   6. b

SECTION 6 MUSIC APPRECIATION

Unit 18 Performances

A.   1.   a. They take children away from activities that are better for them.
         b. They tend to become the teacher's program.
         c. Many children do not like this activity; programs do not help them.
         d. Programs often take time and money that should be spent elsewhere.

   2.   a. They strengthen fine local traditions.
         b. They can involve parents effectively.
         c. They can help the children work together.

   3.   a. It should grow out of the curriculum.
         b. Every child should take part.
         c. A child should do every part he can, not the teacher.
         d. Costumes, if any, should be very simple.

   4.   a. Encourage children to turn the rocking boat over or build a stage.
         b. Play an accompaniment.
         c. Find a needed prop.
         d. Help the children make tickets or programs.

   5.   a. They will let children participate, sing, clap.
         b. They will play numbers familiar to the children.
         c. They will converse with the children and pause to answer questions.
         d. They will give a short performance.
         e. They will play an instrument that is new to the children.

Unit 18 (continued)

B. 1. a. Tim was helped to overcome shyness.
   b. Tim made a stride forward in leadership ability.
   c. The assistant gained confidence because she saw the possibility of the performance.
   d. Joy's self-concept was built up because she was able to lead.
   e. Lupi was encouraged because he thought of a way to involve the smaller children.
   f. Tim's mother had an incentive to become part of the school-parent program.
   g. Each was happy.

   2. a. Tim's skill of listening to music was recognized. He was given suggestions for developing a performance based on his listening to music on television.
   b. Group singing was given a boost.
   c. Musical dramatization was encouraged.
   d. Rhythm experience came from using the rhythm sticks.
   e. Enjoyment of music — the first goal of a music program — was reached.

Unit 19 Musical Field Trips

A. 1. *Quiet Thoughts, Kum-Ba-Yah, You Tell Me Your Dream, Sleep, Baby, Sleep, Home On the Range.* Others that class members know.

   2. *Monkeys and the Crocodile, Five Little Kittens, Up, Up in the Sky, Here's a Ball for Baby, Two to . . .* Others that class members know.

   3. *For America, For Canada; Popcorn Popping on the Apricot Tree; I've Been Working on the Railroad; Rig-A-Jig-Jig.* Others that class members know.

   4. *Hello, Everybody, Little Wheel a Turnin'.* Almost every melody in the text.

B. 1. d   2. e   3. e   4. a   5. e

C. a. false   b. true   c. false   e. true   f. true

Unit 20 A Practical Approach to Music Appreciation

A. 1. a. Use fine music in other areas such as storytelling.
        b. Ask class performers to include classical music that will appeal to the children.
        c. When selecting music for different purposes, choose some suitable music by great composers.
        d. Develop appreciation activities from music that has been part of the teacher's life.
        e. Bring music from travels to the classroom.
        f. Seek help when it is needed.

    2. a. Choose suitable music.
        b. Plan for this period.
        c. Generally, use familiar music.
        d. Prepare the children to hear the music.
        e. Listen to the music with the children.
        f. Hum when suitable.
        g. Follow the music with comments of your own, and ask the children for their comments.

    3. "Tommy Thumb", "Love Somebody". List of songs from your own travels.

B. 1. e   2. b   3. a   4. f   5. g   6. c   7. d

C. 1. Start with the music you like.

    2. Think about the ages and the needs of the children with whom you work.

    3. Using this information, plan the activity.

    4. One idea will lead to another.

    5. Alter the plans if you need to do so.

    6. Use different ideas, but stay with the plan until the music becomes familiar to the children.

    7. Enjoy the activity yourself.

    8. Repeat the familiar music from time to time.

PART II FUNDAMENTALS OF MUSIC

SECTION 7 UNDERSTANDING THE MECHANICS OF MUSIC

Unit 21 Melody

A.   1. c   2. f   3. d   4. e   5. b   6. g   7. a   8. i   9. k   10. h   11. j

B.   1. d   2. b   3. d   4. c   5. d   6. d   7. b   8. b

C.

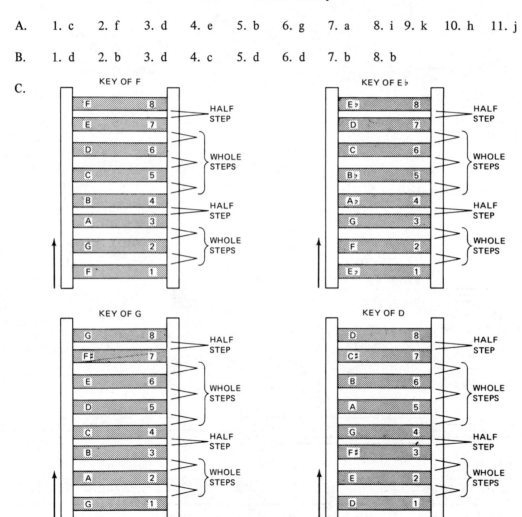

Unit 22 Rhythm

A. 1. a   2. d   3. d   4. c   5. e   6. f   7. e   8. e

B. 1. b   2. f   3. e   4. c   5. a   6. h   7. d   8. g

Unit 23 Harmony

A. 1. g   2. c   3. a   4. i   5. d   6. h   7. f   8. e   9. b

B. 1. B, E, G   3. B, A, G   5. G, A, B   7. B, E, A, D

   2. D, E, A, F   4. D, E, E, D   6. C, A, D   8. F, E, D

SECTION 8 TEACHER SKILLS

Unit 24 Chording

A. 1. d   2. e   3. c   4. e   5. a

B. 1. c   2. f   3. b   4. a   5. e   6. g   7. d   8. h

C.
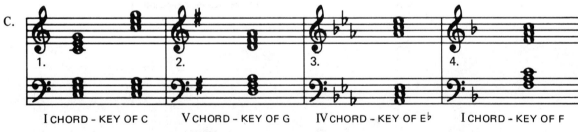

I CHORD – KEY OF C   V CHORD – KEY OF G   IV CHORD – KEY OF E♭   I CHORD – KEY OF F

IV CHORD – KEY OF D   V⁷ CHORD – KEY OF C   V⁷ CHORD – KEY OF G   IV CHORD – KEY OF D

Unit 25 Gaining A Musical Vocabulary

A.   1. d   2. a   3. f   4. h   5. b   6. g   7. c   8. e

B.   1. c   2. a   3. e   4. d   5. f   6. b

C.   1. e   2. b   3. a   4. f   5. c   6. h   7. d   8. g

Bibliography

Andrews, Gladys. *Creative Rhythmic Movement For Children*. Englewood Cliffs: Prentice-Hall, Inc., 1954.

Andrews, J. Austin and Jeanne Foster Wardian. *Introduction to Music Fundamentals*. New York: Meredith Corporation, 1963.

Aronoff, Frances Webber. *Music and Young Children*. New York: Holt, Rinehart, and Winston, Inc., 1969.

Benintendi, Wilma L. *Report of 1971 Early Childhood Kindergarten Program*. Pocatello, Idaho: Idaho State University, 1972.

Berg, Choate, Kjelson, and Troth. *Music for Early Childhood*. New York: American Book Company, 1970.

Bowen, H. Courthope. *Froebel and Education Through Self-Activity*. New York: Charles Scribner's Sons, 1909.

Garretson, Robert L. *Music in Childhood Education*. New York: Meredith Corporation, 1966.

Groesbeck, Lue. *Music for Elementary Teachers*. Provo, Utah: Brigham Young University Press, 1973.

Hackworth, Allen. *Guitar Pleasure: A Study Course*. Rexburg, Idaho, 1975.

Myers, Louise Kifer. *Music Fundamentals Through Song*. New York: Prentice-Hall, Inc., 1954.

Nye, Robert E. and Vernice T. Nye. *Exploring Music With Children*. Belmont, California: Wadsworth Publishing Company, Inc., 1966.

Pugmire, Mary Carolyn. *Songs to Guide Each Day*. 1976.

Richards, Mary Helen. *Threshold to Music*. Belmont, California: Fearon Publishers, 1971.

Runkle, Aleta and Mary LeBow Eriksen. *Music for Today's Boys and Girls*. Boston: Allyn and Bacon, Inc., 1970.

Schubert, Inez and Lucille Wood. *The Craft of Music Teaching*. New Jersey: Silver Burdett Company, 1964.

Slind, Lloyd H. and D. Evan Davis. *Bringing Music to Children*. New York: Harper & Row, 1964.

Stone, L. Joseph and Joseph Church. *Childhood & Adolescence: A Psychology of The Growing Person*. New York: Random House, 1973.

Vance, Barbara. *Teaching the Prekindergarten Child: Instructional Design and Curriculum*. California: Brooks/Cole Publishing Company, 1973.

Acknowledgments

- The ideas and efforts of many persons contribute to the publication of a single book. Although it is not possible to acknowledge every individual who helped, the author wants each to know she remembers, gratefully.

- Without the ideas, encouragement, and constructive criticism of the following, the book could not have been completed.

  Mr. and Mrs. Lynn Weller
  Dr. Lynn D. Weller, Jr.
  Shawn and Joy Miller and Family
  Rose and Mckay Pugmire
  Dr. Chester Hill

- Appreciation for assistance is expressed most sincerely to

  Ardean Watts for ideas used in Part II.
  The personnel and children of the Ricks College Child Development Laboratories, especially H. James Gordon and Helen Lindsay.
  Laurie Rydalch, Illustrator.
  Laurie Genta, Lannae Schwantes, and Nancy Woodland for technical assistance.
  Lynn Thomson, for figure 18-1.

- For the original materials used in the text, thanks go to LaFawn Holt, Allen Hackworth, Rita Robinson, Mary Susan Harker, Karla Livsey, Angie Madsen, Melissa Patrick, Merrill Pugmire, Spencer Southwick, Lyle Ann Virgin, Jubal Eames, and Pam McCallon.

- For the special encouragement given by Alan Knofla and Elinor Gunnerson of Delmar Publishers which kept the project going after it was interrupted by a personal tragedy in the life of the author, a "song of thanks" is sung.

- Every effort has been made to credit all authors and composers of the songs used in the text. If any have been overlooked and can be located at a later time, proper credit will be given in subsequent editions.

Contributors

American Book Company: figures 2-1, 7-3, 10-4, 11-4, and 12-1.
Bowmar: figure 16-1.
Daigger Educational Teaching Aids: figure 1-8.
Deseret Book Company: figures 3-3, 3-7, and 22-9.
Fearon Publishers, Inc.: figure 16-4.
Ideal School Supply: figure 16-3.
Miller-Brody Productions, Inc.: figure 16-2.
Music Education Group: figure 16-6.

Delmar Staff

Director of Publications — Alan N. Knofla

Source Editor — Elinor Gunnerson

Project Editor — Elizabeth J. Eames

Copy Editor — Judith Barrow

Consultant — Jeanne Machado

Director of Manufacturing and Production — Frederick Sharer

Illustrators — Tony Canabush, George Dowse, Al DeBenedetto, Mike Kokernak

Production Specialists — Debbie Monty, Patti Manuli, Betty Michelfelder, Sharon Lynch, Jean LeMorta, Alice Schielke, Lee St. Onge, Margaret Mutka

Materials used in *Experiences in Music for Young Children* have been classroom tested through the Brigham Young University — Ricks College Department of Continuing Education in Idaho Falls, Idaho.

INDEX

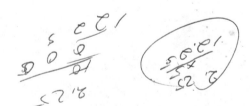

1083(3C82F)